The Psychopathy of
Everyday Life

The Psychopathy of Everyday Life

How Antisocial Personality Disorder Affects All of Us

MARTIN KANTOR, M.D.

PRAEGER

Westport, Connecticut
London

Library of Congress Cataloging-in-Publication Data

Kantor, Martin.
    The psychopathy of everyday life: how antisocial personality disorder affects all
of us / Martin Kantor.
        p. ; cm.
    Includes bibliographical references and index.
    ISBN 0–275–98798–1 (alk. paper)
    1. Antisocial personality disorders.   I. Title.
    [DNLM: 1. Antisocial Personality Disorder.   2. Personality. WM 190 k16pa 2006]
    RC555. K36   2006
    616.85'820651—dc22   2006015393

British Library Cataloguing in Publication Data is available.

Library of Congress Catalog Card Number: 2006015393
ISBN: 0-275-98798-1

First published in 2006

Praeger Publishers, 88 Post Road West, Westport, CT 06881
An imprint of Greenwood Publishing Group, Inc.
www.praeger.com

Printed in the United States of America

The paper used in this book complies with the
Permanent Paper Standard issued by the National
Information Standards Organization (Z39.48-1984).

10 9 8 7 6 5 4 3 2 1

For M.E.C.

Contents

CHAPTER 1.   Introduction   1

CHAPTER 2.   The Psychopathy of Everyday Life   11

CHAPTER 3.   Behavioral Manifestations   29

CHAPTER 4.   Some Psychopaths of Everyday Life   55

CHAPTER 5.   A Few Cases   73

CHAPTER 6.   The Core Personality Structure   85

CHAPTER 7.   Differential Diagnosis: Associated
              and Overlapping Disorders   107

CHAPTER 8.   Social Issues   123

CHAPTER 9.   Successful Psychopaths   133

CHAPTER 10.   Cause   137

CHAPTER 11.   Course and Prognosis   153

CHAPTER 12.   Therapy of the Mild Psychopath   157

CHAPTER 13.   Coping with the Psychopaths of Everyday Life 179

Notes   195

Index   203

About the Author   209

CHAPTER 1

Introduction

Psychopathy is both a serious psychological disorder that threatens our individual happiness and a widespread social problem that threatens our entire civilization. Yet to date the sensed diagnostic unity that we call psychopathy remains a diffuse and poorly drawn entity that comes close to defeating our attempts to precisely describe it, thoroughly understand it, and effectively treat it.

One of the biggest problems in understanding psychopathy is the literature's tendency to lump serious but rare psychopaths like John Wayne Gacy and Ted Bundy with the less serious but common psychopaths, the many in our midst who suffer from a milder and less obtrusive form of what the *DSM-IV* (The American Psychiatric Association's *Diagnostic and Statistical Manual of Mental Disorders*) officially calls "Antisocial Personality Disorder."[1] Martha Stout calls these less serious, more common psychopaths "the sociopaths next door."[2] I call them "the psychopaths of everyday life."

They include men and women like the following composites:

The motorist who is aggressive, narcissistic, and selfish, a man or woman without kindness, empathy, altruism, or regret—the one who honks remorselessly at people who do not move fast enough, bends a fender, then leaves the scene, grabs a parking space right out from under his or her "territorial rivals," and goes through red lights with a narcissistic vengeance that proclaims: "the green, yellow, and red lights are all my own personal go-signals." He or she blames everyone else for his or her accidents, as did the motorist who hit me from behind when I was stopped at a red light and then, instead of apologizing, emerged from her car and severely chastised me for impeding the flow of traffic. The words "It's my fault" were no more on her mind than in the vocabulary of the lawyer who absconds with his clients' escrow money, or in the repertoire of the CEO who bankrupts his company so that he can gratify his personal, very expensive, appetites.

The dentist who, for fame, money, and power, evolves crazy theories with more gusto and greater ease than sensible ones, and who even comes to believe in his theories himself. One such individual was able to build a busy practice and pay the mortgage on his beachfront home by claiming it was necessary to revise all old dental fillings made of mercury lest they cause blood poisoning manifested as chronic fatigue syndrome. When the regulatory agencies caught up with him, and when his patients read about the questionable scientific basis of his theories, he lost most of this practice. So he had to find another way to make a lot of money. He started recommending that all his patients undergo what he called "preventive dentistry," which involved grinding down almost a whole tooth instead of simply filling a cavity, giving as his reason that the tooth would never become decayed again. His motivation was not to preserve his patients' teeth; it was to enhance his bottom line.

The psychiatrist who, when in residency, often made up cases for presentation at conferences and passed the licensing exam by buying the questions and answers available on the underground. When in private practice, he allowed himself to be bought with cheap gifts and free lunches by drug detail men attempting to convince him to prescribe certain medications; refused to prescribe a medication unless it was made by a drug company in which he had a financial stake; and continued to work on a federal panel deciding which drugs were safe without recusing himself, as he should have, on the grounds that he got money from the very drug companies that made the drugs he was endorsing. When referring his patients, he would send them not to the best qualified person available for the job but to his golfing buddies. Though he refrained, he turned a blind eye when his colleagues had sex with their patients, in private agreeing with these colleagues that their behavior was little more than a form of hands-on therapy. At times he would sleep during his therapy sessions and then report his revealing dreams back to his patients, claiming this a particularly effective form of treatment. One of his specialties was treating anxiety, but in reality he was pushing drugs, for he wrote literally hundreds of prescriptions for benzodiazepines without first taking a complete medical history or performing the requisite mental status examination. He also practiced alternative medicine, prescribing nutritional supplements alone for ailments that called for conservative medical treatment. He then deified his trivial interventions as powerful curatives and, to ice the cake, lobbied politically to have his treatment approaches formally recognized and legitimized so that insurance companies would reimburse him. It should come as no surprise that he also cheated those insurance companies that complied by lying about the amount of time he spent with his patients. He would see a patient for a few minutes and then bill the insurance company for a full fifty-minute hour.

The spouse who as a consumer registered his car to a phony out-of-town address in a state with lower car insurance rates, tapped into the cable line to get free cable, and, after becoming a subscriber at a later date, never informed the cable company of its mistake when it gave him premium channels without charging him for them, so that he could continue to get the service without having to pay the bill. He would often buy things, use them, and then return them to the store when he no longer needed them. Once, when he was boarding his brother's dog, he bought a cage from a pet store, used it for the few days that the dog was with him, and returned it, saying that it was cheaply made. When he bought electronic equipment and broke it, he would bring it back to the store and claim that it was defective, and he often returned plants he had killed, saying that they had simply died. When an electronics store had a big sale, he would buy several items and then attempt to resell them at a profit on eBay. He would make person-to-person calls not to reach someone but to alert them that he had arrived without having to pay for the call, and once he even tried sending a letter without a stamp, using as the return address the address of the recipient in hopes that the letter would arrive at its proper destination after having been returned for insufficient postage. When a policeman caught him speeding, making an illegal turn, or using a cell phone when driving, he would falsely claim an emergency that required his immediate presence. Joining the paying crowd at intermission, he would sneak into a show or concert for the second act. In bookstores he would peel back the shrink-wrap from books so that he could read them without buying them, and he would borrow CDs from the public library, make copies of them, and sell them to his friends. He would regularly drop his personal garbage into a public bin, eat his way through the olive bar and otherwise use the supermarket as a smorgasbord, underreport his income on his tax forms, evade sales tax on a purchase by having an empty box shipped to an out-of-town address, buy stolen goods after buying into the excuse that they fell from the back of the truck, and sneak into a gym to which he did not belong. (After telling the person at the front desk that he was just there to meet someone at the cafeteria, he would go into the bathroom, remove his outer clothes to reveal his gym clothes underneath, pack his clothes into a backpack he carried around with him, and unabashedly proceed to the workout floor.) He once altered a medical insurance form after his doctor completed it so that he could increase the benefits due him, often tried substituting stickers on supermarket items so that he would be charged less for an item, and on more than one occasion deprived a real estate agent of an earned commission by teaming up with the seller to purchase the property directly, behind the agent's back.

As psychopathic consumers, all of us give the lie to the maxim that the customer is always right—like those of us who lie, cheat, and steal from the merchants we deal with for any number of financial and personal reasons, among them to pay as little as possible for desirable merchandise, and to get all the fun and excitement we can from putting something over on a bunch of suckers. We are the individuals who borrow a book from the library then "forget" to return it. When leaving a hotel, we try to steal the towels or the bathrobe, and when leaving a restaurant we frequently try to nab souvenirs such as any decorative dishes or salt and pepper shakers that we can lay our hands on. We might claim we had a dinner or hotel reservation we had not actually contracted for, hoping to get the restaurant or hotel to correct an error they had not made by offering us space that we did not reserve. We always correct a waiter or waitress when we are overcharged, but never when we are undercharged. When we think we can get away with it, we eat dinner at a restaurant and then—channeling the old-time comedian's routine, "Waiter, there's a fly in my soup"—complain about the food or service to get comped, to leave a lesser tip, or both. We know that if we send false letters of complaint about a product we can get the company to apologetically send us free coupons good for purchasing more of the same. When applying for jobs, we regularly omit negative information about our past work history, or embellish our résumé, and on credit applications we significantly inflate our income, while in other circumstances we significantly underreport it, for example, to gain admission to a middle-income housing project. Some of us put all our assets under a corporate name so that we will be eligible for benefits available to those with a low income, or apply for Social Security disability benefits on the grounds of having an old back injury, which we falsely claim makes it impossible for us to do any remunerative work whatsoever.

I believe that these individuals are to be classified as mild psychopaths. However, the extant literature would not necessarily agree with me, or acknowledge that such a thing as "the mild psychopath" even exists. Many of my colleagues also do not recognize "mild psychopathy" as an established entity, and the *DSM-IV*, recognizing only the full syndrome, would not classify the individuals I describe as true psychopaths because they generally meet fewer than the minimal number of criteria the *DSM-IV* states must be met before the diagnosis can become official.[3]

In this book I state my belief and present my evidence that a syndrome of "psychopathy of everyday life" actually exists. I then focus on describing it, attempt to determine what causes these individuals to act the way they do, and suggest some doable therapeutic interventions both for them and for the many innocent, and not-so-innocent, victims whose lives they affect.

This, however, has not been an easy task, due to the following factors:

THE DIFFICULTY OF EVALUATING PSYCHOPATHIC INDIVIDUALS EVEN UNDER THE BEST OF CIRCUMSTANCES

Psychopaths are a maddeningly uncooperative group, with a seriously disruptive tendency to be as untruthful with their therapists as they are with everyone else. According to Robert D. Hare, they are even "able to fake the results of psychological tests [such as the MMPI and the Rorschach] without too much difficulty"[4] in order to impress, cow, or manipulate the tester.

THE ELUSIVENESS OF THE DISORDER

Psychopathy is marked by imponderables, contradictions, and paradoxes that make it the subject of some very pointed and legitimate controversy found both in formal and informal exchanges among therapists and in the extant literature. Some of these controversies are listed below.

Controversies About Whether or Not Psychopathy Is Actually a Disorder

Christian Perring states that it is unclear "why being a psychopath should count as having a psychiatric disorder in the first place,"[5] and Dorothy Otnow Lewis suggests that "antisocial persons do not constitute a discrete diagnostic entity, despite their sharing superficial characteristics."[6] Certainly this disorder is different from other psychological disorders in the following key ways:

1. Most observers, before making the diagnosis, require that psychopathic behaviors start in adolescence to constitute what the *DSM-IV* calls a "Conduct Disorder."[7] Other disorders are not so clearly evident by early childhood or so invariably chronic throughout life. Some enduring personality changes can result from catastrophic events, constituting a kind of reactive disorder that appears in the adult after trauma and is akin to, or one subtype of, Posttraumatic Stress Disorder.

2. While most other psychiatric diagnoses focus on individual behavior with only secondary concern for the social impact of that behavior, a diagnosis of psychopathy is heavily imbued with, and fundamentally rests upon, social concepts. A central concept is social normalcy versus social deviation. For example, one of the most important *DSM-IV* criteria of psychopathy is "disregard for and violation of the rights of others . . . as indicated by . . . failure to conform to social norms with respect to lawful behaviors."[8]

3. This focus on social issues necessarily spins off a unique diagnostic preoccupation with superficial behavioral criteria—too often, in this case, a preoccupation with criminality and other "bad" behaviors, not only dehumanizing the patient but downplaying the importance of his or her intrapsychic psychodynamics.

4. Psychopathy is a uniquely here-and-now-oriented diagnosis. But yesterday's social clinical criteria are often today's invalid diagnostic parameters. For example, in the late 1960s the staff of an inpatient service on which I worked attempted to expel a white female patient from the unit for having sex with another patient, a black woman. The staff reasoned that she had broken the rules about patients not having sex with other patients in the hospital, and most of all she unacceptably had crossed the boundaries of race and gender. In those days, we diagnosed the patient as a psychopath. Today the diagnosis would be more applicable to the staff.

5. Defense attorneys often use disorders other than psychopathy to create an "insanity defense," that is, as a reason for lack of culpability. Psychopathy stands virtually alone as a disorder for the prosecution to seize upon in order to convict—a "black mark" on the patient that provides a reason to incriminate and jail him or her based on his or her failure to exercise putative ability to tell right from wrong and to assume and take responsibility for his or her actions.

6. Unlike the symptoms of many other established disorders, the symptoms of psychopathy do not appear to be the product of—that is, a way to handle—anxiety and guilt. While other disorders are characterized by the use of particular defense mechanisms, acting-out is virtually the only defense mechanism that all observers agree is used by psychopaths.

7. While some observers view psychopathy as a true primary diagnosis, others view it as merely a compendium of traits characteristic of other disorders, particularly narcissism and paranoia. Still others view it as normal, mainstream behavior in an "abnormal" society (calling it "sociopathy"). Still others view it as a normal lifestyle characterized by the use of guile as a survival mechanism, a method available to anyone having difficulty making it in the world, and therefore not a maladaptive disorder at all but an adaptive behavior with certain admirable, and even enviable, qualities.

Controversies About the Description of Psychopathy

1. The clinical descriptions we have of psychopathy show exceptional dissonance, to the point of provoking extreme and often vituperative exchanges between clinicians. Theodore Millon believes that the *DSM-III* descriptive criteria of psychopathy are inadequate and, taking "strong exception to the narrow view promulgated in the DSM . . .,"[9] proposes his own entirely different set of diagnostic criteria based on determining fundamental personality difficulties such as aggressivity, a deficit in self-insight, and acting-out tendencies.

2. The descriptive parameters of psychopathy are unclear. As currently defined, the syndrome covers individuals ranging from extreme criminals like Ted Bundy and David Berkowitz to people who fill their cars up with gas and then speed off without paying. The term is often used popularly, and incorrectly, to refer to criminal activity, especially activity with an aggressive or even homicidal bent (e.g., we hear, "I wouldn't let violent video games into my home because they glorify psychopathic behavior.").

3. While some observers see these individuals as charmers, others see them as difficult, ugly people. While some observers invariably view these individuals as

failures in life, others view them, on the whole, as more successful than average, so that their psychopathy is more an asset than a liability. Machiavelli's classic *The Prince*[10] can even be profitably viewed as a self-help book (one of the first) that outlines a step-by-step method on how to become a psychopath—that is, how one can win by developing as many antisocial traits as possible.

Controversies About the Causes and Dynamics of Psychopathy

1. Patients who are psychopathic are said to be both guiltless hedonists and guilty masochists. So, which is it? Do these individuals suffer from an absence of guilt, or are they closet masochists due to being secretly guilty people who live out their intense guilt and shame by becoming self-destructive failures in life?

2. Patients with the disorder are supposedly unable to experience anxiety, yet every so often an article appears that suggests these individuals do in fact suffer from anxiety, only that it is deeply buried in a rock-solid defensive façade. According to some, but not all, observers, the façade can be broken through with the right approach—at least if one could find a way to keep the patient in a hospital long enough to get at the painful things stirring within.

3. Some observers, viewing psychopathy as a throwback to infantilism, suggest that adult psychopaths are like little children in their impulsivity, lack of control, and primary pleasure orientation. Others feel that psychopathic behavior is nothing at all like the behavior of the normal child, but rather goes far beyond normal childish behavior to enter into a realm entirely of its (psychopathological) own.

4. When speaking of the psychopath's early development, some observers suggest that these individuals were overgratified in childhood—so that as adults they want more of the same, and something for nothing. Other observers believe that they were undergratified in childhood—so that they now want what they never had, and soon come around to not caring how they go about getting it.

5. The extant literature cannot decide if psychopathy is an organic or an emotionally caused disorder. While some observers believe psychopathy to be acquired, others suggest that it is the product of an inborn organic/neurological deficit. Some cite in support of the latter theory that certain believed-to-be-specific EEG (electroencephalographic) changes exist. Others view these changes as within the realm of normal and therefore as nonspecific—for example, as the product of characteristic psychopathic disinterest and ennui.

6. Much discussion takes place about whether psychopaths are sick or evil—that is, whether their behavior is conscious or unconscious, calculated by or determined for them, and so whether they are bad, sad, or mad. Debate continues on whether psychopaths are suffering from a disease that needs to be cured or from a willfulness that needs to be tamed; if they are under the spell of inner demons they cannot master or if they deliberately choose to walk not with the rest of us but on the periphery of society, having consciously decided to dwell in a place where the rules of civilization fade, and to enter the realm of the outlaw and the fugitive. (Since these individuals often get into trouble with the law, the question of whether they are sane and bad, or insane and mad, is more

than just an academic one.) Yet there are no easy answers to these questions. More likely there is nothing but confusion about how exactly to define insanity; the differences, which are often considerable, between medical and legal definitions of insanity; and whether in using the phrase "knowing right from wrong" we are referring to a legal or a moral wrong.

7. The identified social causes of psychopathy range from social liberalism to social conservatism. Some observers believe that psychopathy thrives in a lax, laissez-faire society with too few rules, and with those rules inadequately enforced. Other observers believe that psychopathy thrives in a strict society with many rules too heavily enforced.

Controversies About the Treatment of Psychopathy

Some of the greatest and most immediately important controversies involve treatment of the psychopathic patient. Hervey Cleckley speaks of his "own inability to achieve successful results with any regularity in dealing with severe cases of this type."[11] But Lewis disagrees, instead claiming that "their specific neuropsychiatric symptoms, such as paranoid thinking, [are] treatable [though] not curable."[12] In like manner, Benjamin James Sadock and Virginia Alcott Sadock note that under certain circumstances these individuals often "become amenable to psychotherapy."[13]

Many observers who believe that these patients are untreatable using traditional methods go on to state unequivocally that their resistance to treatment is caused by their motivation not to get better, but to con the therapist into thinking that they are improving. Many therapists believe them not only to be passively unmotivated toward, and therefore unresponsive to, treatment, but also actively defiant, forcing their therapists into the unaccustomed role of becoming defensively skeptical and cynical, having to be not healer but detective and inquisitor, with little choice but to abandon the traditional therapeutic stances of understanding, forgiving, and curing, and instead become parental and punitive.

What is certain is that to date, few therapists identify, understand, and then commit themselves fully to treating this heterogeneous and difficult group of patients. If there is one uniting cry in the therapeutic community, it is "They brought it on themselves, so lock 'em up, and throw away the key." As a result, even the mildest of psychopaths are accorded little hope and are given little opportunity to change for the better so that they can start living more lawful, honest, and gratifying lives, in which they use people less and love people more.

Nor are family and friends of psychopaths, or we as ordinary citizens who suffer at the hands of the psychopaths in our midst, much better served. Rather, all concerned are left to their own devices to cope with and protect themselves from the machinations of the psychopaths around us. Most unfortunate of all is that no matter how charitably inclined we might be personally, and how much we want to be of assistance, we have little idea what to do to help these individuals behave more adaptively and act less self-destructively.

My book will not finally resolve these and other related controversies about psychopathy. It will not once and for all solve all the problems inherent in defining, describing, understanding, and treating the disorder. Given the present state of our knowledge about psychopaths, this would be an impossible task. So my main thrust is a modest one: separating out the mild from the severe psychopaths, two superficially similar but spiritually and clinically very different groups of individuals; describing the characteristic behaviors of the mild psychopaths; and articulating what I believe to be a rational, doable, corrective approach specifically meant for the psychopaths of everyday life. In writing this book, it is my hope that therapists will at least attempt to lay their hands on these individuals in a gesture of curing, instead of regularly throwing up their hands in a gesture of defeat, and that we as laypersons can make sense of what is going on with them, and then find ways to cope, adapt, manage, and help them get better.

This is a fascinating and worthy group of individuals. Learning how to cope with and help them change is of more than academic interest. Indeed, for us all, it is a matter of survival, ours as well as theirs. As individuals, they threaten, at the very least, to ruin our lives, and sometimes even to take them. As a group, they threaten to sink society as we know it. Our decline and fall may not come, if it comes at all, solely from the barbarians without, but also from the barbarians within. The con artist who separates the elderly person from his or her life savings or the scam artist who sets up sites on the Internet meant to rake in money for charity that goes directly into his or her pocket does relatively little damage on a global scale. But by the power of sheer numbers, these and other psychopaths of everyday life threaten to return us to the dark ages where the only rules are "anything goes," "if it feels good, do it," and "look out for number one."

We should heed the warnings and decide once and for all if we are going to stand by as our society crumbles, or take individual and concerted action to rescue our civilization before it is too late. Those of you who do not wish to sit by passively as we all go under together might want to consider reading on.

CHAPTER 2

The Psychopathy of Everyday Life

Though the psychopaths of everyday life are everywhere and have a dev-astating overall effect, both on individuals and on society as a whole, as a group they generally escape the notice of the extant scientific literature. If the literature mentions them at all, it is usually merely in passing. It says a few words about the lawyer for whom winning a case is more impor-tant than discovering the truth; the ad writer who uses fragments of infor-mation to put a good face on a bad product; the doctor who touts a costly medication over one that is less expensive but equally effective because he owns stock in the company that produces the drug; the politician who sells out for a mess of concrete, voting for a contractor's new construction project in exchange for a new driveway for her house; and the CEO of a major corporation who decides not to insure his employees, knowing that the taxpayers will have to pick up the bill for their medical care. But sooner rather than later, and all too predictably, the focus shifts from the mild psychopath to his or her more seriously disturbed cousin: the patient properly diagnosed as having an Antisocial Personality Disorder. Ordinary people and real life are left behind as we find ourselves plunged into the extraordinary and fantastic worlds of the likes of Bluebeard, Adolf Hitler, Saddam Hussein, David Berkowitz, and Jack the Ripper.

In my view, the psychopaths of everyday life constitute an important and unique group, one that differs significantly in style, causation, inci-dence, and effect from patients with an Antisocial Personality Disorder. *Descriptively*, while mild psychopathy closely resembles a personality dis-order, severe psychopathy (Antisocial Personality Disorder) more closely resembles a psychosis. *Dynamically*, mild psychopaths are less aggressive, and more anxious and guilt-ridden, than their more severe counterparts. *Therapeutically*, mild psychopathy has both a more benign course and a better prognosis than severe psychopathy and can, unlike more severe, treatment-resistant forms of the disorder, often be managed effectively using an approach consisting of an eclectic amalgam of classic psychotherapeutic techniques.

However, not all observers would agree that mild psychopathy constitutes a discrete diagnostic entity. For example, Hans Toch says that "viewing psychopathy as ordinal (rather than categorical) strikes some as the counterpart of degrees of pregnancy."[1] According to Toch, being a little psychopathic is like being a little bit pregnant. In effect, Toch suggests that we not make the diagnosis of psychopathy unless a specific set of fundamental criteria are *all* in place. Along somewhat similar lines, Henry Pinsker (personal communication, 2004) suggests that in having been applied to anyone who is an opportunist or a criminal, the term psychopath has become too broad and dilute, to the point that it has lost its specificity. As Pinsker says, "I believe [that Cleckley] captured what the profession has meant by the term [psychopath]. [But the term becomes too broad and diluted and loses specificity] when applied to anyone who is an opportunist, or, [when] converted to 'antisocial,' to anyone who does bad things a lot, e.g., stealing to support a drug habit. Cleckley named his book *The Mask of Sanity* because the individuals he described seemed to be sane after they were put into insane asylums. They were put into them in the first place because of behavior so inexplicable that juries decided that they must be insane. If an individual has found that being manipulative and opportunistic is adaptive, there is no reason to diagnose personality disorder unless [that individual] has other characteristics. The behavior must be maladaptive or fantastic to warrant the diagnosis, as I see it. Tony Soprano, the lead in the TV series *The Sopranos*, repeatedly maintains mistresses and has opportunistic sexual encounters on the side. He personally does violence to individuals who "deserve it" according to consistent, predictable standards. We can propose psychopathology to explain the sexual behavior, the bad temper, the apparent pleasure in sadistic violence at times. In other respects, his behavior is regular, predictable, stable, and consistent, so he is not a psychopath. I think that if people are in synch with their society, no matter how depraved we outsiders think their behavior happens to be, we cannot make a diagnosis beyond some evaluation of their eagerness to participate [in and get pleasure from] sadism or submission. "[The world is full of people doing to people who have differing views] what Tony Soprano does to rats."

Other observers do recognize mild, partial psychopathy as an entity. As Donald W. Black says in his book *Bad Boys, Bad Men: Confronting Antisocial Personality Disorder*, "Antisocials are not just muggers, rapists, and violent assailants. They sometimes are embezzlers, tax evaders, fraudulent businessmen, corrupt stock brokers, and conniving attorneys . . . who habitually commit white-collar crimes."[2] The blurb on the back of Black's book includes under the rubric of psychopathy "black sheep . . . con men, or misfits [who] shirk everyday responsibilities, abuse drugs and alcohol . . . and lash out at family members,"[3] and in the book itself Black speaks of "successful bad boys."[4] Robert D. Hare, in his book *Without Conscience: The Disturbing World of the Psychopaths Among Us*, calls mild psychopaths "subcriminal psychopaths"[5] and says of them, "These individuals are every bit as egocentric, callous, and manipulative as the average criminal psychopath; however, their intelligence, family background, social skills, and circumstances permit them to construct a façade of normalcy and to get what they want with relative impunity."[6]

Although the psychopaths Cleckley describes in *The Mask of Sanity* are almost all severely ill, Cleckley discusses mild psychopaths on occasion, without much focus or elaboration, as follows: These individuals "are able to make some sort of adjustment in life."[7] They are "less severely incapacitated"[8] and have a "milder or more limited [disorder that] has not altogether dominated the scene. [Their maladaptive behavior] has not crowded ordinary successful functioning in the outer aspects of work and social relations entirely out of the picture. [They have] strong, [but] not consistent, tendencies and inner reactions characteristic of the group."[9] In them there are "scattered indications of [the] disorder, suggestions of a disturbance central in nature but well contained within an outer capsule of successful behavior."[10] In them there are astonishing differences "between . . . outer adjustment and the indications of deeper pathologic features so similar to those found in the complete manifestation of the disorder. [Their maladjustment is] temporary or circumscribed . . . affecting [them merely] in part and in varying degree [so that as a result] they keep up a far better and more consistent outward appearance of being normal [in areas that] may include business or professional careers."[11] The "motivation [of their asocial or even criminal activity, unlike that of serious psychopaths] can be translated into terms of ordinary human striving, selfish or unselfish."[12] They succeed if only "for short periods [of time]"[13] but they do not "succeed in the sense of finding satisfaction or fulfillment in their accomplishments."[14] "Those of great talent"[15] can even use psychopathic methods "in the successful pursuit of valuable personal and social aims."[16] Not only do they "find . . . better means of adaptation"[17] but they also "profit from what has been learned through the pathological experiences."[18] (The obverse of Cleckley's observations about mild psychopaths reveals what Cleckley means by serious psychopaths.)

I believe that mild psychopaths like the ones of which these observers speak certainly exist and that, however mild their disorder may be, they are still psychopaths. I also believe that mild psychopaths are in some ways even more dangerous to society overall than severe psychopaths.

Since they are more numerous than patients with a formal Antisocial Personality Disorder, their lying, cheating, and swindling is on a more massive scale, so that their resulting mayhem deprives many victims of much. While it is true that these individuals are rarely violent to one person, they perpetrate a great deal of violence on the dignity, identity, and bank accounts of many people. They rarely take a single life, but they have a serious potential for ruining the lives of many.

My central discussion of these individuals and their *psychopathy* of everyday life starts with a general discussion of the *psychopathology* of everyday life.

THE *PSYCHOPATHOLOGY* OF EVERYDAY LIFE

Normal Versus Abnormal

By the term "psychopathology of everyday life," I mean thought and behavior centered somewhere near the middle of a continuum, where "normal" is on the left of the mean and "pathological" is on the right. For example, when it comes to psychopathy, I believe that on the left are those "normal" opportunistic individuals who consider personal gain more important than truth or the collective good, consider winning the only thing worthwhile, and twist logic into obtaining personal advantage by skillfully selecting and misrepresenting facts until even they themselves come to believe in the truth of their distortions. These "normals" on the left contrast with the antisocials on the right, whom we formally identify as full psychopaths based on their psychopathology having crossed the border into the realm of serious lying, cheating, and criminality; they are completely unfettered by anxiety and totally unbound by conscience.

That does not mean that it is easy to precisely define what is normal and what is pathological, especially when it comes to personality disorder. A completely satisfactory answer eludes us for a number of reasons. In particular, many observers believe that for most disorders a continuum exists between normal behavior and pathological behavior, making it difficult to distinguish clearly between the two. These observers, instead of making *categorical* diagnoses (defined below), speak of making *dimensional* diagnoses—that is, they view psychopathologic behavior as consisting of excessive, repetitive, or prolonged normal behavior.

Though the *DSM-IV*[19] generally favors categorical diagnosis, especially when it comes to personality disorders it recognizes to some extent the validity of dimensional diagnoses. For example, it notes that "Personality Disorders represent maladaptive variants of personality traits that merge imperceptibly into normality and into one another"[20] so that the difference between personality *style* and personality *disorder* is mainly one of degree and extent. "Only when personality traits [or styles] are inflexible and maladaptive and cause significant functional impairment or subjective distress do they constitute Personality Disorders."[21] In John M. Oldham and Lois B. Morris' equally dimensional view, personalitydisorders are "exaggerations of . . . personality styles that are present to varying degrees within every individual. It is the *quantity* of each personality style along a continuum, not its quality, that tends to spell problems in life."[22]

To illustrate, we all get angry from time to time. Some of us just accept that anger is one of the normal emotions and get over it. Many of us, however, feel so sheepish about having gotten angry that we beat ourselves up for it, only to then forgive ourselves soon afterwards, albeit incompletely. Technically speaking, this latter sequence of events, although well within the range of normality, is still on a continuum with Masochistic Personality Disorder. Whether we can make that diagnosis depends on how serious the problem is, how frequently it occurs, and if it results in maladaptive behavior—for example, self-punishment that takes the form of seriously defeating ourselves in life, and for as long as we live.

In contrast, observers who make *categorical* diagnoses use a specific rigid set of criteria to distinguish nonpathological from pathological and to outline distinct clinical syndromes with fixed borders within which the syndrome is recognized, but beyond which the syndrome, at least in theory, no longer exists. Virtually all the diagnostic categories in the *DSM-IV*[23] are categorical, specifying a set of criteria and requiring a given number of these criteria to be met before a given diagnosis can be considered valid.

Here are some applicable caveats. As we attempt to assess quantity along a continuum (as above), we have to leave room for personality *differences*. All of us are not alike, so behavior such as introversion or even deviousness is more pathological for some than it is for others. It is also important to distinguish abnormal behavior from behavior that looks abnormal but is normal because of circumstances that make it both predictable and universal. People often behave more "pathologically" when on vacation and at special times of the year, for which we have coined such terms as "spring fever," "midsummer madness," and "winter doldrums," to suggest that cultural allowances be made for intermittent—for example, seasonal—deviation from year-round norms. Job requirements can also make a substantial difference. For example, a checking ritual makes sense for an accountant, for it is "reactive to" or "part of" the work. For an FBI agent a formal, unbending personality with paranoid features can represent not a style of illness but an appropriate or even creative manifestation of health. Additionally, as emphasized throughout, one cannot define social deviance without taking into consideration the variations that exist both within one society and from society to society. We must also take individual motivation into account. The bank robber who intends to be an enemy of the state tends to be a more serious psychopath than Robin Hood, who by stealing from the rich and giving to the poor intends to be a friend of the people. We must also consider differing legitimate points of view that depend on one's position in life. When it comes to determining what constitutes a psychopathic squatter, advocates for the homeless and the landlords of the affected properties are likely to have very different perspectives.

A final caveat is that determining what is normal (and what is abnormal) requires being completely fair. As Cleckley warns, especially when it comes to "our enemies or our neighbors . . . it is not easy to estimate the degree of [their] sincerity [or] the worth of [their] production [and to discern their] real motive[s]."[24]

The Structure of Normal Personality

The "molecule" of personality consists of "atoms" we call *personality traits*. These traits are the building blocks of both (normal) personality style and (pathological) personality disorder.

Personality traits consist of an inherent way of viewing things that is influenced from outside the individual only with difficulty. As such they are inherently and chronically overly rigid, fixed, repetitive, predictable, and inappropriate attitudes leading to specific behaviors that, like the underlying attitudes themselves, are barely subject to the dictates of reality and common sense.

To the individual who possesses them, personality traits can either feel as if they are part of the personality ("ego syntonic,") or feel like foreign bodies in the personality ("ego dystonic").

Dynamically speaking, personality traits are composed of fantasies that tend to originate in infancy or childhood and persist into adulthood. A persistent fantasy typical of psychopaths is the fantasy that everyone will take advantage of them like their parents used to way back then. These fantasies readily become attitudes and behaviors dogmatically retained throughout life, simplistically embraced, and compulsively acted upon, even when circumstances and common sense—the threat of punishment, for example—indicate that the rigid behavior be either modified or completely abandoned.

Wilhelm Reich[25] noted that personality traits are like symptoms in that both are composed of such signs of intrapsychic life as wish, fear, and conflict. However, they are unlike symptoms in that they are less discreet, making them like mild yet pervasive dilutions of symptomatic presentation. For example, the dilute equivalent of "obsessive-compulsive scrupulosity" might be "excessive, scrupulous honesty." To this presentation Reich applied the term "character 'armor,'"[26] which he contrasted with the more concentrated presentation of a symptom of a major disorder, such as a hand-washing compulsion or a paranoid delusion.

Personality traits can be compared in subject matter and style to proverbs and related sayings like maxims. We can think of them as a lifetime overvaluation and realization of a proverb or maxim manifested clinically as an overvalued idea, e.g., one that grabs hold and resolutely guides thought and behavior. Because personality traits are like proverbs and maxims, proverbs and maxims can serve as headlines to the "story" of one's personality traits, and ultimately of one's personality type or style—being apt, pithy summaries of the individual's core personality. Thus the individual who lives by the sayings "Cleanliness is next to godliness" and "Never postpone to tomorrow what you can do today" tends to be an overly scrupulous but still normal obsessional type. "We have nothing to fear but fear itself" describes the propensity for denial found in those with a hypomanic bent. The maxims "There's no business like show business," "A sucker is born every minute," and "Caveat emptor" are the rallying cries of the individual with the potential for developing a psychopathic personality style.

Everyone has a personality style—that is, is of a given personality that consists of multiple personality traits. Two things that differentiate normal from abnormal personalities are the *selection* of personality traits and the way that they are *combined*. In the realm of *selection* of personality traits, while many of the traits that go into making up normal personality are as pungent—that is, as marked by a degree of piquancy or "character"—as the traits that go into making up abnormal personality, the personality traits of normal individuals tend to be more adaptive than the personality traits of those individuals who are abnormal. An example of an adaptive personality trait might be ambitiousness, and an example of a maladaptive personality trait might be overambitiousness.

Depending on content and context, the same trait can be either adaptive or maladaptive. The personality trait of *adaptive* evasiveness is illustrated by the behavior of the familiar political figure who evades one question by answering another. When asked, "When is this war we are in going to be over?" he might answer, "We have to persevere and pursue the enemy for as long as it takes to win." Thus he ducks by answering not the question he was asked but instead the somewhat related question: "Should we give up now or persevere and fight to the end?" In contrast, the personality trait of *maladaptive* evasiveness is illustrated by the behavior of the individual recently at the center of a widely publicized scandal who was punished not for his actual misdeeds but for lying about them to the government.

In the realm of how traits are *combined*, in personality style, as compared to personality disorder, the traits, though pungent, are somewhat muted by the way they are strung together, embedded as they are in a significant amount of benign, neutral, inactive matrix. One might say that they are combined with a good deal of interstitial grout, anastomosed into a composition that contains a great deal of bland, inert filler that dilutes and softens even the "bad" traits, making them less objectionable and resulting in a less than rock-solid presentation.

While there are significant differences between personality style and mental illness, and while individuals with a distinct personality style are not by our usual standards suffering from an emotional disorder, there is something to be gained by viewing individuals with a distinct personality style as if they were "mentally ill." The illness model of emotional difficulty offers us the opportunity of judiciously selecting and employing here, with normal (though difficult) individuals, many of the psychological and social remedies we use elsewhere—when we are dealing with true emotional disorder. We now have a scientific method for managing the troubles that can and do arise from the operation of normal personality, both in ourselves and in our normal, though problematical, fellows.

Seminormal Personality

Statistically speaking, few individuals look or are markedly abnormal. The vast majority of the "abnormal" individuals whom we run across in our daily lives suffer from mild psychopathology, making them "seminormal." In the case of psychopaths, seminormal or mild psychopaths have to be differentiated from normal individuals who are, like most of us, "merely somewhat morally challenged," and from individuals suffering from severe psychopathy, who have a diagnosable "Antisocial Personality Disorder." Millon gives the name aggressive personality nonantisocial type[27] to a category of individuals who closely resemble what I call mild, e.g., seminormal, psychopathic individuals. Hare refers to mild (seminormal) psychopaths as "white-collar psychopaths"[28] and speaks of "subcriminal psychopaths"[29] and "successful psychopaths."[30] Stout speaks of the sociopaths next door.[31] Robert I. Simon might call my mild psychopaths "passive psychopaths [individuals who] tend to be parasitic and exploitative of others [unlike the] aggressive psychopaths [who] commit major crimes."[32]

In seminormal psychopaths the past manifestations of the disorder, while overt, were attenuated—that is, qualitatively mild and quantitatively partial. Thus, speaking of the past manifestations of Antisocial Personality Disorder, the *DSM-IV* suggests that as adolescents, adults diagnosed with an Antisocial Personality Disorder routinely showed signs and symptoms of a "Conduct Disorder with onset before age 15 years."[33] But while adult seminormal psychopaths may as adolescents have been dishonest girls and boys who lied, cheated, and stole, they were probably not recklessly impulsive truants who ran away from home, serious brats who regularly acted in an intimidating, aggressive, and physically hurtful manner, devilish fire-setters, serious bed-wetters, or sadists who relished hurting and maiming animals. If they were arrested it was more likely to be for misdemeanors than for felonies, and if they were punished they were more likely given community service and a fine instead of jail time.

In the seminormal, the personality traits are mostly negative and maladaptive, as are the defenses used. For example, seminormals tend to favor aggressiveness over kindness, and projection over sublimation. This rule, however, has exceptions, notably the fact that being excessively clean can occur as often as being excessively dirty.

Structurally, these individuals use multiple defenses that result in multiple maladaptive traits. In turn, the multiple defenses and the multiple maladaptive traits that consequently prevail in these individuals tend to coexist, and coalesce, based on conceptual and behavioral similarities. For example, in the seminormal psychopath, narcissism has an affinity for and so coalesces with rabid acquisitiveness, and aggressiveness coalesces with rebelliousness. Sometimes the different traits coalesce via learning, especially the negative kind of learning exemplified by the psychopath who discovers at random that throwing garbage in front of his house (the trait of soiling) goes nicely with his wish to upset his neighbors (the traits of aggressivity, rebellion, and sadism).

Overall, seminormal individuals are rarely what we think of as "salt of the earth" people. They may have almost as many difficulties as those people we officially recognize as disordered. Negative thoughts and behaviors such as selfishness prevail over such positive ones as caution, honesty, and altruism. They do make waves, ruffle feathers, and call significant attention to themselves. However, their difficulties, for one reason or another, are undeveloped or otherwise held in abeyance to the point that they fail to develop into a true full pathological personality disorder. As a result their disorder is less chronic, unremitting, immutable, pervasive, and troublesome both to themselves and to society. This is because they:

- Retain some capacity to feel love and to display such derivatives of love as pity and altruism. "Loving" others typically kicks in at the last minute to slow the pathological process down a bit and keep it from taking over completely. For example, these individuals begin to feel sorry for those they are about to hurt, and so go a bit easy on them.

- Retain some capacity to feel guilt. For example, they might apologize to those they have wronged, even though their apologies have no practical effect on their subsequent behavior.

- Tend to display fewer than three of the *DSM-IV's* defining characteristics.[34] Sometimes they only display two, and even only one. For example, they are deceitful and aggressive, but not impulsive, reckless, irresponsible, or thoroughly lacking in remorse. Unfortunately, as we shall see, they sometimes come to represent social norms instead of failing to conform to them.

- Consciously or unconsciously pick and choose only the less objectionable and dangerous traits and defenses found in the related major, objectionable, and dangerous disorder. For example, they con more than they stalk, and they use the defenses of rationalization and denial more than they use the defense of projection.

- Are less single-minded about their use of defensive character mechanisms than patients with a true "pathological personality disorder." Indeed, they tend not to use one mechanism exclusively and resolutely, but to use several mechanisms, and different mechanisms that mostly pertain to different personality disorders, simultaneously. Since they almost certainly use at least two mechanisms at once, it is unusual for them to exhibit characteristics of fewer than two personality problems at any given moment, and they often exhibit more. For example, in seminormal psychopaths, paranoia, histrionic behavior, narcissism, impulse disorder, and addiction are often associated with the primary antisocial psychopathology.

- Use major mechanisms discontinuously, making their deviant behavior somewhat less than persistent and repetitive. One episode might subside long before another appears. One year a seminormal psychopath cheated on his final exam. Later in life he cheated at cards, later on his taxes, and later still on his wife, so that the individual pathological traits, even though maladaptive in and of themselves, did not completely deform, distort, and usurp his entire personality by becoming regular and predictable features of his behavior.

- Display pathological traits selectively in some areas but not in others, with the result that their disorder is not characterized by a full diathesis. Their problems only show in certain facets of their thought and behavior and are limited to certain arenas, and to only one or two parameters of functionality. For example, one seminormal psychopath stole from work in order to better provide for his wife and children at home, making him an embezzler who was, however, also a loving husband and father. His psychopathy was selective because he was especially "social" in every area but the one in which he was "especially antisocial."

- Manage to turn, or "sublimate," a maladaptive trait such as cheating into an adaptive trait such as getting ahead—whatever the means—and winning—whatever the method. Indeed, when it comes to seminormal psychopathy, being successful may be as much the rule as the exception. Successful seminormal psychopathic individuals function effectively and creatively within the mainstream, but they do so in a clearly psychopathic mode.

- Have a disorder that is reactive—that is, is a more or less transient response to external, often traumatic, life events. Included here are those seminormal psychopaths who loot not for fun and excitement or because they are so insatiable that they have enough of everything but want more, but because they have little to eat. In such cases the psychopathic symptoms can be transient and subside with an improvement in circumstances.

- Have some control over the pathological self to the extent that they can keep their worst aspects from emerging and taking over the personality completely and destructively. For example, a seminormal psychopath whose professed goal was to be more like a saprophyte than a parasite, used people for nefarious ends but deliberately steered clear of harming them seriously or fatally. He cheated on his expense account at work and embezzled from his company, but stopped short of draining his company dry, though he could easily have done so. In his interpersonal relationships he was narcissistic and lacked empathy, but he carefully avoided destroying these relationships completely. Instead he deliberately maintained them—but only in order to manipulate them.

- Sometimes undergo a positive change when they are caught in wrongdoing or when their schemes fail. While they rarely admit to being bad people who have sinned and need to be forgiven, they will at times, and without batting an eye, simply change course, as did the individual who when caught in a criminal act fled to private life with the declared intention of writing a book about his experiences.

My discussion next turns from the *psychopathology* of everyday life to a discussion of the basic characteristics of *psychopathy* (Antisocial Personality Disorder; Psychopathic Personality Disorder; or Sociopathy), whether mild, moderate, or severe in degree.

PSYCHOPATHY

There are two general ways to define psychopathy. One can define it according to its core characteristics:

- *dynamically* in terms of a relative or absolute absence of anxiety and guilt and an inability to experience remorse;
- *interpersonally* as an incapacity for feeling empathy and an inability to be altruistic, and an absence of clear and understandable human motivation;
- *cognitively* in terms of the individual's illogical thinking: for example, the belief that "what I want is what I should have."

There are at least two advantages to defining psychopathy according to its core characteristics. First, this way one can generally avoid making value judgments, and second, one does not have to rely solely on measuring deviation from social norms, which are rarely standardized and are mostly elusive. One serious disadvantage involves the difficulty of achieving interrater agreement about dynamic, interpersonal, and cognitive criteria. Another serious disadvantage, according to Heidi Hansen, is that the psychologist's "tendency to focus on drives and conflicts"[35] is inappropriate in these cases, for, as she sees it, psychopaths are best viewed as individuals with "defects,"[36] that is, theirs is a problem not of presences but of absences, a concept well expressed in the biblical: "for they know not what they do."[37]

Alternatively, one can, as does the *DSM-IV,*[38] define psychopathy *behaviorally*, in action-oriented terms imbued with concepts of social deviance. Behavioral constructs emphasize maladaptive actions such as unpredictability, impulsivity, irresponsibility, ruthlessness, and criminality. The major advantage of defining psychopathy according to behavioral rather than dynamic criteria is that interrater reliability is greater, for it is easier to agree about what constitutes criminality than it is to agree about what constitutes true empathy and altruism. However, there are several disadvantages to using strictly behavioral criteria. They tend not to go to the heart of the matter, they tempt the making of value judgments, and they are highly dependent on social standards that vary both from society to society and within one society, leaving us without a fixed platform in space from which to measure deviation: bad from good, acceptable from unacceptable, social from antisocial. Who is the psychopath: the individual who sneaks across the border through the desert to get into the United States illegally, the posse patrolling the borders and mercilessly hunting down and shooting trespassers, or the person who in defiance of the law puts water out so that the "illegal immigrants" don't die of thirst in the hot sun? Who is the psychopath—the gang member in a crime-ridden neighborhood, or the person who refuses to go along with the gang in power and join in? As bizarre as it sounds, in Nazi Germany the SS guards would not, strictly speaking, be the psychopaths. The psychopaths would be the people who in defiance of official regime policy tried to save the Jews. For most teen-agers, and in the teen-age societies that they and some of their adult compatriots form, being countercultural is not a problem but a goal. Certainly the *DSM-IV* "disregard for and violation of the rights of others"[39] is an awkward criterion considering how greatly culturally dependent rights happen to be. Thus, in a totalitarian collectivistic society it is not antisocial but prosocial to deprive others of the right to speak freely, and those who insist on demanding that right in such a place are the ones most likely to be branded as psychopathic enemies of the state and locked up. Today the Boston Tea Party would, strictly speaking, epitomize antiauthoritarian sociopathic acting-out, and it is ironic that according to legend the repressive Russian dictator Joseph Stalin considered not himself but the modernistic nose-thumbing brilliant composer Dimitri Shostakovich to be the psychopath!

Another serious problem associated with defining psychopathy behaviorally is that behavioral definitions tempt the emphasis of the negative over the positive features of a disorder, for example, psychopathic criminality over psychopathic cleverness. Yet the core personality characteristics of psychopathy do not necessarily result in negative behaviors but rather can lead to positive behavior. For example, the psychopath's lack of guilt can spin off either negative lying, cheating, and stealing, or socially valuable ambitiousness and extreme productivity. Thus the socially valued behavior of the doctor who speaks euphemistically (that is, who lies) in order to put a good face on a bad prognosis is in a way just as psychopathic as the socially destructive behavior of the quack healer who uses sophistic skills to sell the public an entirely worthless nostrum. Clearly, not all aspects of a personality disorder, or even the personality disorder itself, are self-destructive and maladaptive. Personality disorder has its beneficial side. Therefore, the concept of positive psychopathy does not actually challenge our basic concept of what it means to have a disordered personality.

In turn, it is not surprising that many people who are accounted successful, e. g., in business, are actually suffering from what can be termed "temporally effective" psychopathy—one in which well-defined sadistic and amoral elements are efficiently controlled because otherwise they could compromise everything that has been gained. When psychopathy is harnessed this way for the appropriate service of self in a socially useful activity, it begins to look more like a virtue than a vice, to the point that many of us wish that we were more psychopathic than we already are. Conversely, we all sometimes need to think and act a bit like a psychopath, for not being a little psychopathic can constitute an impediment that makes it hard to protect our well-being and get ahead in the world. Not being able to tell a white lie to spare others' feelings, or to save our own skins when we are cornered, can, after all, be detrimental to our ability to function effectively—personally, socially, professionally, and politically. It is not surprising, then, that many of us secretly identify with psychopaths and admire and want to become like them. At least in our dreams, we find ourselves enjoying being ruthless and hard-hearted. As we see it, with fewer scruples holding us back we could reach the highest pinnacles of achievement. We could get more and win bigger and better by being less guilty. Thoroughly rid of our inhibiting scruples and completely unfettered by retrospective or prospective angst, we would remain totally unconcerned about matters of wrongdoing, and so be free to victimize others, and to do so if not with impunity then at least with little or no regret.

Examples of positive psychopathy in our society include the pleasant, harmless, acceptable, even "fun" psychopathy of Fritz Kreisler, the violinist and composer who wrote music in the old style and then, rather than attributing it to his own hand, said he had found it, and that of the composer Charles Ives, who, otherwise not obviously psychopathic, may have backdated his compositions to make them seem more avant-garde. Less acceptable but still within the realm of what is generally tolerated in our society is the psychopathy of the realtor who becomes rich and successful by selectively underplaying the flaws of sub-par properties in order to inflate their price. For example, in calculating the amount of income a small apartment complex brings in, this realtor simply "forgets" to say that one of the tenants is a nun who pays considerably less than market value rent, has a lifetime lease, and has no plans to leave. Many successful salespeople can point to their psychopathic ability as one important reason for their success. This was the case for a patient of mine, a life insurance salesman, someone who had previously signed himself into a mental hospital just to beat a drug rap. During treatment with me he tried to take out a life insurance policy on *my* life to protect his investment in *his* therapy in case *I* died or was killed—a clever, though self-serving and, for me at least, potentially dangerous idea, but one that illustrates the close relationship that often exists between narcissism, psychopathy, and creativity.

A final disadvantage of using behavioral criteria to define psychopathy is that psychopaths well know how to hide their psychopathic behavior. After all, these are individuals who are famously untruthful. In particular they know how to manipulate mental health professionals, and the entire system, to create the impression that they behave well, or, if they behave badly, that their bad behavior is justified by their circumstances.

After discussing first normal and psychopathological personality and then psychopathy in a general way, I go on to focus my discussion on the subject of this text: mild psychopathy—the psychopathy of everyday life.

THE PSYCHOPATHY OF EVERYDAY LIFE

The psychopaths of everyday life are among the forgotten people of psychopathology. These are the individuals who appear to the casual observer to be upright, honest citizens whose reputations are "merely" marred by a touch of dishonesty. To paraphrase J.C. Prichard as quoted by Millon, Erik Simonsen, and Morten Birket-Smith, their "power of self-government is [not] lost or greatly impaired [because they are still capable of] conducting [themselves] with decency and propriety in the business of life."[40] Yet in "the moral or active principles of the mind [they are still] strangely perverted or depraved."[41]

Mild psychopathy might be said to stand in the same relationship to major psychopathy (Antisocial Personality Disorder) as Obsessive Compulsive Personality Disorder stands in relationship to Obsessive Compulsive Neurosis—a dilute, partial, attenuated, subclinical, transient variant of the severe form, with essentially the same content presented in a new, different, less intense, and less pervasive style, and—in the society in which we live—as likely to be prosocial as antisocial.

Mild psychopaths can be differentiated from patients suffering from Antisocial Personality Disorder as follows:

Patients with an Antisocial Personality Disorder:

- Resemble hardened criminals. Their crimes often involve direct aggressive acts toward individuals and may even go beyond committing mayhem to committing murder. *In contrast,* mild psychopaths are more like ordinary schemers and conners. Their crimes tend to fall into the gray area of criminality, such as the "crimes" of opportunity of ad writers who speak partial truths that effectively mask whole falsehoods, emphasizing the positive and eliminating the negative to sell a nearly worthless product—quite possibly stealing more from an unsuspecting and gullible public than the armed robbers of this world collectively take from banks, or than the crooked CEOs of the business world collectively steal from their companies.

- Are commonly found in jail or in forensic psychiatry units. *In contrast*, mild psychopaths are more likely to be found either "on the streets" or in the courts, and to be given suspended sentences or sentenced to community service. If they go to jail, it is often because they miscalculated or experienced a run of very bad luck.

- Mostly lack discernible anxiety, are short on empathy, and are incapable of feeling guilt or remorse, either at the time or after the fact. When convicted of a crime, they do not even try to fake guilt or remorse because they lack the ability to know what these emotions feel like and cannot even play-act them. *In contrast*, mild psychopaths often become somewhat anxious, are capable of feeling some guilt and remorse, and retain some ability to empathize. In court mild psychopaths have enough residual empathy and ability to feel guilt and remorse to be able to apologize to the people they hurt—although they usually do so less because they really mean it, and more because they are out to get a shorter sentence.

- Tend to be extremely impulsive, now-oriented individuals. *In contrast*, mild psychopaths are often quietly and resolutely calculating, and desire and retain the ability to think about the future and plan ahead.

- Completely lack loyalty. *In contrast*, mild psychopaths often retain a sense of loyalty to select groups—the familiar "honor among thieves."

- Tend to be completely oblivious to feedback, without audience sensitivity or much, if any, concern about the effects of their actions on others—all part of an overall tendency to show poor conditionability. In contrast, one can often approach, get through to, and influence mild psychopaths, at least to an extent. While they could care more, it is not entirely true that they couldn't care less.

- Hurt people for the sheer fun of it. *In contrast*, mild psychopaths often hurt people as much for profit as for fun. They are more opportunistic than purely sadistic. They may enjoy making their victims writhe, but they also enjoy making themselves rich. [An important caveat, as the *DSM-IV* notes, is that "Antisocial Personality Disorder must be distinguished from criminal behavior undertaken for gain that is not accompanied by the personality features characteristic of this disorder."[42] Thus while a psychopath is likely to be an opportunistic crook, an opportunistic crook would not necessarily be a psychopath. (The *DSM-IV* suggests diagnosing the likes of the opportunistic thief as an individual with Adult Antisocial Behavior.[43])]

- Often show little or no improvement as they get older. *In contrast*, mild psychopaths may, and often do, grow up and out of their psychopathy. They frequently have an epiphany later in life and suddenly and seemingly inexplicably begin to feel guilt and remorse for their past actions, even to the point that they actually achieve a measure of reform. This rule also has its exceptions, for serious psychopaths can improve and mild psychopaths can stay the same or get worse. As an example of the latter (taken from the behavior of someone who may very well not have been a psychopath) I cite the "mere" antics of Truman Capote's youth (he allegedly impersonated an editor at the *New Yorker* when he was just a copy boy). These antics seem to have hardened into a serious mistreatment of his best friends, whom he offended and badly hurt by criticizing and exposing them—for what appears to have been a combination of professional and personal gain, and possibly even just to have some great immoral fun at their expense.

- Produce mainly negative responses in us. We invariably dislike, refuse to tolerate, and are afraid of them. *In contrast*, we (too often) tolerate, embrace, and even love the mild psychopath, taking him or her into our hearts and homes— one reason why we call these individuals "confidence men"—and view them not as infrahuman but as superior life forms.

- Often live as outsiders in society. *In contrast*, mild psychopaths are often "insiders," in many senses of the term, including in the sense conveyed by the use of the term "insider trading." Instead of completely removing themselves from people and society, mild psychopaths keep close relationships going with others, but mainly so that they can manipulate them for their own ends. We might say that while patients with Antisocial Personality Disorder, as well as all serious psychopaths, remind us of (dangerous) outlaws, mild psychopaths remind us of (troublesome) in-laws. That is, they are less like hard-core criminals and more like those difficult people we all know who live among us, those who spit on the floor, throw apple cores out of the window of a moving car, blast their horns at drivers who do not get moving when the light changes, turn up their personal stereos on public conveyances, yell into their cell phones calculatedly oblivious to the discomfort of others around them, rev up their motorcycles at night in quiet residential neighborhoods, or put their dogs to sleep because they bark too much. Here is a typical difficult behavior of a mild psychopath. A man breaks into a line of people waiting to check their coats. When his wife reminds him, "There is a line," he retorts, totally oblivious to her concerns or the feelings of the others he has cut off, "I know. I'm on it."

- When caught and exposed make things worse for themselves by becoming reflexively angry, vindictive, and confrontational. *In contrast*, mild psychopaths seem to know how to avoid being caught, or when caught in the act and chastised and punished know just what to do to get out of a difficult spot. For example, instead of becoming angry, they become reflexively more ingratiating.

Mild psychopaths are not, however, completely benign. Behaviors characteristic of those with an Antisocial Personality Disorder, such as selling drugs to children or joining murderous gangs, are not entirely unknown in the mild psychopath, and under some circumstances mild psychopaths can even find themselves admitted to mental hospitals. Mild psychopaths are rarely extremely violent and usually do not maim or kill with knives and guns, but they can, and often do, murder people, although they mostly do so indirectly. For example, they might skim money off a building project, putting up a structure that ultimately collapses and injures or kills its occupants. This could have been the outcome when one builder erected a high-rise structure over inadequate pilings. He then went bankrupt, leaving behind a skeleton that another builder tried to salvage but at the last minute found he could not. Instead, to his surprise, chagrin, and great expense, he discovered that he had to demolish the structure completely.

Mild psychopaths can certainly be destructive in epidemic proportions. As con artists and confidence "men" they can fool, mulct, and even destroy the lives of many, many people. In the ranks of the widely destructive, we find our usual suspects: the ad writer who fleeced hoards by touting the superiority of one aspirin over another based on an elusive purity falsely claimed to be exclusive, but doing so in terms carefully calculated not to break the law; the ad writer who convinced the poor to overspend during a discount sale by persuading them that they would save more if they spent more; and the ad writer who compromised many people's eyesight by touting a cure for nearsightedness, representing as scientific truth the flawed hypothesis that glasses never cured anyone's eyesight and invariably cause myopia in people who wear them. The ad urged people to throw away their dangerous glasses and learn how to see better without them—for a price. Belonging here, too, are the actions of politicians who ultimately harm us all by destroying perfectly good opposition candidates with attack ads that make victims not only of their opponents but also of the truth; reporters and book reviewers who destroy reputations by omitting facts that might save or enhance them; realtors who steal other realtors' exclusive listings then offer customers cut-rate commissions to switch to them; crooked telemarketers who con and intimidate people into buying worthless products; Internet phishers who empty bank accounts and steal identities; shady corporate CEOs who fake balance sheets to artificially enhance the value of their stock; office workers who regularly call in sick when well, rationalizing their behavior as "taking a mental health day," and cheat on their time cards by leaving early then getting someone else to sign out for them, as well as office workers who steal large amounts of office supplies and then sell them on eBay; and used car salesmen who turn back the odometer, or sell cars that have been in a wreck or flood without mentioning this information .

However unfortunate, a certain amount of psychopathic opportunism, greed, distortion of reality, bullying, and cheating must be taken for granted in the world. Even the most "normal" individuals among us have some mildly psychopathic traits. This is because, to some extent, we "all" use psychopathic methods to cope, achieve, and succeed. All of us have the potential to be aggressive when that suits our purposes, and all of us have a lax enough conscience structure to make us, when that suits our purposes, selectively morally reprehensible—selfish, unloving, and unempathic, at will, and free from guilt. All of us can be unreliable when we see an opportunity to feed ourselves a little forbidden pleasure or to go for ill-gotten gain. All of us can be much too willing to compromise our ideals, for, as they say, "every person has his price." However, though we can all become at least somewhat evasive, tricky, and dishonest when the lure and prospect of instant gratification looms, some of us, the normals and milder psychopaths among us, recognize and control our potential for deviltry better than others. Either a compulsive morality kicks in to set limits on how evil we permit ourselves to be, or our better judgment kicks in and we watch what we do—simply because we are afraid of getting caught.

CHAPTER 3

Behavioral Manifestations

The behavioral manifestations of psychopathy generally offer the first diagnostic indication that the disorder exists in both its mild and severe forms. However, none of the behaviors described below, when taken individually or even together, are by themselves indicative of the existence of psychopathy. This is because:

First, we may only diagnose psychopathy when, as George E. Vaillant and J. Christopher Perry state, the behavior "involves many areas."[1]

Second, almost any given behavior has a differential diagnosis. Therefore, it is quite possible to act in what appears to be a psychopathic fashion without actually being psychopathic. What looks at first to be a psychopathic personality trait may on closer inspection turn out to be a manifestation of an entirely different problem. As mentioned throughout, many people are opportunists without being psychopaths. A dishonest homeowner told potential buyers that the black wall in the basement of a house he was trying to sell was the result not of the mold that was in fact creating it but of a bad paint job. Parsimony requires that before we think of him as a psychopath (rather than as little more than a dishonest salesman) we obtain more information about his psychological history, his inner life, and his interpersonal relationships.

Third, all, or almost all, of the personality traits I label as psychopathic occur in normals. Some can be manifestations of health rather than of illness.

Fourth, the significance of any given behavior depends on the nature of the society in which the individual in question lives. Therefore we must always heed the *DSM-IV* caution: "in assessing antisocial traits, it is helpful for the clinician to consider the social and economic context in which the behaviors occur."[2]

Fifth, the essence of a given behavior depends on more than its descriptive elements. It also depends on its core characteristics, such as the motivation for the behavior, the presence or absence of specific types of disturbed thinking behind it, and the overall quality of the individual's object relationships both within and outside of the power area. (I describe these criteria in Chapter 6). Within the realm of motivation, it is one thing for a doctor to lie about a patient's prognosis in order to push unnecessary expensive treatments, and quite another for a doctor to lie about a patient's prognosis in order to be able to keep secret that the patient is about to die. A store manager can put too high a price on a product either by mistake or because he is out to mulct the public. A man was not being psychopathic when he conned his mother-in-law into being on time by telling her to arrive one hour before he actually wanted her to be there. She forced him into this (little) lie, for she was a passive-aggressive person, and the more he pleaded with her to be prompt, the later she came.

All the behaviors I focus on in this chapter fall far short of rape and mass murder. I am concerned here not with the behaviors of the likes of Ted Bundy or Adolf Hitler but with the behaviors of smooth and shady operators "disguised" as "normal citizens." These individuals range from criminal types such as bunko operators and con artists who sell snake oil, to minor criminals such as the woman I recently saw at a salad bar in a supermarket ladling a very large scoop of a very costly appetizer into a plastic container provided for takeout, then proceeding to eat it with her fingers until it was gone. I then overheard her explaining her behavior away not as stealing but as sampling—in preparation for a possible purchase, but one that she clearly never intended to make. The behaviors I describe may not be of those individuals who operate outside of or even in the gray area of the law, but of those individuals who operate legally but immorally. The latter range from the crusading columnist who disguises personal vendettas as just and valid causes for all to espouse to the successful politician who makes it to the top by being a vicious competitor, drawing inspiration from a quote by the erstwhile bodybuilder-turned-politician Arnold Schwarzenegger, one I found on a poster displaying not only his brawn but also his brain: "My instinct was to win, eliminate anyone who is in competition, destroy my enemy, and move on without any kind of hesitation at all."[3]

APPEARANCE

It is both unrealistic and dangerous to assume that psychopaths will advertise their true nature in their appearance. There is no single characteristic look for either mild or severe psychopaths, and certainly only a few fit the popular stereotypes of jailbirds, multiple parolees, or specimens of picturesque riffraff from the boondocks—men with bad teeth and tattoos emerging from obscenely emblazoned T-shirts; individuals who look as if they have just come from a falling-down shack strewn with empty beer cans; lounge lizards; old-time porno stars with hair parted in the middle over a handlebar mustache; or women who are street-corner temptresses with short, tight skirts and too much cheap makeup.

These types fit only one milieu, and such descriptions rarely characterize successful psychopaths. In fact, successful psychopaths often look appealing and have a great deal of superficial charm—an asset for anybody who chooses to live by first impressions. Successful psychopaths dress and groom in accordance with the kind of influence they wish to have on people, and the kind of people they want to influence. The psychopath trying to pass as an honest stockbroker will look like a stockbroker, not like a paste-up of lowlife. The psychopath wanting to hide out and the psychopath wishing to maintain an air of mystery will not necessarily display a marked fondness for sunglasses. Recently two doctors received the worst kind of publicity when they were suspended from practice for falsifying their credentials and for other fraudulent abuses in connection with prescribing drugs and participating in Medicare. One was inclined toward chinos and open-collared shirts and wore a large caduceus on a thick heavy chain damping down the abundant hair on his chest. The other went in for pin-striped suits and an attaché case. Many savvy psychopaths are inclined toward an elegant simplicity meant to obscure the true, often complex, nature of their motivations. This was the case for the woman attempting to fake business credentials. She avoided calling attention to herself by wearing her hair straight, donning a simple hat, and dressing in a superficially featureless but in fact highly styled suit.

A trademark of some psychopaths is to be found not in the particular style of dress and grooming that they adopt but in the impression they convey of time and trouble expended on their appearance. (Considerable allowance must, of course, be made in evaluating the appearance of actors and certain other professionals constantly in the public view.) For example, hustler types often not only use, but overuse, makeup, with both sexes much given to primping and mirror glancing. After a certain age the stigmata of prior plastic surgery may be seen. In the later stages of psychopathy, a rapid deterioration in appearance resulting from surrender to physical appetites is not uncommon. Some individuals become obese and display the familiar signs of heavy alcohol use or drug abuse. In the subtropics, leathery wrinkled skin may be a clue to the fact that one is dealing with a psychopath aptly characterized as a "beach-bum type."

SPEECH

Psychopathic individuals are often voluble, not because they are suffering from a bipolar disorder and are on an emotional high; not because they are so depressed that they talk compulsively in order to get all the poison out of their systems; not because they are so obsessional that they need to include every little detail of what they are thinking about in what they say; and not because they are so anxious that they just cannot stop talking; but because as shysters, hucksters, and con men and women from all walks of life—crooked lawyers, shady politicians, cheating CEOs, and faith healers, among others—they talk fast and smooth as part of their predatory natures. Their fast smooth-talking arises from the belief that if their speech is seamless there will be no cracks through which their lies can be detected. As part of the belief that offense is the best defense, they figuratively machine-gun others verbally in order to intimidate them effectively. As part of their attempt to complicate an issue in the hope that they can thus confound their detractors—they flood them with so much information that they become confused to the point that they lose focus and can no longer think of an effective comeback or adequately mount any other form of self-defense.

Sometimes psychopaths misuse words. But unlike the schizophrenic who often uses neologisms, the psychopath often uses malapropisms—a sign that he or she is attempting to feign being an intellectual or an expert, but falling short. For example, one psychopath failed in her attempt to appear sophisticated because she erroneously Anglicized the pronunciation of the French word "rendezvous."

Many psychopaths favor the use of hyperbole, which they particularly like to employ in order to manipulate others. We are all familiar with how psychopaths exaggerate their pain and suffering when attempting to get a monetary reward. At trial they can outdo the most theatrical of individuals in their attempts to impress and stun the judge and jury into believing and pitying them—and, when applicable, offering them the largest possible settlement or shortest possible sentence. While a nonpsychopath wanting to appeal a court verdict that went against her might say, "I was shocked," the psychopath, out for sympathy and seeking a retrial, might not be content with anything less than "When it came to the outcome of my trial, I was outraged, dismayed, utterly shattered, and totally horrified."

Almost all of these individuals have a tendency to speak in what I call the *narcissistic* mode. They monologize, with the focus not on others but on themselves. They are the star and others are relegated to the background. They often overuse the first person singular, and refer to others in a belittling way as part of their attempt to enhance their image. However, when they are trying to manipulate others psychopaths may shift the focus onto others in order to act as if they are interested in them personally. Now they profess a polite concern for their listeners, but that does not go beyond meaningless small talk, perfunctory questions along the lines of "How are you doing?" or hollow unsubtle compliments, the latter really self-advertisements and statements of self-appreciation. For example, "You look great!" really means, "I had the good taste to associate with you," or (as one applauding opera lover admitted) "You sing great!" really means, "I had the good taste to be your fan." More artful individuals may tone down these practices, but few are able to conceal their egocentrism entirely.

Some psychopaths share with some individuals with Multiple Personality Disorder the tendency to alter their speech in order to fully develop a new identity. Others change how they speak in order to fit in, infiltrate, or control and influence a given group or social stratum. Depending on which group, there are four types, or styles, of psychopathic speech.

The first is the *normal or conformist*. Practitioners of this style wish either to go unnoticed or to fit in. Sometimes the only indication that they are fabricating is to be found in the movement of their hands, which pantomimes a message that is the opposite of the one they hope and plan to convey and gives away how they are deliberately falsifying their presentation.

The second is the *elegant/polished*. Practitioners of this style are characterized by a highfalutin vocabulary, diction, and tonality, with the last two often given a British flair. Many con artists develop this style of speech in order to convey, or obviously attempt to convey, superiority in character, abilities, and trustworthiness.

The third is the *demotic or popular*. Practitioners of this style aim at securing the confidence of the less educated. Their speech is crude and highly flavored, with the use of many terms current on the streets and in the underworld. Psychopathic politicians sometimes talk down to, really "down with," their followers, acting like "just one of the guys" or "a member of the masses" in order to gain the acceptance of their electorate.

The fourth is the *emotional*. Practitioners of this style make every effort to arouse others by an appeal not so much to their intelligence as to their feelings. Gifted individuals can do this by measured eloquence without special effects, but most practitioners of this style are show people. Their speech is marked by deliberate excess—exhortation, bombast, menace, pleading, etc., and by various artifices of manner using inflection, intonation, rhythm, and volume. These qualities are widely associated with the speech of political demagogues, but when suitably toned down they can be detected at every level of psychopathic interpersonal relations. Beggars, con artists, phony healers, and some used car salesmen are adept at this kind of speech, as are those religious leaders who use bombast or unctuousness in a manipulative fashion. Thus a noncredentialed preacher intending to sway a group made the tone, inflection, rhythm, and content of his speech sound in a way that he imagined to be sublime and holy. He opened his mouth wide in a shriek of passionate sincerity, raised his voice either "up to the heavens" or spoke as if what he was saying was coming down from them, purred softly to envelop those around him in a shared secret, spoke seductively so that he and his flock might rapturously merge, or gradually crescendoed in order to arouse his audience's heretofore suppressed sexual passion until it was climactically discharged in a burst of affirmative "amens." (As was true of this preacher, emotional speech like this is often combined with a degree of sincerity. This preacher was, like many such individuals, not simply bowing to the expectations of a flock known to respond better to "preacher-talk" than to ordinary everyday speech. He was also living up to a personal ideal and realizing his self-image, which in his case involved being a "messenger of God.")

BEHAVIOR

In the following discussion I try to distinguish strictly behavioral characteristics of psychopathy from the core manifestations of the disorder. However, as will soon become clear, such a distinction cannot always be made, or if made, often soon breaks down. For example, I have chosen to include certain aspects of aggressivity, like "demolishing others," with behavior, although behavioral aggressivity is clearly akin to the core psychopathic "interpersonal hostility." Therefore, some readers will find it useful to read Chapter 6 on core manifestations of psychopathy along with this chapter on characteristic superficial psychopathic behaviors.

Violation of the Rights of Others

Psychopaths are notorious for their serious disregard for and tendency to violate such rights of others as their rights to life, liberty, and happiness. However, at the same time, they characteristically believe that their own rights must remain inviolable. A favorite maneuver of psychopaths is to say something mean, hurtful, and aggressive and then, overlooking that others have a right to be treated kindly and with respect, claim their Constitutional right to say anything that happens to be on their mind. This is essentially true, but it is not the only point, for while they have virtually a full right to speak freely, they have only a limited right to speak wrongly and hurtfully. For example, consciously misquoting for purposes of character assassination is not fully protected by the Constitution. Nor is incompetence, for the right to freedom of speech does not cover a doctor's obligation to give correct advice. Here, failure to do so is called not "free speech" but "malpractice."

Failure to Conform to Age-Appropriate Social Norms

The "failure to conform to [age-appropriate] social norms" *(DSM-IV)*[4] consists in the main not of a failure to conform to *negative* but of a failure to conform to *positive* social norms. Psychopaths usually do not conform to the norms governing being a Good Samaritan, but they mostly do conform to the "norms" governing cheating on one's income taxes, or sending empty boxes out of state to save on sales tax. As emphasized throughout, this is an awkward criterion because norms vary from society to society; it does not make much sense to call someone mentally ill when he or she is in fact well because he or she is *not* conforming to the norms of a *sick* society.

Unreliability

Psychopathic individuals tend to be erratic, unpredictable, reckless, impulsive people unconcerned about the effects of their actions on others. For example, a victim of a psychopath became depressed when her new boyfriend cancelled out on her for July 4 weekend on July 3, leaving her nothing to do for the entire holiday. He did not care at all that she had turned down desirable invitations from others that could not be retrieved because by then all her friends had made other plans.

Impulsivity

Theirs is a lack of foresight based on a lack of forethought and a lack of desire or ability to plan ahead. If it feels good, they do it, and they do it now, unconcerned about the future consequences of their present hedonistic actions.

Treachery and Disloyalty

As treacherous individuals, psychopaths even give the lie to the expression "honor among thieves." Many have never had a monogamous relationship but have rather used their lovers, wives, and husbands sexually when they suited that purpose, then cheated on them when they wanted someone else, then cheated on the ones they were cheating with. They also typically justify their cheating along the lines of "everybody does it," or "he or she deserved it," or "I am being not disloyal, but seeking variety," or "I am only human," or, the cry of some highly promiscuous homosexuals, "Having a string of partners is the essence of being gay."

Many such individuals are disloyal not only to their mates but also to their friends—people whom they favor one day then, when they no longer find them useful, drop the next, entirely without guilt or remorse. They might ask their friends, "What have you done for me lately?" and then turn on and abandon anyone who has not been continuously forthcoming.

Also, and without giving it a second thought, they backbite or backstab anyone in order to ease their own way to the top. Here is how a college professor stabbed a musician in the back: This musician had entered a musical comedy contest open only to undergraduates. Though this was strictly an undergraduate competition, the music professor used his position of power to preempt the competition with a musical of his own, pushing out the student's entry and using as his excuse that the book was weak. The book was not nearly as weak as the professor's morality. It is especially ironic that the so-called "weak book" was written by a man who later on won a prize for another book—an Oscar for a screenplay he wrote for a famous movie.

Aggressivity

Both the following are true: Aggressive people tend toward being psychopaths, and psychopaths tend toward being aggressive people. Characteristic of aggressive psychopaths is their tendency to demolish people, which they do for several reasons. First, they are by nature hostile people in need of an outlet for their anger. They find getting their anger out intensely pleasurable, and they also like the feeling of superiority they get from being hurtful and full of disdain. I once asked an antiques store owner about a piece of furniture. "What is it?" I inquired, excited and curious. "It's a settle," he said. "How much is it?" I asked. His reply: "If you have to ask what it is, you can't afford to buy it." Second, they are out to manipulate people, and with this in mind seem to know that some people will do just about anything to please, and just about nothing to further antagonize, people who do not like them, willingly doing the bidding of the master in the (usually vain) hope that the master will come around to love the slave. Third, they demolish people as part of the process of blaming others for their own shortcomings. I once had a large painting installed in our apartment. A few days later the frame cracked, and it fell. When I reported this to the people who installed it, their reply was, "We always, always, do perfect work. Either you knocked it down yourself or your kids did it when you were away." Instead of feeling guilty when brought up short, the gay man discussed throughout this book who infected a host of strangers at sex clubs with AIDS called his victims stupid for not protecting themselves—from him.

Psychopaths become especially aggressive when crossed. A psychopathic patient asked me to falsely claim that his girlfriend was qualified to receive Social Security Disability benefits. When I, quite naturally, refused, he cursed me out, telling me, among other things, that I was an incompetent so-and-so. Then he refused to continue with me in therapy because that would mean having to "speak to me again."

Sometimes psychopathic aggressivity takes the form of setting people up on a one-to-one basis. For example, when one psychopath got angry with his social worker for refusing to make a personal date with him, he tried to ruin her, first by plausibly denying suicidal intent and then by making a gestural suicidal attempt in the hopes of getting her censured for malpractice. Another time he set her up by saying that he was too depressed to come to the clinic to get his medication. He pleaded with her to deliver antidepressants to him at home so that he could avoid having to make what he considered to be a long, difficult trip in to see the clinic psychiatrist. After smooth-talking the social worker into doing his bidding, he used the medication to make another gestural suicidal attempt. The crux of his actions was to create difficulty for both the social worker and the psychiatrist for ignoring clinic rules and behaving in an unprofessional manner.

At other times the setup involves triangulation used to hurt their enemies and defeat their rivals. For example, employing guerrilla tactics, they tell gossip Y that their hated rival Z was critical of their boss X, knowing that gossip Y will tell boss X what hated rival Z supposedly said about him, thus sealing Z's fate.

Behavior That Indicates an Apparent Lack of Anxiety, Guilt, and Remorse

Most observers state their belief that psychopathic individuals act as if they are unable to adequately experience anxiety, guilt, and remorse, and that seeming feelings of anxiety, guilt, and remorsefulness are a sham. However, other observers disagree. They cite the commonly found self-destructive tendencies seen in the psychopath and analyze these as signs of severe anxiety and guilt about being successful, leading to significant remorse, leading to massive self-punishment. These observers suggest that, far from being incapable of feeling anxiety and guilt, psychopaths feel these things deeply and poignantly. But they do not admit that they feel them, either to themselves or to others. Instead they hide them by covering them up—by acting out, either against themselves or against society; by "regressing," e.g., returning to a state of proclaimed infantile-like learned helplessness; or by denial, creating the familiar hypomanic "who cares" caste often associated with this disorder.

Sigmund Freud's paper "Criminality from a Sense of Guilt" describes individuals for whom guilt does not arise from a transgression, but for whom "the transgression [arises] from the sense of guilt . . . so that [bad] deeds are done precisely because they are forbidden, and because by carrying them out the doer enjoys a sense of mental relief [from] oppressive feelings of guilt . . . ."[5] Psychopaths so motivated are reminiscent of masochists who act out of a need for self-punishment. They look self-serving, but they are instead being deliberately, if unconsciously, self-destructive.

Some observers who note this paradox—that in psychopaths an apparent absence of anxiety and guilt lies side by side with anxiety and guilt that appear to be excessive—have suggested that these individuals are well characterized as having "superego lacunae"—figuratively, holes in the conscience—so that they might allow themselves seven years of good luck but then, much like Faust, make arrangements to "go to the devil." However, just because these individuals are self-destructive does not mean that they are guilty masochists. In an alternative interpretation, their ability to lie guilt-free is predictably a recipe for disaster given that, as the popular expression goes, "all lies have short legs."

The issue of lack of anxiety, guilt, and remorse as core difficulties is discussed further in Chapter 6.

Criminality

While not all criminals are psychopaths, all psychopaths are criminals—at least in the broadest sense of the term. Mild psychopaths' crimes fall far short of the serial murders of a Ted Bundy or David Berkowitz and the mass murders of Hitler and Stalin. Mild psychopaths commit crimes more of deceit than of violence and tend to confine their lawlessness to the gray area that exists between legality and illegality, operating as they do in the realm of contradictory laws and legal loopholes. They know how to bend a good law to justify their bad behavior, as when they claim, with some justification, that their bigoted actions are protected by the first Constitutional amendment. When they clearly break a law, they count on lax law enforcement to see them through and get them out of trouble.

Characteristic, too, is the reason they break the law in the first place. They typically do so both for practical and for emotional reasons—because they are hostile to the establishment and want to goof on it; because they are sadists who like to create suffering in innocent victims; and because they just want to prove to themselves once again that their elevated self-esteem is not irrational but justified by their above-average abilities and accomplishments.

Flamboyant Sexuality

Sexual wildness, including multiple marriages and divorces, is often part of the psychopathic picture. While some sexual wildness can be understood as hormonal in origin, as the product of overactive neurotransmitters, or as just ordinary philandering, some is symptomatic of psychopathy. This is particularly applicable to sex that is fantastic and grotesque, e.g., sex involving that form of triangulation where a man arranges to get caught having sex with his brother's wife. It also often applies to cheating on a partner where an abuse of trust is involved and sadistic pleasure is obtained from hurting someone who wants and has been led to expect a conventional monogamous relationship. In these cases the subterfuge is often as pleasurable as the sex, with much of the so-called fun arising from the cloak-and-dagger fear, and promise, of getting caught.

Of course, cheating is less psychopathic in those cultures where it is permitted or even valued. Some members of the gay (and straight) community consider promiscuity to be both normal and admirable scene behavior. As Pinsker notes (personal communication, 2004), many gay men are simply doing what many testosterone-driven males would do if freed of responsibility for perpetuating the species and given opportunities for non-committed sex in a way that simply isn't available for straights. However, gay scene behavior moves closer to becoming psychopathic when drugs such as methamphetamines are used, when the sexual relationships take place without much positive feeling for the other person, when there is an indiscriminate failure to discriminate between objects, and when there is a lack of sensitivity to others' needs, as manifested in a refusal to practice safe sex with no concern for the consequences of doing otherwise. According to Pinsker, as a growing concern about AIDS brings about significant change in the community's behavior, it becomes more reasonable to consider individual diagnosis in the risk takers, and psychopathy in particular in the risk donors.

Finally, psychopathic sex is often in great measure mainly a power play—a way to dominate people, ranging from employees to patients. Here the rush comes in great part from the triumphal maneuvering—getting, or forcing, another person to do one's bidding, turning a "no" into a "yes." The emotional raping that employs the telling of tall tales is an alerting sign here. For example, an older man regularly selected impoverished youths to impress into bed by telling them the lie that he was an important CEO who just happened to be looking to hire an assistant.

Psychopaths characteristically know how to justify their wild sexuality after the fact. They might attempt to normalize their cheating by blaming their spouse's inadequacy, e.g., by saying that anyone would look around when one's marital partner becomes too old to be attractive. They often convince themselves that they can be unfaithful sexually and still be loyal and loving personally. Many have their own self-serving definitions of what does and what does not constitute cheating. The ancient Romans believed that sex with a prostitute was not cheating. Just recently a boy of about 12 years old approached me at a bus stop in a tourist Mecca and asked me if I were with my wife. When I said nothing committal he continued on, trying to convince me to try a strip joint down the block—I guessed one with which his family was affiliated. When I finally protested that I was not interested, he pushed on, trying to convince me that going to a strip club was not only a good idea, it also did not in any way constitute cheating on my wife.

Hypocrisy

Psychopaths typically do not do what they say they are going to do. They instead make and break promises. They set down rules for others but do not follow them themselves. Belonging in this category are the for-the-record antigay legislator who turns out to be a closeted homosexual; the council member who lobbies for integration of disadvantaged youth into the public school system and then sends his own children to out-of-town private schools (because he secretly believes that only there can they get a good education and be protected from the criminal element); and the city council member who fights against gays being on the school board on moral grounds, while he is accepting under-the-table bribes from contractors in the form of a free roof in exchange for voting in favor of their projects before his planning board.

Manipulation

Psychopaths manipulate others in order to attain nutriment and power. In their manipulations they are indifferent to ethical and social restraints, and have no real attachment to their marks, so that when one does not provide them with what they want, they try another, then another, until they achieve their goals.

There are three types of manipulation—oral wheedling, anal controlling, and phallic seducing. Therefore, there are three types of manipulators.

Oral manipulators, or wheedlers. Central to this style of manipulation is a sense of narcissistic entitlement that forms the basis of extreme inappropriate expectations and leads to excessive demands along the lines of "my need is your command." The objective is predominantly nourishment, which may be sexual, material (the acquisition of money or property), or purely emotional (e.g., kindness, solicitude, and reassurance). When oral psychopaths seek nourishment, they can, like anal psychopaths, seek it through such crude forms of pressure as intimidation or stubbornness. More characteristically, they seek it through such subtle means as pleading, nonthreatening cajolery, and subterfuge. They often favor getting what they want by using loopholes in the law originally meant to protect innocent people in trouble. For example, as tenants they sign a long-term lease, declare bankruptcy, and then continue to live, rent-free, until the long eviction process can wind itself out. Often they coax the desired responses from others by an appeal to their better natures—to their altruism, compassion, and forbearance. Thus one alcoholic begging for money for drink regularly started his con by saying, "I am trying to reform . . ."— his way to get money for alcohol in the guise of asking for money for therapy. When their accustomed ruses fail, they often switch over to the guile of self-abasement—as in one (in fact well-heeled) beggar's: "Please, please help me out; I am just a poor suffering wretch."

Also belonging here are some squatters preempting privately held property and refusing to leave on the "unassailable" grounds of needing a place to live; and the opportunistic coffee shop owner discussed throughout who tried to beat her landlord out of rent owed by an appeal to the landlord's compassion. She stopped paying rent, even though she had plenty of money, but she convinced herself she needed to stash the money away "for emergencies." She should have felt guilty about stiffing her landlord. Instead, she first complained to him about all the dunning letters he was sending her demanding the rent, and then threw herself on his mercy. As she put it, "Just because I am a couple of months behind in my rent is no reason for you to continue to treat me like an animal."

A man approached me in the town in which I live, saying that he was a worker at a building project next door and that he had accidentally locked himself out. He said that because he had left his wallet and keys inside he needed money for a train ticket to get back to his house a few towns away, retrieve his spare keys, and return to pick up his things. He was so persuasive that I gave him some money for the train fare. I later discovered that his story was a lie and that he had told it, or a variant of it, tens of times to different people, many of whom, like me, felt sorry for him. Convinced that he was telling the truth, they also gave him handouts of a few dollars.

Some oral manipulators are full-time small-time swindlers. Included among these are the individuals who deliberately prolong their injuries (and may even deliberately incur them) not only to bring on the welcome attentions of doctors, family, or friends, but also to attract the welcome, and profitable, ministrations of trial lawyers. The big-time swindler can also be included in this category. One big-time swindler with a philanthropic bent stole millions from his business partners—just so that he could continue to get accustomed accolades for contributing large sums of money to science, and to have a room in a science museum named after him.

Oral manipulators who are simultaneously paranoid often use paranoid mechanisms to rationalize and be excused for their actions after the fact. Their prevailing cry is "It's not me, it's you." Caught with their hand in the cookie jar, they disavow personal responsibility and instead blame others for leaving the cookie jar where they can find it. For example, a woman who dumped lover after lover after finding someone else with more money and a better apartment would regularly deflect criticism and avoid taking responsibility for her hurtful behavior by putting the blame on her lovers, saying, "I left them because of what they did to me, and I can prove it, for they were so guilty about how they treated me that they didn't even try to get me back after I walked out on them."

When caught in criminal actions, paranoid manipulators conveniently blame authority. For example, a psychopathic patient claimed police brutality when in fact the police had only treated her harshly because she had tried to steal their police car. Later she went through a phase of life when she was so down on her luck personally and financially that she started begging in the subways. She told her marks that she needed money because she was pregnant and hungry and that there was no one she could turn to for help because what little official help was available was unacceptable. Here is what she omitted: She had trouble staying in shelters because she became abusive to the other residents when she was high on drugs. Childhood abuse, a broken home, racial profiling, and a malicious justice system certainly were a big part of her history and had their impact, but for this oral manipulative paranoid psychopath these had become easy excuses to justify her bad behavior. She blamed externals in order to avoid taking any responsibility for and suffering any guilt over her own actions. When it came to her complaints of child abuse, she was mostly blaming her parents for being abusive in order to deflect responsibility from herself for being a difficult child and an irresponsible adult. As such, her assessment of the effects of early abuse did not arise out of a search for truth. Rather, they arose out of her need to hand her parents the rap that she herself partly merited.

Anal manipulators, or controllers. These individuals have a modus operandi that is coercive and one whose objectives are power, control, and material supplies as obtained through such cruder forms of pressure as intimidation or stubbornness. The intimidation often involves making threats or bullying, often conveyed in authoritarian know-it-all proclamations advanced in the hope, often justified, that they can cow others into submission. Alternatively, they can be stubborn people who use muted, veiled, and subtle pressures with a passive-aggressive caste meant to wear others down until they stop fighting with them and eventually yield.

As predators they are particularly likely to rationalize their unilateral actions as provoked and therefore as consensual. For example, sexual predators might say, "She wanted it anyway, which is obvious because of the way she dressed seductively," or "I thought she wouldn't mind being forced into it; after all, she has a long history of promiscuity, so why stop before me?"

Machiavelli's *The Prince* can be viewed as a book on how to gain power and achieve success by being a psychopathic anal manipulator. While the introduction to the book calls the volume a "basic handbook of politics, statesmanship, and power . . . and a guide for efficient democratic government,"[6] to me it seems to be really a brilliant outline of the ageless anal game of how to win by playing dirty. *The Prince* is discussed further in Chapter 10.

Phallic manipulators use sexual allure for gain, ranging from landing a job to cajoling someone for sex. These individuals stress appearance—good looks, dress, grooming, social accomplishments, and, if men, such props as prestige automobiles, yachts, and other phallic symbols. In their catalog of desirable traits are handsomeness, beauty, and charm, all three of which outrank intellectual depth, creativity, and impeccable morality. The handsome con artist who preys on lonely older women and steals their money falls into this category. Also fitting the mold are good-looking gay hustler types who hook up with older men with money, exchanging sex, or perhaps at most the promise of sex, for lodging and other material things. A gay male hustler I once treated used his good looks to charm and his promises of undying love to convince an unending stream of older patrons that he loved them and wanted to spend the rest of his life with them. More than once he got them to give up their jobs and homes and run off with him, only to then suddenly tire of them without any real pretext. He would then leave them without notice—sometimes when they were thousands of miles away from what used to be their home. He did this not for practical reasons but because of all the fun he got out of "watching the faces of a bunch of suckers as they finally wised up to the fact that I was screwing them." He was able to repeat this stunt over and over because he kept a home base with an old lover, now his roommate, a man whom he could bamboozle into taking him back whenever he chose to return. The men he suckered, however, were not always so fortunate. Often they had no place to return to. Not a few of them were ruined financially, and one even attempted suicide.

These individuals are particularly persuasive when trying to smooth-talk their way out of being punished. They know how to convince a judge to go easy on them, or a parole officer to intervene on their behalf, often inappropriately. They spot and then select the therapist with the strongest rescue fantasies and seduce him or her into becoming their advocate and getting them off easy. Typically they con therapists into making unilateral decisions about punishment instead of leaving these up to a court of law. In one of my cases, with the aid of "psychiatric counsel" an identified thief with an annual six-figure income went free several times by pleading "irresistible impulse." Charges of computer fraud were shelved indefinitely because a psychiatric aide wrote to the prosecutor attesting that the individual's problem lay not in larcenous inclinations but in an obsessive fixation with numbers. This man had convinced the aide that he was responding to unconscious forces beyond his control when in fact he was mostly in it for the money. Many of these individuals know how to play even the most experienced mental health professionals exactly the way they want. It is completely within their capacity to skew their history, fake their mental status exam, and even put one over on supposedly fool-proof psychological tests in order to put on the mask of insanity and get into treatment when that suits them, or to put on the mask of sanity and be released from treatment when it suits their purposes.

They often rely on brinkmanship, bluffing just short of provoking a rebuff. The more successful psychopaths are equipped to deal with the consequences of losing the resulting gamble. The less successful psychopaths, given their narcissistic hypersensitivity to the untoward, fall apart and become at least transiently depressed due to being emotionally incapable of absorbing defeat.

Charming and Conning

Many psychopaths are charmers. As such they depend on the use of flattery and offers of friendship to enchant and hypnotize their marks, cobra-like, putting them into a state in which they readily relinquish responsibility for themselves and let others take over their lives more or less completely. A paradigm is the neighbor who turned on the charm, freely using the words "dear" and "love," and was everywhere to be found when she wanted to borrow some freezer space, only to suddenly become too busy to stop and talk when she no longer needed the extra room. A couple having their apartment redone, a half-year process, started speaking to their next-door neighbor for the first time in years so that they could butter him up in preparation for asking him if they could store their grand piano in his small apartment for the duration. When he refused, they pouted and whined that they would have no place to put their baby grand. They gave no consideration whatsoever to how he might feel about having a large piano occupying his small apartment for months on end. Just recently an editor eagerly sought a blurb from me for a client's book. He was all flattery and availability until I was forthcoming and it was too late to take my submission back. After that he stopped responding to my friendly e-mails and to date there has been nothing but complete silence from him.

Charmers often find their milieu in the world of the scam to become con artists. Con artists are among the most successful psychopaths of all. They are often creative, effective people who make their way to the top less through good luck than through the skills they have refined.

I ran across a man in the supermarket. He was receiving food stamps, which were not good for the cigarettes he wanted to purchase. So he asked me to buy him cigarettes with my cash and in exchange he would buy me my grocery items with his stamps. A worker in this country illegally manipulated his boss into marrying him so that he could get United States citizenship. This man had a mistress whom he also manipulated into waiting for him for the several years that it took to get his citizenship, when, as he promised, he would divorce his wife so that he could marry his mistress. A man used his ability to con to become a successful entertainer. This man advertised himself as a mind-reader, although he was just a magician. He would have the members of the audience sign in before the performance and would then use the personal information they gave out on the sign-in sheets to make himself look uncannily knowledgeable. When on stage he would wear an earphone and have a shill relay the previously obtained personal information to him by radio so that he could seem to be pulling facts about a complete stranger out of the air. In Coney Island many years ago, a man touted his act as one in which he risked his life to descend into a tank of water to bring up an octopus. That he did, and exactly as promised, only what he emerged with was a baby octopus, which also happened to be dead. For the climax of his act he said, in all seriousness, and with plenty of psychopathic chutzpah, "If this had been a big live one, my life could have been in real danger."

When asked about dates for finishing projects, a contractor simply made them up and persuasively strung people along, intending to keep not his promise but hope alive (and deposits in place). Then he blamed outside forces for the delay and offered new, equally implausible dates with other, firmer, equally made-up promises. His intention all along was to collect a substantial amount of deposit money from a number of marks in anticipation of running off to Canada before anyone could catch up with him. Unlike some other con artists who count on loopholes in the law to save them from the consequences of their illegal actions, this man relied heavily on how the cost of full justice was more than his victims would choose to pay or even be able to afford. One of my almost-publishers, a woman I knew personally from having done my residency with her, also relied upon the high cost of litigation to render herself judgment-proof. She told me my work was exemplary, but that it needed some editing. The editor she recommended to me was her friend, and the price of the editing significant. When the editing was complete, at a cost of many thousands of dollars and a year's worth of time, she turned down the book, even though I was under a contract with a no-escape clause. Later the editor, with whom I had now become friendly, confessed to me that right from the start the publisher never had any intention of publishing the book. Her real and only intention was to create business for her editor friend! A patient whose psychopathic personality disorder was the "talented author" of his neurosis used an easily manipulated and inexperienced student therapist to write letters on his behalf, knowing that letters work even when written by students not yet credentialed, because the qualifications of the writer are not carefully checked.

Con artists often use selectively enhanced empathy and phony altruism to effectively worm their way into the hearts of others—to fool most of the people most of the time into thinking that even though they are being handed a lemon, they are being served lemonade. They also depend heavily on self-assured narcissism to make themselves seem satisfyingly heroic to the many individuals who need someone strong to attach themselves to. Simultaneously, they harness their inbuilt sadism to appeal to those who are masochistic enough to seek punishment for past sins, often less real than imagined.

They also know how to get their way by using reverse (manipulative) psychology, the kind the psychotherapist Jay Haley used as a valid therapeutic tool. For example, Haley (personal communication, 1960) described treating a patient who slept through his alarm clock every morning and as a result was about to be fired from his job. Haley suggested that the patient throw the alarm clock away and instead plan on waking up on his own steam. Haley correctly expected that his stubborn and oppositional patient would do exactly the reverse of what the doctor ordered. As it turned out, Haley was right, for the patient, perversely becoming healthy by undermining treatment, decided to spite the therapist. He kept the alarm clock and started setting it correctly, getting right up when it rang, and doing so, without fail, every morning. On an everyday basis, realtors do the equivalent thing when they make it difficult for a client to see or purchase an apartment or home, anticipating that people will want most what they think they might not get at all. The pitchman's cry of "Walk, do not run, because they are going fast" belongs in this category of manipulation—making fruit desirable by making it look forbidden.

Some con artists ensnare third parties to help them with their schemes. For example, an administrator in a clinic where I used to work greased his way to stardom by winning the admiration, affection, and support of the patients even though that involved compromising their medical care. Using the patients as stepping stones on his way to the top, he played the role of the savior whose main and only goal was to protect the patients who attended his clinic from all the "bad doctors." The doctors were very good doctors, but were perceived by the patients as bad because they offered treatment that, though necessary, was unpalatable. To illustrate, once I told a patient that he had to be hospitalized because he kept insisting that he was going to kill himself. The patient appealed to this administrator, hoping for a rescuer. As a ploy, when the patient, a psychopath himself, approached the administrator he changed his story, saying that he was not suicidal after all. The administrator, motivated to fall for the patient's ploy, decided that the problem was not that the patient was sick but that I was overreacting. Next the administrator kept me away from the patient and released him. The patient, who was in fact seriously depressed and truly suicidal, got what he wanted rather than what he needed. The administrator got both what he wanted and what he needed: a reputation around the clinic of being on the side of the underdog, the hero advocate who would protect all the misunderstood patients from repressive medical authority—in exchange for the patients rallying around him at promotion time.

Some con artists actually pay third parties to help them with their schemes. They pay for testimonials from official-sounding individuals, or from a regulatory group that has an impressive name but no real standing or, if it even exists, was created for the express purpose of giving the testimonial. In one case a chiropractor using infomercials to sell a device for relieving back pain paid her mother, acting under an assumed name, to give the testimonials for her.

Of course, so often the effectiveness of the con depends on the vulnerability of the victim. We all contribute to being conned. We all need manipulative con artists. They offer us all hope. They fan the flames of our fading desires and our tired imaginations. They stoke the fires of our secret, and often sinful, passions.

Unfortunately, in the world we live in today, it can be difficult to impossible to climb high without some ability to manipulate, charm, and con. Manipulators, charmers, and con artists are a major presence among the politicians who win elections, card players who regularly beat the opposition at poker, and generals who triumph by foreseeing an enemy's weaknesses and using them for their own benefit.

Lying

Psychopaths, more than those suffering from any other personality disorder, depend on telling lies chronically and with conviction.

Of course, as psychopaths almost always point out, everybody lies at times. Honest people lie for a good cause, such as to protect someone vulnerable from having to hear a painful truth. Sometimes circumstances, other individuals, and society compel us to lie by making self-protective lying preferable to all other alternatives. When asked about past drug usage, a public official who smoked marijuana when he was young reasoned, "If I admit to smoking marijuana, my career is over before it starts. If I deny it and the world finds out about it later, I will have been elected, so only my reputation will suffer. So it would appear that I have a choice between being a liar who succeeds and being a masochist who fails. Guess what I am going to do."

Here are some vignettes someone I know personally, someone who is not a psychopath, told me about the liars in her life, and about her own lying:

"About those two I met over the Internet: Each lied when he insisted I was his only Internet courtship, and not well. They were always letting slip info to the contrary. It turned out the one I actually visited also lied about our guest accommodations. He had played it like he, I, and my daughter would be sightseeing and so forth family-style, while in reality he had arranged 'babysitters' for her so that he could be alone with me. He saw it as romantic and, to be fair, I think he was lying to himself as well, for it was preposterous of him to suppose I would leave my daughter alone with strangers. The other one, the one I never met in person, sent me lewd photos of himself and wanted some from me in return, and used his poor health as an excuse, like not knowing how much longer he'd be around, to pressure me in a charming and affectionate way into engaging in a bit of cyber-foreplay, that is, until I caught on when he once let his guard down and showed me his true, nasty, colors.

"My favorite charlatan is an older man I ran around with in college. He was sort of a campus-subculture hero, and I knew him as a college radio disk jockey. We did bold stuff together—such as making love while he was broadcasting—although among his campus following we were not a secret. But this whole side of him was a secret to his other following, that is, to his students and colleagues at the school where he taught and to the students he advised to whom he apparently was another kind of hero. I think his wife knew about me, but not his children.

"When I got out of my abusive first marriage, I ran around with most of the married men in town. I reckon they all were liars (to their wives), except one who bade his wife be friends with me. She was pretty polite.

"Another little tale of deception: Did I ever tell you I gave our piano away to a fellow who hid it from his wife in his garage? He got away with playing it out there for the longest time before she found out."

Psychopaths often start their lying early in life. With practice they get so good at it that they learn to lie spontaneously without having to think twice about what they plan to say. An adolescent boy would call strangers up and suggest a sexual encounter over the phone. He often wrote down the directions to the assignation, for example, "Take the subway to Kingsbridge Road and look for the six-foot man with a ponytail and a bandanna." When his parents found one of his slips with these directions written down and they asked him to explain himself, he lied to them so spontaneously and cleverly that he actually appeared to be telling them the truth, to the point that they believed him: "A classmate and I were just kidding around, passing notes to each other, imagining that we were part of an important covert cloak-and-dagger operation."

Lying is a trademark of our familiar list of shady professionals from all walks of life. An ad writer advertises a product by saying "there is nothing better of its kind" in order to give the impression that his product, though in fact it has no virtue over any of its rivals, is nevertheless distinctly superior. A lawyer lies for his client, proclaiming the client's innocence even though he knows he is guilty (to quote a renowned attorney, "all lawyers lie"). A doctor gives his patient a certain medication and says it is the best one for her illness, but completely forgets to mention that what is really best is the free Chinese food the drug detail man pushing the product buys and brings for the doctor. A book reviewer "unconsciously allows herself to be swayed" and gives a negative review of a book because she has a personal vendetta going against the author, or because she is about to come out with a competing book, or has a friend who wrote one. There are whole tracts on the Internet devoted to how one can lie—whether on an employment application or to the Justice Department—and get away with it. Apparently one can even find on the Internet a set of instructions on how to remove a house confinement bracelet. The only things that keep us from recognizing and admitting that these writers, editors, doctors,

lawyers, reviewers, and the rest of us are willfully lying are their social status and personal charm—and our own low ethical and moral standards.

Characteristically, psychopaths advance a number of euphemisms for
their lying, such as "telling white lies," "puffery," or "hyperbole," but
these are, as the psychopath will no doubt only reluctantly admit, lies
nevertheless. For example, musicians, using the positive spin we call
euphemism, steal songs then call it not thievery but "sampling."

As expected, psychopaths lie defensively. When caught and cornered,
they shamelessly plead "not guilty" to crimes they know perfectly well
that they have actually committed. They are also prone to lie in further-
ance of a calculated practical purpose, such as gaining power or getting
material things like creature comforts. Some alter their medical history to
benefit from entitlement programs, while others feign emotional or physical illness to seek hospitalization in order to get a place to stay for the
night. Some assume false identities, as when a dishonest stockbroker who
is just a salesperson passes himself off as a trained financial advisor, or
when a doctor who is in fact a foreign medical school graduate—seeking
cachet, and with it a large practice—passes himself off as the graduate of
an American medical school. Most psychopaths also lie purely for emotional gain, for example, to extract love, pity, or sympathy, or to protect
their self-image from damage. Some lie just for the fun of it to see if they
can sucker someone into believing one of their outlandish stories, into
falling for one of their crooked schemes, or into buying into one of their
ridiculous excuses.

The lying of mild psychopaths is as likely to be distortive as categorical. Categorical lying involves radically changing reality to fit. Distortive
lying involves playing somewhat loose with the facts. Often distortive
lying relies on selective suppression of the facts in order to accentuate the
positive and eliminate the negative. For example, an ad writer trying to
make a rival's long-acting antacid pill look inferior to his short-acting pill
emphasizes how his pill gives immediate relief—while "forgetting" to
mention how transient that relief happens to be. A columnist gives a former New York mayor a deserved compliment so that she can look as if
she is being fair, but glides over it so that it detracts as little as possible
from the real goal of her column—a critical attack on him. Distortive lying
may also rely on part-to-whole logic, as do headlines created out of non-
stories like the tabloid headline that screamed that a famous psychologist
was involved in a child-beating scandal. The only substance to the report
was that the psychologist had once referred a client's adolescent son to a
school where a child-beating took place much later on.

Successful psychopaths get away with their lying for a long time. Either
they are very clever liars or they know how to escape the consequences of
their lying when exposed. After being exonerated at trial, the men who
killed the black youth Medgar Evers sold their true story to a national

magazine. They admitted their guilt, secure in the knowledge that they could not be tried twice for the same crime. Less successful psychopaths' lies have particularly short legs, leading to predicable short- and long-term negative consequences. For example, a psychotherapist in training analysis made up a supervised case. She said that her patient came four times a week and was seen on the couch when in fact the patient came three times a week and was seen face to face. Her first comeuppance was that she felt no joy when she got her diploma. She felt "strangely unmoved" due to a combination of underlying feelings of guilt and shame and a fear of being exposed. Her second comeuppance was that her lack of training showed—to the point that she was asked to leave the psychoanalytic institute because of her poor performance.

When exposed in a lie that they cannot cover up with other lies, or when they run out of excuses for their lying, psychopaths may attempt to sweet-talk their way out of a tight spot. Or they may become evasive or vague. Or they may try to defend themselves using even more sophistic distortions of fact, as did the individual who asserted that his right to initiate a chain letter was protected by the First Amendment. (We should always suspect psychopathy when we find ourselves recoiling because someone is making excuses for questionable behavior by distorting what it means to have the privileges of living in a free country.) Or they may instead become angry. When such is the case, they may hold in the anger they feel and assume a posture of restraint in order to appear reasonable, patient, and conciliatory. Or they may sublimate their anger into intellectually argumentative debates meant to get us to see things their way. Or, as often happens with less successful psychopaths, their anger may explode as their façade crumbles and they attack their accusers verbally or physically. When the response is extremely blind or crude aggression, there is reason to suspect an underlying paranoid tendency.

Severe lying is sometimes called *pseudologia fantastica* to indicate that the individual has become florid in his or her lies, lacks a degree of insight into what the truth is, and no longer appears to have his or her lying under control. Patients with pseudologia fantastica may not be psychopaths. They may instead be suffering from a Histrionic Personality Disorder; as a result, they become so caught up emotionally in their needs and wishes that they actually find themselves unable to distinguish fact from fantasy. Or they may be suffering from hypomania, where they lie in order to avoid being knocked off their emotionally induced high, something they fear might happen if they stopped and realistically assessed what they were saying.

Many observers have noted how psychopaths, especially psychopaths in trouble, malinger by feigning or exaggerating illness. Those who feign or exaggerate illness can simulate emotional illness, emotionally caused physical illness, or actual physical illness. In the realm of *emotional illness*, the psychopath may feign a new emotional disorder or exaggerate one that previously exists. In an entity that used to be called "prison psychosis" or "Ganser's syndrome," and is now in the *DSM-IV* called "Factitious Disorder With Predominantly Psychological Signs and Symptoms,"[7] the individual "acts crazy" to avoid incarceration entirely, to be sent to a mental hospital rather than to jail or, if already in jail, to be transferred to a mental hospital. The individual who acts crazy often feigns a psychosis, more rarely a neurosis, and almost never a personality disorder. Some individuals do a good job of feigning psychosis, but often the feigned psychosis has a much too simple, childlike quality to appear genuine, at least to the experienced eye. Instead, it resembles what a layman might merely imagine a psychosis to be—for example, "I feel I am being attacked by birds." One convict did a bad job of feigning hebephrenia by rarely bathing or shaving, and by acting regressed by always wearing a bathrobe and pajamas instead of street clothing. Some contrive a suicidal wish and others go beyond that and actually make a gestural suicidal attempt. Unfortunately—for us, for them, and for society as a whole—tactics like this can, and often do, succeed.

In the realm of feigning or exaggerating *emotionally caused physical illness*, psychopaths often feign pseudo-organic memory problems, either hypomnesis (memory loss), for example, amnesia, or hypermnesis (remembering everything with great clarity), for example, a concocted traumatic memory from a past life, often of childhood abuse, but also of any other remembrance whose usefulness is all too apparent in circumstances where the facts cannot be either proved or disproved.

In the realm of feigning or exaggerating *physical disorder,* the individual might feign abdominal pain or an organic memory deficit. This feigning used to be called "Munchausen's disorder" and is now in the *DSM-IV* called "Factitious Disorder With Predominantly Physical Signs and Symptoms."[8] The intent may be to get hospitalized—to get a bed for the night or to be transferred from jail to a hospital; to get a drug, as when a patient feigns a heart attack or other physical pain in order to obtain opiates; or to deflect criticism or avoid real trouble. Sometimes a physical illness is both feigned and given concrete form. The individual puts a thermometer before a light bulb to fake a fever, or tears the skin to fake a skin ulcer. Once a doctor had a patient's leg encased in a plaster cast so that she would not hit and traumatize her healing leg ulcer and accidentally reopen it. Needing the care, concern, and disability payments that went along with having and keeping the ulcer, she twisted a coat hanger open, pushed it under her cast, and poked a hole in her newly healing lesion.

Individuals who exaggerate a *previously existent but mild physical disorder,* for example, whiplash, may be best classified as having either a Histrionic Personality Disorder or a compensation disorder, or both. Individuals applying for disability benefits and those suing for personal injury sometimes fall into this category.

The ability of individuals who feign illness to enlist other psychopaths to aide and abet their doings—ambulance-chasing trial lawyers, for example—is legendary. They are also good at seducing some of us, including those of us who sit on juries, to make the preposterous assumption that when a successful lawsuit is the goal, distorting the facts will never be the means. In general, the process of determining eligibility for disability benefits is inherently flawed, for the patient is really not a patient but a self-advocate, and as such is likely both consciously and unconsciously to distort the presentation of his or her symptoms. With symptoms like back pain, it is particularly difficult to distinguish true suffering from consummate faking.

Some methods exist for therapists to use to fake out the faker and determine the truth. For example, we used to spin a revolving drum with vertical stripes before the eyes of someone who was complaining of blindness to rule out "hysterical blindness" by seeing if the eyes automatically followed the spinning wheel. In cases of partial or complete sensory anesthesia, it is sometimes possible during the neurological exam to "trick" the patient into "confessing" by putting one finger on two places in the supposed area of anesthesia and asking the patient which one he or she feels more intensely. (Naturally, if the patient answers by saying one or the other, he or she is caught admitting being able to feel in an area previously claimed to be anesthetic.) We are all familiar with how individuals who claim total disability due to back pain have been flushed out by being filmed lifting heavy parcels on a full-time job they hold on the sly.

However, to the best of my knowledge, no one has developed an acid test to uncover all malingering. "Trick" questions on psychological tests are supposed to expose the malingerer, but, and as previously mentioned, Hare has pointed out that many psychopaths know, or can learn, how to "fake the results of psychological tests without too much difficulty."[9] Their answers to all the test questions, including to the ones meant to expose the faker, are inherently consistent, but questionable overall.

It is unfortunate but true that disability determinations by doctor, judge, and jury are often made, at least in part, on irrelevant aspects of a case, particularly the nature of the countertransference to the patient, client, or victim (e.g., on the basis of the therapist's or other concerned individual's feelings about the patient/client). In an example of a positive countertransference response, a clinic where I used to work had an unwritten policy sometimes put into effect with patients who were suspected of malingering in order to obtain new, or to get an increase of old, benefits. The policy was: Compromise—if they ask for 100 percent compensation, bend a little—and give them 50 percent.

Because both actual and exaggerated illness can, and often do, occur together, "feigning" illness, like so many of the issues discussed in this chapter, is not a precise scientific concept that refers to a readily identifiable process. It is usually difficult to impossible to be certain who is really sick and who is faking, and if indeed the need to fake is itself a sickness, so that the need to fake is not entirely conscious—under the individual's control—but is also, at least in part, unconscious—beyond individual control and done not opportunistically but for such intrapsychic benefit as relief of anxiety. Some psychiatrists have said that anyone who fakes illness for monetary gain is indeed ill for that reason alone, irrespective of the manifest symptoms that take center stage. One cannot ever be certain if it is "sick to feign being sick" or if that view represents an unduly permissive take on an exceedingly unacceptable behavior. Each case must be judged on its own.

Some psychopaths resort not to maximizing but to minimizing illness—to pass a life insurance examination or a job interview. A surgical resident said he wanted to switch over to a career in psychiatry because he loved the field. In fact, he was aware that he was developing multiple sclerosis and knew he had to give up his surgical career immediately, though he could practice psychiatry for a while longer.

In the gray area are those prisoners who feign not emotional illness but emotional health by undergoing a religious conversion in which they assume an uncharacteristically saintly demeanor. We are all familiar with the story of the felon who is released early for good behavior or spared the death penalty because he or she has found God and is helping others to find Him too. Our suspicions are usually aroused because the temptation to convert for gain is so great that the end can all too clearly seem to be motivating the means. However, while some exalted states are mainly opportunistic, others seem sincere, and some individuals even change their ways permanently and for the better. I believe that the end of a religious conversion can be a good thing even when reached via questionable means. However, we may only assume true reformation if the reformation continues after the spoils for the good behavior have been collected, and it is still not too late to demand their return.

CHAPTER 4

Some Psychopaths of Everyday Life

In the last chapter I described some important behavioral characteristics of mild psychopaths—for example, manipulativeness, opportunism, and sexual flamboyance. In this chapter I catalogue the behaviors of some psychopaths grouped by class. Not all the individuals I describe are true psychopaths. Some just behave psychopathically in a limited way. For others, the manifest traits may only look psychopathic, but not be so at all. In technical terms, there is a differential diagnosis of most traits. However, while a trait such as dishonesty can turn out to be simple carelessness, if there is such a thing, it often holds true that where there is smoke, there is fire. I believe that when psychopathy is suspected, it is better to be proved wrong in assuming (and treating) it than in underestimating (and neglecting) it.

CUSTOMERS

The homily "the customer is always right" does not apply to customers who act immorally and unethically—buying clothes to wear for a night's event and then returning them to the store in the morning, or being difficult restaurant diners for the fun of dominating hapless waitpersons to impress their dinner companions with their prowess or masculinity, or for the sadistic amusement they get from watching the helpless staff suffer as they trammel them, secure in the knowledge that the staff are in no position to adequately defend themselves. Just recently the proprietor of a restaurant complained to me about people who first wait an hour to order their food and then want it served immediately after they order it. A waiter complained to me that a group of four ran up a breakfast bill of over a hundred dollars and then left him a dollar tip. He then described a difficult lunch-time customer as follows: "This man came for dinner at 3:30 P.M., two hours before dinner was to be served, then complained that the kitchen was refusing to accommodate him because it would only serve him lunch. Then, after perusing the luncheon menu, he became angry and called me over to complain that five bucks was a ridiculous price to pay for soup and a sandwich. But he didn't let it go at that. He demanded to speak to and take his complaints to the management. He then groused when I told him that I was also the manager, meaning that that there were no higher-ups to complain to. Then he threatened to write to the Better Business Bureau, and a week later returned to tell me that he had done just that, and showed me the letter he had written and actually sent. As I look back now, from the hints he was giving out, I think that this time around he was angling to get a rake off on his bill."

HEALTH PROFESSIONALS/PATIENTS

In the health professions we find psychopathy manifest both in practitioner and in patient syndromes. In the realm of practitioner syndromes, doctors sometimes subvert the Continuing Medical Education requirements that dictate a certain number of hours of additional training be obtained for license renewal. They claim that they are spending the time reading journals, and they attend one conference after another on the same topic just because the drug companies offer the conferences free of charge. Cheats in the medical profession also include:

- the senior surgeon who lets a junior doctor do the operation the senior doctor was retained, and is being paid, to do, under the guise of training students;
- the diet guru who accepts being on the payroll of a fast-food franchise that serves unhealthy food, denying a conflict of interest and instead justifying his actions, he believes plausibly, by saying that his only goal is to repair the damage from within;
- speech therapists in nursing homes who bill Medicare for vocabulary and diction lessons they give to patients whose Alzheimer's disease is so far advanced that they are unlikely to benefit much, if at all;
- medical drug salespeople who advertise their products as falsely as some beauty companies advertise their remedies, and then bribe doctors to prescribe them using free trinkets like snazzy ball-point pens as the bait;
- chiropractors who focus more on stage dressing than on medicine, such as the one in solo practice whose office had twelve darkened examining rooms and piped in soft music to accompany the burning candles;
- forensic psychiatrists who can argue just as easily for as against an insanity defense in the same patient, depending on which side is paying for their testimony; and

- nonmedical quacks who tout worthless cures and then handle accusations of fraud by postulating an unholy alliance between drug companies and federal regulators while affirming how *they* are the heroes out to bust such trusts.

Patients can, of course, be as psychopathic as their doctors. In this category I include:

- patients who intercept the insurance form the doctor submits and alter it to receive a higher reimbursement;
- patients who hide income to increase eligibility for entitlement programs;
- patients who see more than one doctor in order to get more than one prescription for a medicine they like and want;
- patients who consciously intensify their pain and suffering to sue and win a large monetary settlement; and
- patients who fake illness in order to get drugs or a desired hospitalization, such as patients who fake mental illness to get themselves hospitalized when they need a place to stay and then fake mental health when they want to leave the hospital. For example, they fake hearing voices when they want to be admitted, and then deny hearing voices when they want to leave. They might fake depression and make a manipulative suicidal attempt when they want in, and then claim that they feel fine and are ready for discharge when they want out— either so that they can return to their daily lives or, perhaps, to make another suicide attempt—perhaps one primarily meant to embarrass their therapist.

MEDIA PEOPLE

Psychopathic media people include the columnist who rises to the top by writing sensational stories, fictional creations concocted out of part truths that are just fragments of information; editorial writers who use repetitive harassment to defeat someone they do not approve of personally or politically (I currently get the impression that almost every day a respected newspaper's editorial page has an antiestablishment "you can never do anything right" editorial); and editorial writers who make their point by first developing a conclusion and then forming their argument around it instead of weighing facts, evidence, and both sides of an issue in order to reach the conclusion.

EDUCATORS AND STUDENTS

Teachers become psychopathic if they turn a job whose essence it is to give (to their students) into an opportunity to get (for themselves). For example, it is psychopathic for a teacher to attempt to enhance her own self-image by competing with her students, viewing and treating them as rivals and then covetously and consciously arranging for them to fail in order to score a competitive win over them. Too many teachers, blurring the distinction between teaching and proselytizing, use the classroom as a forum not for ideas but to win converts to one of their special causes. Particularly psychopathic are teachers who try to seduce their students for sex, either indirectly, by using their own position of power to elicit a compliant parental transference to have their way, or directly, by bribing their students with promises of good grades or a little professional push in return.

However, sometimes the student is the psychopath and the teacher is the victim. We all are familiar with students who willingly lie on the casting couch or actively attempt to seduce their professors to get a good grade. When the relationship is exposed, it is completely psychopathic if the student attempts to foist blame entirely on the teacher for seducing him or her, "the innocent one," when in fact both the attraction and the seduction were mutual.

RELIGIOUS LEADERS

Psychopathic religious leaders use religion, and especially the concept of the sanctity of religious freedom, insincerely, as a cover for manipulating, intimidating, demolishing, and stealing. As the cliché goes, they set out to do good, and they do very well indeed. Such individuals may manipulate by using religious tenets to assert their authority and seize power, to justify bad behavior philosophically, or in the service of opportunistically buying and running businesses for profit without having to pay taxes. For others, religion offers the opportunity to be safely aggressive, as they avoid the personal consequences of their hostility by giving a personal vendetta a religious caste, justifying their own anger by citing God's principles to deflect attention and blame from their own lack thereof. A case in point is that of a religious man who fumes over another's blasphemy and hides how he is out to "get him good" by giving his vengeful fantasies a religious twist: "I can only sympathize with him because of the punishment that he is going to receive from the heavens." Especially psychopathic is using religion to express and act on sexual feelings by sublimating them into unbridled heavenly religious love, what one observer called a horizontal desire displaced vertically. Here religion becomes a vehicle for base sexual instincts that are presented as having lost their earthly tether to become not at all worldly, but entirely sanctified.

Machiavelli summarizes this concept tersely: a person seeking to be a prince "should seem to be all mercy, faith, integrity, humanity, *and religion*" (italics added).[1]

BUSINESS PEOPLE

We are all familiar with how psychopathy takes hold in business practices. Of course, many businesses succeed through honest, sophisticated, creative practices. But a certain amount of opportunism, greed, lying, bullying, and cheating must be taken for granted in the business world. Many businesses succeed through modest deceit or fraud, having become the philosophical equivalent of the grubby or "schlock" lawyer, the corrupt politician, or the "media bully" newspaperman. The people running the businesses, though accounted successful, actually suffer from a Psychopathic Personality Disorder in which the well-defined amoral elements are contained and efficiently controlled because they would compromise everything if allowed to get out of control—an apparent adjustment that challenges our concept of personality disorder as necessarily self-destructive and maladaptive.

Here belongs the all-too-familiar story of the psychopathic CEO who ran his company's for-the-record profits up by manipulating the stock in order to cover how he was stealing from his company to benefit himself and a few of his old-boy network cronies. When he was caught he claimed, "I didn't know what was going on; it never got up that high, to me." Also belonging here is the story of a charitable organization's CEO who appropriated for herself an excessive amount of the money collected by the charity, then rationalized her behavior by pointing out how much money she raised overall and how little would have been collected without her good works. Belonging here too are shyster brokerage firms that advocate quack get-rich-quick schemes such as how to make a profit by trading the same stock over and over again, buying low and selling high, overlooking that the strategy only works when the stock accommodates by following a friendly pattern, without tanking permanently.

A competitive narcissistic builder and realtor claimed that he was the only honest builder and realtor in town. He touted his own properties by saying that all the other local realtors were crooks, and by knocking the properties of rival builders, even those that were actually superior to his. He libeled one builder in town, saying that his buildings were in defiance of the local codes, his roofs leaked, and he used indoor wood (cheaper than outdoor wood) for the façade. To ice the cake, he then swore that everyone the builder sold property to was suing him. This realtor/builder attempted to falsely enhance the value of his own properties by painting an unduly rosy picture about the future of a neighborhood that was actually in decline. When all else failed, he created sham sales to colleagues, who bid up the price and then backed out at the last minute without actually signing up to buy anything.

In this category too are art dealers who conceal how much they paid for an item in order to sell the item at an extremely inflated price—whatever the market will bear. Just recently I asked two partners in an art gallery the price of a painting. They replied in perfect concert: only one said "$4,000"—exactly at the same time that the other said "$4,800."

Business failure as well as business success can be an unrecognized symptom of Psychopathic Personality Disorder. This can be the case when the failure is the expression of maladaptive psychopathic masochism, where the unconscious masochistic goal is in the forefront right from the start and we wonder, with predictive justification, "How can he ever hope to succeed under such circumstances?" or "How can she ever think that she will get away with that?"

Masochistic determinism is not to be confused with system failure due to bad luck or simple judgmental deficit that leads a person to honestly err because of poor planning, say due to attempting the impossible. System failure can also result because the person running the business has met his or her match: someone as shrewd or shrewder—like a rival who wins simply because he or she is a more successful psychopath.

LAWYERS

Psychopathic lawyers are manipulators who are adept at knowing how to make any means justify their self-serving ends. They cover up their true intent with sophistic reasoning.

A case in point is the attorney who sued a doctor who visited a patient who was also his friend, just to say hello. In his lawsuit, the attorney claimed that the bad results the patient ultimately experienced would not have come about if this doctor "had expedited" his friend's medical care during his personal visit.

In some ways, lawyers who can argue both sides of a case using two opposite, inherently consistent but totally specious arguments, resemble con artists who are adept at putting their lies over as the truth. We are all familiar with the lawyer who uses selective abstraction (discussed further in Chapter 6) to make the case that he is motivated strictly by an altruistic search for justice and truth and by concern for the suffering of his clients, when he is really out for the money, status, and power that a big win would bring, and perhaps also wants to become famous and build a large practice on the reputation he acquires from getting a high-profile criminal off on a technicality.

We are also all familiar with the lawyer whose ethics go beyond being merely shady. A case in point is the judge in the news recently who was censured for continuing to preside instead of recusing himself when a close friend sued for an alleged personal injury (for sixty million dollars, just for falling off a chair!). He had previously been censured for giving the same friend the most lucrative fiduciary appointments—not the first time he gave these to someone with whom he maintained a close personal contact.

We are perhaps less familiar with lawyers who try to shame the opposition into giving up all their demands for a large settlement. A man had just lost his daughter because she drowned after getting stuck in a poorly maintained whirlpool bath in a posh foreign hotel. The lawyer tried to intimidate the father into sheepishly pulling back—by asking him, "Exactly how much do you want for her anyway?"

This said, many lawyers are as much the victims of psychopaths as they are psychopaths themselves. They become victims when they actually buy into their psychopathic clients' shams and believe their clever protestations of innocence. I believe that some judges get the reputation for being too liberal less because they take that position philosophically and more because, being only human, they are conned by psychopaths able to talk them into meting out ridiculously small sentences. The psychopaths elicit the pity they know how to arouse in us all, as well as the misplaced altruism they know how to bring forth so successfully from the hardest of hearts.

POLITICIANS

Psychopathic politicians are known for being manipulators prone to presenting partial truths as whole truths in political campaigns that focus on the opposition's negative qualities. They sacrifice presenting a fair and accurate picture to the voters in order to present one that sways voter opinion and gets their votes. In the news recently was an attack ad that claimed the opposition candidate had voted for a 200 percent rise in personal property taxes, when all he had done was rubber stamp a small town's previously agreed-upon temporary property surtax meant to pay for a needed public works project. Psychopathic politicians are also famous for altering their personal convictions to appeal to the voters, changing like "rubber band men" what they really think into what they anticipate others want to hear. They take one stand when they believe it will get them elected, take another when the climate changes, and then excuse their waffling in various creative ways, such as "I have a right to change my mind," "I have become more mature," or "The times have changed, and so have I." The most successful politicians know how to rescue themselves after misfiring—how to back themselves *out* of a corner using gems of self-justification consisting of clever and persuasively illogical formulations that originate in the distortive premises discussed throughout. Two of the more familiar ones are "I didn't have sex with her because what I did wasn't sex" (e.g., similar things are not in any way the same thing), and "I didn't smoke marijuana because I didn't inhale" (e.g., the absence of a part completely invalidates the presence of a whole).

AUTHORS AND ARTISTS

Some authors who are not necessarily psychopaths nevertheless promote their books aggressively, in a manner reminiscent of the way con artists promote themselves. For example, one garnered media publicity by handing out free copies of his book in places where the TV cameras were running. Crossing the line are particularly opportunistic authors who feed their egos and enhance their finances by misusing public trust attained from prior good works. I found it especially appalling that a well-respected financial guru misused his status as someone who helps people budget when he promoted, no doubt for a hefty fee, a specific brand of computer.

Some of the more psychopathic authors fit too well the (personally highly original) composer Ned Rorem's characterization of artists: "All artists steal, but if you know you are stealing, you try to disguise it."[2] They plagiarize a little here and a little there, hoping that no one will notice, and that they will get away with it. Composers too often freely and shamelessly plagiarize folk tunes without marking them. I have often been startled to discover that some of Igor Stravinsky's better-known tunes were unmarked appropriated folk tunes, and to hear the major tunes in the composer Aaron Copland's works in the works of the composer Carlos Chavez, and vice versa. While many observers note the differences between borrowing (e.g., stealing) folk tunes, sampling rock and dance music, forging art, appropriating someone else's text, taking a term paper from the Internet, copying a neighbor's papers during the exam, and thieving someone's identity, I instead see mainly the similarities.

Other artists are fakers more than they are thieves. In my opinion, some of the composer John Cage's works are little more than instructions to players to "play something, anything you like," leaving it up to the players to decide exactly what and for how long. He calls this "aleatory." Others call it a "con job."

Publishers sometimes act in a psychopathic fashion to create a product that sells or to promote one already written. A well-known publisher releasing a multi-authored volume listed first the name of the man with the biggest reputation and second the name of the man with the most expertise—the one who also happened to have actually written most of the book.

FAMILY

A writer describes a "self-absorbed sister dethroned by her youngest sister, who decides that all family members can visit her swanky San Francisco apartment free of charge, but asks a hundred dollars for a one-night stay for the sister and husband, as they attend events. They never come to San Francisco otherwise, so it is not like they're constantly asking for this favor. Sister claims: 'a. it's expensive to live in San Francisco and b. she must clean, and it costs sixty dollars for that.' Her brother-in-law's comment is, 'Geez, charge me an expense, but don't try to make money off of me. My cousins own a hotel in Europe but never charge me and when they come to visit I do the same.' To top it off this sister wanted gratis 'room at the inn' one holiday season with the sister she chose to charge. Of course, youngest sister and hubby said 'forget it' and got a room in a hotel with a pool in a nearby town, driving into the city. Charging for one night to sleep in a sofa bed is a pretty lame excuse I thought, and it's her choice to live wherever, despite cost of living. Why make someone else pay for that choice?"

NEIGHBORS

Many so-called "*neighbors* from hell" are actually psychopaths who happen to be living next door. A neighbor who did not like the sound of his neighbor's pool filter would simply climb her fence on a regular basis and turn it off. A selfish neighbor who was renovating piled his garbage up on the side of his house instead of using a dumpster and let it sit there for weeks on end. Once, wanting to take the most direct and convenient route to his own house, he simply drove his heavily loaded truck across a neighbor's lawn, in the process completely destroying some of the lawn's infrastructure. When intoxicated, he hurled personal insults at all his neighbors. He beat his wife, sold drugs to children, and more than once in a fit of rage hit his own children—bashing one so hard on the side of her head that he destroyed her hearing in one ear. He also let his dogs run wild to defecate on and tear up his neighbors' yards. He adopted cats and then let them run free, even though he knew from personal experience that they would ultimately be run over. He regularly parked in his neighbors' driveways, making it impossible for his neighbors to park their own cars in their own garages; created a neighborhood eyesore by leaving discarded objects all over his lawn; and, envious of a neighbor's new car when he only had an old, beat-up one, keyed the car and then hit the hood with his fist, putting a large dent in it that seemed to proclaim, "I don't want you to have anything better than what I have."

FRIENDS

Many friends, good as well as bad, tell little white lies even to their best friends. For example, they might follow the advice of cooking show hosts and invite friends over for dinner, buy prepared food, add a little spice or two, and act as though they cooked the meal from scratch. Just recently a national Internet provider ran a story that in essence spoke of how to buy a friend or family member a cheap gift and then pass it off as something expensive. Truly psychopathic friends take their dishonesty one step further. Some sleep with a friend's lover and snatch him or her right out from

under. Traitor types, willingly thinking ill of a friend without first checking the facts, buy into a negative story about their best friends in essentially the same way that Othello bought into Iago's accusations about
Desdemona, Othello's wife.

GYM PEOPLE

The gym seems to bring out narcissistic psychopathic behavior in many
people. Some leave a machine they are currently using, all the while holding it in their fantasies as theirs, and fully prepared to complain when
anyone else thinks the machine is free and tries to use it. Others use the
machines as lounge chairs, holding long conversations from what they
have made into their thrones, entirely oblivious that people are waiting
their turns. Seeking an unfair advantage, body builders use steroids illegally, a behavior somewhat in keeping with such antiestablishment body
tattoos as pictures of the devil and representations of skulls and cross-
bones. In some cases, however, as with many of the psychopathic stigmata I describe throughout, these behaviors are not indicative of
psychopathy. They may at most indicate the presence of sociopathy; that
is, they are part of a socially approved costume/behavior that a countercultural subgroup—in this case, people who go to the gym—wears as a
kind of collective antiestablishment logo.

TENANTS

Becoming a tenant brings out latent narcissism and extreme acquisitiveness in some people. I once had a tenant who asked specifically if I would
leave one of my rugs, because she admired it so. She then promptly threw
it into the basement, where a flood from the water heater ruined it. Next
she moved out and installed her unsupervised teen-age children in the
house. They proceeded to tear up the floor and walls and spray the ceil-
ings with obscene logos. As a tenant in an apartment, the coffee shop
owner discussed throughout withheld rent payments for months because
of a small ceiling leak, which she claimed made her dwelling entirely
uninhabitable. When her landlord had her evicted for nonpayment of
rent, she retaliated by vandalizing his property—stuffing the toilet, putting glue in the locks, and cutting out square pieces from his wall-to-wall
carpeting. She next found another apartment where they did not check
references as carefully as they should have and repeated the pattern while
expanding on it. This time after not paying the rent, she declared bankruptcy, part of her conscious plan to stay in her place rent free for the considerable amount of time it took her landlord to have her evicted. She
easily could have worked harder to pay the rent, but instead she closed
her coffee shop on most days and quit a lucrative part-time job so that she
could spend more time with her dog. Her new landlord started legal

action, and once again she played the role of the innocent victim and assigned him the role of Shylock. This time she hired a lawyer. But when he could not prevent her from being evicted, she tried to sue him for malpractice.

WORKERS

Dishonest psychopathic employees are unreliable individuals who come into work irregularly, call out sick even when they are well and know that others will be hard-pressed to cover for them, work when they are being observed and slack off when no one is looking, fall asleep on the job, make long distance phone calls on the employer's line, and steal office supplies for home. As highly vindictive individuals, they become whistle-blowers who avow that they are exposing questionable business practices that have to be changed, when really they are acting out of a disgruntled aggressiveness toward and envy of those who are in power and are more successful than they are.

When psychopathic workers make mistakes, they blame everyone but themselves. For example, a doctor who overslept did not call in a request for a lab test before the daily cutoff time. Next, instead of taking responsibility for her error, she criticized the lab technician for being uncaring and incompetent simply because he (rightly) insisted that the test be deferred to the next day.

Paradoxically, some of the apparently best workers can be the most psychopathic of all. For example, embezzlers often have the best job attendance, but they come in every day so that the boss will not hire a substitute who might uncover their shady bookkeeping.

Some acquisitive opportunistic psychopathic workers look for and find ways to sue the company, often with the help and guidance of an equally psychopathic attorney. A CEO was practically in tears when he told me the story of how, after he sold his business, a lawyer "got on my case" and recruited some of his ex-workers to start a class-action suit against him—for making his employees work under poor conditions. He was particularly hurt that these workers, men and women whom he previously had counted as his friends, were now too ashamed of themselves to even talk to him. He had two main consolations: he was well insured, and he knew that the lawyer would get almost everything—and as payback the workers the lawyer was using to further his own ends would get just about nothing.

Some administrators are psychopathic in the sense of having double standards—one for themselves and another for their staff. For example, an administrator on the same time clock as her employees cracked down on the employees when they were even a few minutes late, while simultaneously cajoling her secretary into falsifying her time records so that she could come and go as she pleased. She frequently ran up large monthly bills for personal use on the cell phone the hospital provided her—meant, however, to be used only for business purposes.

Some administrators are sadistic psychopaths who stress their employees to the breaking point by giving more priority to making money for themselves than to treating their employees fairly. One doctor hired out his employees to work for his golfing buddies at unaffiliated outlying hospitals, both for the money and in order to please, satisfy, coddle, impress, and reward those who were in a position to refer him patients and advance him politically. A psychiatric administrator wanted the psychiatric residents to make home visits in dangerous neighborhoods without a guard for protection. He did not seem to care that the residents might get physically hurt. What he mainly cared about was the savings he would realize by not having to put an extra person on the payroll.

Finally, there are those nepotistic administrators who use their positions as an opportunity to hire family members. When I was in psychiatric training, a big boss, a social worker, hired his wife, a nurse, to run one of his clinics. He cited as his only reason for hiring her, her invaluable contribution to science and the community. Left entirely unmentioned was another invaluable contribution—to his household finances.

THE MANIPULATIVE DISENFRANCHISED

A small proportion of disenfranchised individuals and groups choose manipulative psychopathic mechanisms to compensate for personal and collective weakness and to give themselves strength they might not otherwise have to stand up, protect, and assert themselves. They gain unfair advantage by beating others over their heads with their bloody bodies as they overplay the role of the long-oppressed and marginalized to the hilt. Some hold later generations completely responsible for what earlier generations did. Others level partly or entirely false accusations of here-and-now racism or sexism, purely for purposes of remuneration and retaliation. Such disenfranchised psychopaths pay a disproportionate price for their psychopathy when they go too far in the direction of sacrificing present functionality for the (undoubted) advantages that accrue from continuing to live in a painful past.

PSEUDO-ACTIVISTS

Psychopathic (pseudo-) activists are motivated less by the true activist's pressing need for reform and more by their own personal need to actively do battle with the establishment. (Possibly this is why there at least appear to be more liberal than conservative activists.) The reasons false activists give for why they defend, promulgate, and push an issue tend to be of minor importance compared to the real reason for their activism: It serves as a vehicle for shocking and outraging the bourgeoisie. (This helps explain why false activists so often tend to side more with the victimizer than with the victim.) Many have learned to hide their negative personal motivation as positive socially valuable activity. For example, in the news recently was a group of bigots who burned down a housing development because the units were being sold to blacks. To justify their actions, they claimed that they were not committing a bias crime—they were just protecting environmental wetlands.

False activists may go beyond debating fairly to unfairly intimidating others by proclaiming special knowledge, ability, and understanding. They are often hypocrites, too, claiming as they do the very rights that they deprive others of—the familiar "I want to be free to take away your freedom." Often, they simultaneously use manipulative paranoid mechanisms to convince others to do their bidding. For example, in an election year they conjure up a common enemy, such as physicians who perform abortions, for the sole purpose of whipping the electorate into frenzy in the hope of creating an anti-abortion coalition—not for the practical and moral reasons they put forward, but to establish a block vote that goes in their favor.

However, who is and who is not a psychopathic (false) activist can be a matter of whose side you are on and what is, or is not, in it for you. Oskar Schindler—the hero of the movie *Schindler's List* and a German who hired Jews during World War II in order to rescue them from the gas chamber—may or may not have been a psychopathic activist. What appears to be certain is that some of us ignore behaviors that seem to fit him into the mold of a psychopath so that we are able to continue to view him and his good deeds in a completely favorable light. Still, there are some apparently accurate descriptions of his erratic inconsistent behavior, inexplicable motivations, heavy drinking and promiscuity, spying, and embellishing his heroism, perhaps motivated as much by greed and excitement as by any altruism he might have feigned.

THE WILDLY OUTLANDISH, FIENDISHLY, FLAMBOYANTLY SEXUAL DON JUAN OR FEMME FATALE CHARACTER

Hypersexuality, while certainly driven by nonpsychological forces such as hormones and neurotransmitters, can also have psychopathic elements. This is particularly the case when the sex involves an absence of feeling for the other person, associated with the philosophy that any orifice of any object will do, associated with a willingness to hurt someone else for one's own orgasmic pleasure, all in the setting of a lack of concern for the personal and social immediate and long-term consequences of one's actions and behavior.

Sometimes what is psychopathic about sex is not the sex itself but its public display intended to shock and appall. A colleague described what might be considered to be a paradigm of such sexuality, which occurred at a birthday part she gave for her son: "Last night, Christmas Eve, was a trip and a half. I had a house full of people. The celebration was no longer an Xmas Eve celebration. Since my son Greg was born around that day, I have turned it more into a yearly birthday celebration. Let's say for the first time I really got to know his girlfriend and her mother (he is usually at her house every night and despite my pleas to have her hang out here, he insists that hanging out there is better. I now know why.) My son, who has barely said more than 75 words in this house in the past few years, suddenly came alive as his "mother-in-law" (a tall, obese, hirsute woman who talks as if she is preparing for reality television) came in and kissed him long and hard on the lips, showered him (and us) with presents, even though I just met her the night before and of course hadn't had her on my Xmas list, and generally acted as if we were all going to be in this life together from here on in. Mother tells me she has been cooking all of my son's favorite foods for the past year, and buying him his favorite boxer short underwear (I'm wondering what else she might be doing to service him). Then, when Mother finally left to go to her cousin's place she told daughter that my son Greg could keep her daughter out all night if he wanted to (not OK with me, so nix that one). Daughter, who is the opposite of mother in appearance (slim, long beautiful hair), and is equally eager to please, comes in wearing bare midriff skirt and a little black shell which covers only up to the top of the nipples of her boobs, which she promptly begins shoving into my son's face as she grabs his crotch IN FRONT OF EVERYONE. There is mention of a phantom father named "Charles" who is never seen but somehow exists and lives with mother and daughter. As we all settle in before the tree to drink hot cocoa, daughter takes a dive and goes "searching" for the buttons which run across the crotch-line of my son's new boxer shorts and then proposes to eat the last one in the line. I didn't know whether to slap her hand or drink a bottle of antacid. Instead I dragged my son off to another room and told him it looked like he would have to be the responsible one here and went into an extra detailed discussion on condoms, AIDS, pregnancy, being too young for any of this, and the like. As I am talking to him his cell phone rings. It is her from the other room, in front of the tree—checking on him. Throughout my son is acting like an idiot who just won the Lotto and hasn't a clue what to do with the dough. Not quite a typical Xmas eve blessed scene. But if it was impious it was at least colorful."

SUBSTANCE ABUSERS

Of course, not all mild psychopaths abuse drugs and alcohol. But substance abuse problems do often occur in patients who are psychopathic. When this is the case, as the *DSM*-IV states, "both a Substance-Related Disorder and Antisocial Personality Disorder should be diagnosed if the criteria for both are met, even though some antisocial acts may be a con-sequence of the Substance-Related Disorder (e.g., illegal selling of drugs or thefts to obtain money for drugs)."[3]

Characteristically mild psychopaths who also both drink and take drugs do so less to get pleasurably high than to disinhibit themselves so that they can behave wildly and have fun, or become aggressive, and then excuse their misbehavior as drug– and alcohol–related. Also, as Stout sug-gests, theirs is an "inclination to dilute boredom chemically for a while."[4]

Psychopaths who are forced into rehabilitation programs for drug use and heavy drinking often fail at all attempts to get them to go straight. This is in part because they actually want to relapse, and they want to relapse in order to defeat an authority that wants them to be, or demands that they stay, sober and drug free.

Drug addicts who are also psychopaths tend to push as well as to take drugs. Sometimes they do so so successfully that they climb rather than descend the social ladder. In a typical scenario, an English teacher seemed to be the antithesis of a drug pusher type. He was not a tattooed, snaggle-toothed individual who looked like he had just gotten out of jail and was on the verge of being sent back. Rather, he was a handsome, charming, sophisticated person, an excellent host, with many friends who were all proud to be associated with him and to be seen in his very distinctive company. He was kind to his parents, especially close to his mother, and had a great love of the arts, particularly opera, which he regularly attended wearing an elegant formal opera jacket. But on the side and on the sly, he ran a popper (amyl nitrite) business out of his apartment, syn-thesizing the aphrodisiac and selling it to a constant procession of men coming and going all day and night and hanging out in the halls of his apartment building trying to meet each other for sex. He also bought and sold cocaine and other drugs, and after he moved from Boston, his home base, to California, sent parcels of drugs through the mail back to his cronies, omitting the return address so that if the package were inter-cepted it could not be traced back to him. On the side he learned how to feign back pain due to spasm and went from doctor to doctor asking for prescriptions for benzodiazepines, which he would then sell on the street. To further supplement his income, he took a night job in a boutique pre-cisely so that he could steal merchandise from the store and then return it for cash or credit to another store in another town.

A nursing home aide supplemented his income by stealing drugs from the nursing home for which he worked and then both using and selling them. A handsome hustler type, he would move in with older wealthy men and then use their homes as drug headquarters. Soon enough he would be turned out, but he did not care, for he was getting restless and wanted to move on once again. He was good-looking enough to easily find someone new, and moreover he was looking for fresh "suckers" to put one over on.

When I asked him why he acted the way he did, he replied, "I am just having fun; there is no particular downside to it for me, and think of the good times I am having screwing those stupid idiots who think that I love them and will let them take care of me for the rest of my life."

CRIMINALS

Most mild psychopaths are criminals, but not *hardened* criminals. Mild psychopaths characteristically commit certain kinds of crimes only. They tend to commit crimes of guile, like embezzlement, against institutions, more than they tend to commit crimes of force, like breaking and entering, against people. Acting more with their wits than with their fists, they steal not automobiles but ideas, or figure out ways to hack and spam without getting caught. They also know how to stay within the gray area of illegality and how to rationalize any criminal or criminal-like behavior after the fact in order to maintain a charade of honesty. In this regard they especially favor the misuse of Constitutional protections that were probably never meant to apply specifically to the likes of their personal behavior. In particular, they favor the Constitutional protections of freedom of speech, the right to privacy, and the prohibition against illegal search and seizure—good principles that they corrupt by applying them to their egregiously bad actions. Furthermore, they are adept at confusing their marks with sophistry, as in, "I am only creating, not actually spreading, a computer virus, and that is no different from a mystery writer's creating (not committing) a perfect crime." (Many people intend to put a clever computer hacker's new virus into operation, but few if any intend to play out the scenarios Agatha Christie created.) They are also especially adept at hiding out from the law, retaining their anonymity by covering their tracks behind multiple layers of camouflage.

Some of the mildest "criminals" confine their crimes to those that affect others' quality of life. For example, on moving day they might fill a construction site's dumpster not meant for household garbage with broken furniture and old mattresses, urinate in public (sometimes but not always behind bushes), or change in the men's room at the beach. Others confine their criminality to antisocial actions done specifically for modest financial gain, such as borrowing software and installing it on their computers, or giving and taking small bribes in the form of friendly repayments, e.g., a dinner out in a fine restaurant as return for some illicit political favor. Just recently a patient was selling his home. The appraiser came. When the patient and appraiser were alone, the appraiser asked the patient, "Do you have any money for me?" This question led the patient to suspect that the appraiser was asking for a tip so that he would appraise the property high enough to assure that the buyer would get the full mortgage she applied for.

Mostly the crimes of mild psychopaths are committed both opportunistically—that is, for secondary gain such as money—and for emotional reasons, for primary gain, such as the feeling of self-esteem-enhancing power (without practical use) they get from cleverly one-upping a victim.

Mild psychopaths, should they get caught, usually know how to avoid hard jail time. They know what to do to instead be sentenced to community service, and even how to turn that to their distinct advantage, e.g., by getting themselves hired out as enforcers who make certain that others never commit the same crimes that they themselves just pulled off, got caught at, and were recently convicted and sentenced for.

FICTIONAL CHARACTERS

Psychopaths as fictional characters make for some of the most interesting reading. Sometimes we shiver in horror at their behavior, as we do at Madame Bovary's lover's conning her for sex, destroying her marriage, and then leaving her. Others we identify with as we admire their pursuits—forgetting in our admiration of their antics that they are the very same crooks and charlatans that we roundly condemn should they enter our lives in reality and affect our daily living. We forget that Robin Hood became a hero by being a thief. We overlook how the Music Man, the "star" of the show by the same name, falsely promises to teach the children how to play in order to get their parents to purchase expensive instruments from him in a role more villain than hero. Even though she murders the man with whom she was having an illicit affair, we clap in delight as Roxie Hart, the star of the musical *Chicago*, winds up in a successful sister act with another performer, also a murderess. We refer to pirates as swashbucklers, a term with a positive connotation that would certainly be out of place when applied to the run-of-the-mill crook who holds up and robs people. It is unlikely, for example, that we would seriously consider speaking of "the swashbuckling Mr. Willie Sutton (the bank robber best known for the quote reproduced in Chapter 5)." Alas, only in fiction, not in real life, do most psychopaths come to unhappy ends. Faust, for example, succeeds for seven years. Only then does his life unravel as all comes crashing down at payback time when the devil comes to collect his soul. This is, unfortunately, not always a parable of what actually happens in the real world, to the psychopath of everyday life.

CHAPTER 5

A Few Cases

To illustrate many of the behavioral characteristics I have described so far in this book, I first present some composite case vignettes of psychopaths of everyday life and then present an actual case of a mild psychopath. In the latter I have altered details that would reveal his identity and have added anecdotal illustrations for purposes of clarity and emphasis.

SOME COMPOSITE CASES

A psychopathic newspaper reporter regularly made telling the truth secondary to selling his copy. Each week he wrote about a new miracle breakthrough diet of the "eat what you want and still lose weight" variety, none of which worked at all. Once he wrote a headline in a scandal sheet shouting that someone famous who had so far gotten away with murder was finally caught red-handed, and at last would have to pay. In the body of the article we learned: the individual was caught—for parking illegally, and would have to pay—a very costly parking ticket.

A covetous ambitious editorial writer for a large eastern newspaper frequently expressed his negative feelings about political figures by haranguing them obsessively. Just as obsessive patients, by perpetually expressing the same worry, or compulsive patients, by perpetually performing the same ritual, unconsciously aspire to drive their families to distraction, this psychopathic media harasser consciously set out to accomplish something similar by presenting and re-presenting his point in the manner of Chinese water torture. He acted as if his was a real interest in clarity, and presented himself as a savior with the sacred trust of protecting us all from harm by exposing the one and only truth held in his possession alone. In fact, he was acting out a sadistic vendetta, hoping to keep his victims under a complete and perpetual siege.

An aggressive ambitious sadistic music critic set out to use his vocation as a vehicle for gaining status within the academic establishment. He attempted to accomplish his goal by writing biting reviews of contemporary composers who created music that did not exact an emotional price. He knew these reviews would sit well with the inner circle of an academic establishment he wanted to impress—an establishment whose members characterized the highest function of music as "the power to give joy through pain." So he made the theme that happiness was less meaningful than sadness a recurrent one in his critical writings. Expressions like "almost unbearably intense" and "emotionally draining and exhausting" became conspicuous in his vocabulary of approval, while at the same time he damned all joyful, melodious music, however well made and sophisticated, as completely trivial because it was not sour, dissonant, or darkly foreboding. As he put it, hoping to be accepted by the tenured professors, and then tenured in his turn, "Because in our society suffering and failure are life-enhancing, joy is an expression less meaningful than tragedy, and an emotion far inferior to sadness."

He also sought out other critics strongly susceptible to the psychology of the herd and got them to join him in forming "gangs" of critics who would, with one voice, pick on some tacitly selected victim. Along the narcissistically manipulative lines of "I know better than the great unwashed," one gang he formed set out to smear with a single voice the composer Charles Camille Saint-Saëns, especially his opera *Samson and Delilah*. It was classified among the weakest of works—even though (as even he would grudgingly admit) it remained a favorite of opera lovers all over the world. His gangs were no more guilty about depriving their victims of their right to peaceful existence and professional success than the psychopath who left his grandmother penniless by remorselessly stealing her pension and using it to buy drugs. I know of at least one composer who gave up writing after being trammeled by this violent herd. In fact, I once hinted to the critic that my definition of a great artist is someone who can survive the onslaught of narcissistic, covetous, destructive psychopathic critics like him without developing a serious and sometimes professionally fatal case of writer's block.

A self-styled critic used book critiques on the Internet site Amazon.com as a way to act out his personal vendettas. He put talented people down, first to further his own career by hurting the careers of those he perceived to be his rivals; second to make himself feel less like a personal failure when others thought of or did something he believed he should have thought of or done first; and third when a book spoke negatively of someone with a personality trait that described him to a "T". His critiques used the same tricks of logic favored by psychopaths for dealing summarily with their victims. A favorite method of attack involved the use of selective abstraction, where he quoted out of context in order to attack and destroy effectively. For example, wanting to make an author look like the antifeminist that he had already decided she must be, he quoted her inexactly. He used the simple psychopathic expedient of leaving out qualifiers, turning her statement "Some women never marry because they have emotional problems" into "unmarried women have emotional problems"; then, after misquoting her, he concluded that she had said that single women are all flawed. Often writing one negative review was not good enough to satisfy his sadistic needs. So he would write as many as three or four, and post them from different friends' computers using pseudonyms to hide their true origin.

He once confided to me: "In my opinion, Amazon.com is itself no better than I am for not letting authors respond in self-defense to the negative reviews of reviewers like me. I have always suspected that the bookstore is catering to the buyers, whose numbers are much greater, than to authors, a typical self-serving behavior along the lines of Willie Sutton's famous explanation (which he probably never said) of why he robbed banks: 'Because that's where the money is.'"[1]

CASE HISTORY OF A PSYCHOPATH

The following case, of a doctor suffering from a mild form of psychopathy, illustrates the typical psychopathic behaviors discussed throughout, as well as matters discussed more specifically in later chapters: such as the course and prognosis of mild psychopathy, and some options for treating the less severe form of the disorder.

For the first forty or so years of his life, a physician suffered from a relatively mild form of psychopathy. I judged his disorder to be mild because it permitted him to function effectively in his profession, albeit on a lower level than his training, intelligence, and experience might have otherwise dictated. He was able to function effectively because even though he was ill, his illness spared important aspects of his personal and professional life, in part because it was partial and incomplete and had a favorable prognosis. As we shall see, the illness essentially ended completely later in life with, as commonly happens, an apparent epiphany.

As a *young child* he was diagnosed as suffering from Conduct Disorder, Child Onset Type that was mild, for the symptoms of his disorder were not such that he stood out markedly from his peers. He was a selfish child, likely to act without much if any concern for the effects of his actions on others, mainly his parents. For example, on more than one occasion he threatened to run away from home and several times actually did disappear for hours on end to a neighbor's apartment, where he had gone to visit a childhood sweetheart who lived in the same apartment building.

One day when he finally returned home after disappearing for some hours, his mother went into a panicky rage and beat him severely with a horsewhip, leaving him from that day on fearing retaliation and bodily harm should he act spontaneously and in a heterosexual manner. Such action, as he came to see it, would mean "upsetting her by going after some girl other than herself."

After this incident, and partly as a result of it, he became an aggressive child prone to temper tantrums. These tantrums often consisted of expressing anger and frustration in a self-destructive way—for example, by burning his clothing and tearing up his favorite books. He also started wetting his bed on a regular basis, partly out of anxiety and partly to get back at his mother—first by soaking her fine linens in urine and second by frustrating and defeating her in her attempts to get him to stop.

Early in life, one of his favorite activities involved sticking caterpillars into a roaring campfire and watching them writhe. He also enjoyed pulling the legs off daddy longlegs spiders. When he went fishing he particularly delighted in catching blowfish, tickling their bellies until they blew up in response, and then, without giving a thought to how the fish might feel, sticking a knife into their bellies. He rejoiced at letting the air out and watching as their eyes glossed over as they died. Notably, he regularly did this in his father's presence—a father who, although not apparently psychopathic himself, made no attempt whatsoever to stop him. Though he found stories of cats put through washing machines and into microwave ovens highly amusing, he stopped short—barely—of actually doing that himself.

As an *older child* he would organize small groups of children to steal from five-and-ten-cent stores. In one case he developed a solo scheme for grabbing candy bars from a candy shop. He would ask the proprietor to go to the back of the store for something he knew the proprietor stored there, and then, when the proprietor was out of sight, run behind the counter and grab a candy bar from the shelf.

In *high school* he went on with his cheating. He regularly translated *Julius Caesar* into English using a ready English translation. Before a final examination he went through the secretary's wastepaper basket looking for cast-off copies of the typed exam. (He found one, but his conscience kicked in, a bit late, and he stopped reading it halfway through—though he never told anyone before the exam that he had read the first half.) He did not seem to care that he might have been severely disciplined had he been caught, and possibly even thrown out of school without getting his diploma—four years wasted because of one foolish mistake.

Around this time, in the rush of budding homosexuality, he would pick out names at random from the telephone book, call them up, sight unseen, and make sexual proposals to them, his attraction based on little more than their having names that sounded sexy. He especially liked men who were named "Testa." That excited him because the name brought up images in his mind of "testicle." A few times the older men he preferred found themselves accused of child molestation, yet he was really the one who seduced them as much as the other way around.

Also around this time he started drinking, smoking pot, and becoming highly promiscuous sexually. To support his appetitive pleasures, he stole cash from his father's wallet and his mother's purse, and to get to his assignations he even drove off with the family car before he had obtained his full driver's license.

He often faked illness to stay home from school, and when he did go to school he would hang out with unsavory companions, get into fights, and then lie to his parents about who his friends were. On a number of occasions he and a pack of his friends set small fires on the front lawns of neighbors. Once one neighbor caught him egging her house, and another time a neighbor observed him destroying her lawn ornaments with a baseball bat. He was about to twist the neck off a swan, but he stopped just short when some passers-by appeared and interrupted him. Around this time he was thrown out of the Boy Scouts for cheating on a survival course. He said he made a fire the Boy Scout way. Actually he made it in what was, for Boy Scouts, the psychopathic way: by using a match.

When he was *sixteen* and in summer camp, without even imagining that he was doing anything wrong, he broke into another camper's room to get some sheet music he just had to have. When caught rifling through her drawers, he used as his excuse that he was stuck in the country, where there were no music stores to supply him with what he needed. As far as he was concerned, that alone entitled him to go for anything he wanted, and to try to get it in any way he could.

In his *late teens* he began to become argumentative and unpredictably aggressive. He was especially apt to have a temper tantrum when he felt someone had deprived him of what he needed or crossed him in some way, however insignificant. Once a dealership told him that a bicycle he had brought in for repair was ready, but when he went to pick it up it was not done. So he had a rage reaction in the showroom, refusing to leave until they fixed his bike, ultimately becoming so obnoxious they had to call the police to drag him off the premises.

As he grew into *adulthood*, his psychopathy continued to be manifest, but intermittently. Though he often acted shamelessly in a way that created serious problems for others, he usually stopped short of getting into big trouble himself. When he did get into trouble, he knew how to charm and manipulate his way out of it. His behavior, while often atrocious, could at times be paradoxically acceptable and sometimes even admirable. For example, he abandoned one dog to the land and had another put to sleep because her barking bothered him. But he spent a month's salary on having a third cured of mange so that he could adopt her out to a loving family.

In *college* he became known for his sarcastic and often morbid sense of humor. In particular, he became a jokester who specialized in goofing on authority. One of his pastimes consisted of telling mean-spirited anecdotes about the administration. A favorite story of his, which he repeated incessantly, was a tale involving a string quartet in residence at the school he attended. This quartet was giving a young person's concert for television. Each member of the quartet was asked to demonstrate what he played—whereupon the lead violinist, speaking in an unwitting double entendre, looked directly at the camera and proudly said, in all seriousness, and to the consternation of the show's producers, "Now I am going to show you my instrument, the one I play with."

Unfortunately, when he went to *medical school*, he continued to goof not only on the higher-ups in the administration but also on his patients. For example, during medical school he regularly and publicly referred to the flashbacks from which veterans with Posttraumatic Stress Disorder were suffering as "flushbacks." While not a practical jokester himself, he did nothing to stop others from pulling off practical jokes that he knew to be hurtful and even dangerous. For example, while on service in a psychiatric hospital, he discovered that one of the patients was slipping her medications into the water in the kettle he and the other doctors were using to make their morning coffee. He himself stopped drinking the coffee, but he never told his colleagues what was happening, preferring instead to sit back and have a good laugh at their expense as they stumbled around wondering why they were feeling so dizzy. Another time he invited some colleagues to a party on the North Shore of Long Island in New York. When they asked him for directions, he suggested in all seriousness that the best way to reach the house was to drive to the south shore of Connecticut, rent a boat, and then sail across Long Island Sound.

Around this time he always seemed to need money to fly around the country to visit his various sexual partners. He extracted this money from his relatively impoverished parents by telling them that he was so hungry and the food at school so expensive that he had to buy more food coupons just to survive. These he promptly sold for the cash he needed to feed himself his rich little pleasures.

While in medical school, he avoided taking assigned night calls whenever he could. Instead he hid out, refusing to answer his pages. He did not seem to care that the service he was on needed him, that he was not doing his job, or that his irresponsible behavior might earn him a failing grade. Instead he bragged to all his friends that he could get away with avoiding calls because "First they have to find me, and second they have to make me understand what they want." He completely forgot to mention that "Third they can fail me and have me kicked out of medical school."

As an *intern* after medical school, he regularly bounced checks on the hospital for the money he needed to go drinking and cruising. He also developed an elaborate scheme to save money by not paying for his food. He would fill a tray with a big meal, put the tray down in a place where the cashier could not see it, go back for a small item, pay for that, and then sneak back to pick up the full tray and waltz right past the busy and pre-occupied gate-keeper.

When he was on two services at once, he would tell one that he was working for the other, then leave them both and take a nap. Once he stole a rubber sheet from the hospital to protect a valise on the luggage rack of his car from the rain. When a housekeeper reported the theft, he threatened her life. He finally got out of a jam by lying—saying that the nurse who had given him the sheet had told him that it was torn, and that they were going to throw it out anyway.

During *residency*, after internship, he would phony up medical cases to present at grand rounds, in order to make himself look good. His tendency to be an iconoclastic countercultural antiestablishment person who, to use his own words, liked to "goof on everything and everybody sacred" continued now with potentially and truly severe consequences for his career. He thought it amusing to pick as the topic for a grand rounds presentation to the big boss three cases that had one thing in common: The people who had asked him to consult on them had fired him, writing in the order book, "D/C (that is, 'discontinue') the doctor." Also in residency he would identify those lecturers he disliked and attend their lectures just so that he could deliberately and obviously stand up and stalk out of the room after five minutes—his way to show the lecturers his displeasure.

When he was on call he would often act in a completely irresponsible manner. He once went for a flying lesson at an airport on a Sunday while he was on duty. He insisted that his action was not wrong because "I told the nurse when I'd be back." Another time, totally without guilt, remorse, or fear of consequences, he went to a party when he was on duty, and then came back drunk when he was still on call. His excuse: "I had asked for the night off but they didn't give it to me, so I decided to take it anyway, and the hell with them." One night when he was covering the emergency room, a woman called up to say that she had accidentally overdosed with a substance and wanted to know if it was toxic. Without bothering to check to see if it was (and it most certainly was), he told her that it was not, just so that she would not rush in for care, waking him up in the middle of the night. He never knew, or even cared, what had happened to her.

Now, as throughout life, he continued his old ways of mistreating animals. Once he got a puppy just so that he could give it a name he thought clever, "Gargle." When that amusement value wore off, and he found that the puppy inconvenienced him by interfering with his lifestyle, he let the dog run free in the rural neighborhood in which he lived. Finally, when it returned over and over again in spite of his efforts to be rid of it, had it put down when it was just a few months old. He beat another dog for losing control of her bladder and bowels, though as a physician he should have known that her partial paralysis from a slipped disk made her unable to hold on. He found her pain from the disk a serious inconvenience for him, and later, as she lay slowly dying, saw her gradual demise strictly as a matter of her putting him through changes. He found it particularly annoying that she was about to put him through the emotionally unpleasant (for him) process of having to put her down. Eventually she died. But really, she was killed when he covered her up with a towel that impeded her breathing, for she was too paralyzed to move from under it. He carelessly let her smother. Afterwards, a friend trying to help him get over his grief, gave him a purebred Siamese cat, but he did not take care of it and let it escape. When his friend asked him what had happened to the cat, he shrugged his shoulders and said that she had gotten out and that he was too tired to go looking for it—and besides, since this was her second escape, he wanted to teach her a lesson. Another time a friend with several cats complained that she could no longer take care of them because of her allergies. This time he was the one to generously offer his help. "I can get them a good home," he said. Then, thinking it uproarious, and needing some spare change for himself, the day after she left her cats with him he brought them to an experimental lab and sold them for a few dollars apiece.

After residency, even though he had a somewhat lucrative practice, he made a habit of never correcting cashiers when they made a mistake and gave him back more than he was owed, or waiters when they undercharged him for dinner even though he suspected or knew that they would have to pay for the error themselves. Once he accepted $5,000 a bank had mistakenly credited to his account. He did not protest. Rather he waited a few years before taking the money out, and then, when he felt they had forgotten all about it, had the money transferred to another account thinking that they would not be able to find it if they bothered to look for it.

Throughout his *adult life* he lost one friend after another, mostly for two reasons. First, they spotted him as a phony putting on airs. He admitted that he put on airs because he wanted to be the exact opposite of his parents, whom he saw as "low-life immigrant types" who dressed unstylishly and misused English. He felt he had no alternative but to do what he could to dissociate himself from them—adopting a British accent and wearing only Ivy League clothing, just so that he would not be identified in any way with those "schmucks." Second, he was nice to his friends when they were around but then talked about them negatively behind their backs and to people who would predictably report back what he had said. He would demean them by putting them down and ridiculing them. This one was a stupid redneck who belonged in a pickup truck, that one a dumb blonde with dark roots that showed her true colors, and the like.

Around this time he was beginning to drink heavily and simultaneously take high doses of benzodiazepines. When intoxicated he would have even worse temper tantrums and become even more verbally abusive than before. Once when drunk he made fun of a lover's father for having committed suicide by hanging. He staged a mock hanging of his own, with the necktie he wore. One New Year's Eve he drank too much and took too much Valium. When his lover warned him against walking into traffic, he blew up at him, told him to stop being so controlling, and walked off into the night to go cruising alone in the bars and baths. He would frequently drive while drunk. One time he had an accident that almost totaled the car. Afterwards he managed to convince the police that he was not unable to drive because he was intoxicated. What had happened, to hear him tell it, was that the brakes had failed. He also managed to convince his parents to pay to have the damage repaired by telling them that student loans and other harsh expenses made it impossible for him to swing the repairs himself. Another time when he was drunk the police picked him up before he got into his car, but they let him go because he charmed them with smooth talk about how he worked the emergency room in the local hospital and how nice he would be to them when they came in and had to wait for a patient they had brought in by ambulance.

As a *gay adult man* he had a string of lovers, with no affair lasting more than a few months. He cheated on all of them. He typically found himself attracted to low life, that is, to rough trade, whom he admired for their earthiness and lack of refinement, and because they were "the way I would like to be if only I weren't stuck being a professional person." One of his lovers died of cancer. Knowing that he was about to go, the lover asked him to use his life-insurance money to take care of his sister. Instead he used it to take care of himself—by putting the exact sum down as a deposit on a luxury condominium apartment, one he bought the day his lover died. (He did retain some guilt about his actions, however. Even though the will stipulated that his lover's father's royalties were to go to him, he graciously had them transferred to his lover's sister.) Not surprisingly, he never bothered attending his lover's funeral but instead stayed at home—just so that he could have sex with someone new and attractive— a young man he had met just the night before.

In his *early thirties,* after yet another attack of gonorrhea, he experienced a brief episode of guilt. Disgusted with himself for "being such a whore," he became seriously depressed, stopped his wild behavior, and, trying to go straight, sought psychoanalysis. After a few years of celibacy he decided that it was not working, so he became actively and openly hypersexual once again and restarted all his old unreliable, hurtful, self-destructive ways.

During this period he began to drink even more heavily than before and use, in addition to alcohol and benzodiazepines, excessive amounts of poppers as aphrodisiacs and marijuana to get high. He often misused these substances to the point that his judgment was effectively suspended. For example, once he got drunk and had sex with a man in the bathroom of his apartment when the man's wife was sleeping in the adjacent living room. He was never careful about whom he took back with him. He would pick up a stranger in a bar and then drag him home without knowing anything about him. Several pickups gave him a Mickey Finn and then rifled his apartment. He also started going to the baths every night—and picked up multiple cases of gonorrhea, a case of scabies, and venereal warts. All this behavior he excused as "that's what all gay men do, isn't it, so how can it be wrong when I do it too?"

The lying and thieving that started in childhood continued into adulthood in the form of serious stealing from his newly widowed mother. He stole from her because he felt entitled to have all the good things in life, and because he felt that his mother, like everyone else, had been so unjust to him that it made sense to avenge himself upon her. When his mother first became mentally impaired due to early stage Alzheimer's, he cleaned out her apartment. Even though he knew how much she loved her personal treasures accumulated over the years, he unlovingly moved all her things to his place. He reasoned that they were valuable and that he did not want her to ruin them because they constituted his inheritance. Next he cleaned out the money in her accounts so that his present lover would inherit her money in case anything happened to him—a dangerous thing to do because if he had died before his mother, she would have been left completely impoverished. Later, when his mother became mentally disorganized, and forgot that she had left him almost all her estate, he used the fact that she had left a few of her personal things to her relatives as an excuse to get angry with, and back at, her by putting her in a nursing home—before she really needed to be institutionalized. When she finally did die, he had so few feelings and experienced so little grief that he did not even cry. As he put it, "I felt more grief when I lost my hamster than when I lost that bitch of a mother of mine."

In therapy we got past the manifest maladaptive behavior to work on some of its possible causes. One thing we worked on was his tendency to avoid taking responsibility for his actions by blaming them on everyone but himself. For example, he rethought his claim that if his behavior were immoral, which he would occasionally admit that it was, it was because he was quite naturally rebelling against his parents' extreme, excessive morality. As he had put it, "Anyone in my shoes would do what they could to avoid being the passive compliant wimps they were."

We also worked on his selfishness, which he saw in the beginning as both understandable and inevitable because it was a way to love and take care of himself in a world where no one else cared about him. Ultimately he was able to understand that he had reversed cause and effect: He was not selfish because no one took care of him; no one took care of him because he was selfish.

We also focused on his apparent lack of guilt around such things as stiffing the hospital cafeteria and sending dogs he adopted to the pound without considering the responsibility he assumed when he first took them home. Underneath this apparent guiltlessness we uncovered a great deal of guilt around his manifestly pleasurable and self-serving but mal-adaptive behavior, and noted how this guilt led to his constantly and self-destructively defeating himself overall. I noted by way of example that though he was a brilliant student who graduated *cum laude* from college, and though he finished medical school with a decent average and in spite of his maladaptive behavior was able to get good recommendations from his professors, he went through life constantly pulling the rug out from under himself. The remedy then was to stop knocking himself off all pin-nacles as soon as he reached the top and to instead start discovering and putting into action more constructive ways to behave, in order to achieve success and attain permanent happiness.

In parallel fashion, we analyzed how his excessively high self-esteem was a cover for his excessively low self-esteem. We focused on the grandiose belief that he could get away with absolutely anything without getting caught because God was watching over him, and would not cru-elly let a nice guy like him suffer a fate that was only for the undeserving. We came to view this as a denial defense against its opposite: the feeling that he was a poor wretch abandoned by God who could do no better than grab at anything good that came his way in the certainty that he would not be around to enjoy life for very long. After uncovering his basic low self-esteem and poor self-image, we traced it back to the beating his mother gave him for being in love with the little girl next door, and the belief that if his father had cared for him more, he would have stopped him from doing bad things like sticking knives in fishes' abdomens. He also came to recognize that his maladaptive behavior was in part a test to see if someone would love him enough to try to ignore the bad part of him, and to stop him from misbehaving instead of just sitting idly by as he destroyed his life and himself.

His psychopathy began to peak as new insights developed, all at about the same time that his reflective powers increased with age. His hormones leveled off, and his interneural transmitter firings decreased—all starting around age forty, and just in time to keep him and his career from being completely ruined forever. By the time he was forty-five, he had had what amounted to an epiphany. He gave up his wild and fantastic behaviors and swung to the opposite extreme, going from sinner to saint, to become something even more than a solid citizen—an arch conservative whose "good behavior" not only met but exceeded the standards and requirements of even the finickiest members of the establishment.

Simultaneously he began to feel some retrospective guilt long after the fact. It particularly pained him to look back on his previous actions and see how all along he had been drowning in selfishness, lacking empathy for others to the point that he would wrong and badly hurt the humans and animals in his world without a care for how they felt, and without any compunction whatsoever.

One day he told me, "I was able to feel anxious, then cry for the first time in my life." We took this as a sign that he was getting better, at least enough to consider leaving therapy. During his last sessions he vowed to go through life making amends to the animals, people, and institutions that he had tried to destroy in his younger, more ebullient, and less responsible days. On follow-up he told me he had adopted a number of stray cats and dogs to try to make up for his mistreatment of animals earlier in his life, had a long-term committed relationship with a man much his junior whom he cared for deeply and took good care of emotionally and physically, and had developed a successful and lucrative practice, as well as a career teaching students—the children he wanted to bring up right—so that "they wouldn't become psychopaths like me."

CHAPTER 6

The Core Personality Structure

In Chapters 2 and 3, I described the characteristic behaviors of mild psychopaths. In this chapter I describe those fundamental, or core, characteristics of the disorder that outline its basic structure and reveal some of its causes. It is only when we take the behavioral manifestations and the core personality difficulties together that we have a complete picture of the full syndrome. In turn, psychopathy should only be definitively diagnosed when characteristic behavioral and core features are present together and to a significant degree. For example, opportunism is not by itself psychopathic. A money-mad newspaper owner who instructed his staff to write positively about his advertisers and negatively about those who refused to put an ad into his paper may or may not have been a psychopath. His actions may merely have been those of an unduly ambitious striving businessman. Before we seriously entertain the diagnosis of Psychopathic Personality Disorder in him, we would need to examine his life closely, looking to answer some important questions. Outside of the business realm, did he treat everyone not as individuals but as objects, in effect narcissistically? Did he demand that not only the business people he dealt with, but also his family and friends, "pay up or shut up?"

The material here is once again presented using the classic mental status examination format as a convenient way of giving organization to the clinical picture of psychopathy. The two parts of the mental status of psychopaths that describe their more superficial attributes, their *appearance* and *behavior*, were discussed in Chapter 3. In this chapter I discuss those parts of the mental status of psychopaths that reveal the more basic aspects of their personality. These are:

- Difficult-to-ascertain or actually incomprehensible *motivation;*
- Problematic *affect;*
- Compromised *insight;*
- Variable *intelligence* ranging from below to above average;
- Sometimes poor and sometimes better-than-average *judgment;*
- Unreliable *memory;*
- Mildly compromised *orientation;* and, perhaps most importantly,
- Disordered *thought content* and *process.*

In particular, thought content and process disorder are, in my opinion, as characteristic of psychopathy as loosening of associations is characteristic of schizophrenia or flight of ideas is characteristic of mania—so much so that as criteria they distinguish psychopathy not only from other character disorders but also from the "normally flawed character of everyday life."

Some of what follows about the mental status of psychopaths is inferential, given how these individuals are generally uninsightful, have much to hide, are not averse to hiding it, and can be unappealing to the point of discouraging the prolonged close contact that is necessary for understanding them in depth. Nevertheless, a combination of careful and intelligent observation and listening, good guesswork, and reliable third-party information can provide the experienced observer with substantially meaningful and accurate depth material that can, at the very least, help him or her spot, understand, cope with, manage, and treat the psychopathic condition. As an example of good guesswork, a number of astute observers have described making the diagnosis of psychopathy countertransferentially—when the patient tells a concocted hard luck story that is nevertheless so piteously convincing that they feel compelled to reach for their wallets—and then feel stupid afterwards for having been suckered in. These observers have learned by (sad) experience that this is a clinical sign, or a warning, that they might be dealing with a psychopath. They have also discovered after having been burned more than once that the best "twice shy" response in such cases is to not give these individuals what they ask for but to simply, but firmly, demand to know why exactly they feel justified in requesting it.

DIFFICULT-TO-ASCERTAIN/INCOMPREHENSIBLE MOTIVATION

Cleckley notes that it is characteristic for the antisocial behavior of serious psychopaths to be "inadequately motivated,"[1] forcing both therapists and lay observers to ask themselves what the person could be thinking. Delving into their unconscious can be unrevealing, and even their dreams can seem to say little if anything about what is going on in the deepest layers of their minds. (Cleckley qualifies his formulation by saying that "causal factors do . . . exist [but in psychopaths they are very] deeply rooted"[2] and so quite difficult to uncover.)

In contrast, the motivation of mild psychopaths, while hardly transparent and not generally admirable, is often somewhat comprehensible in human terms, both emotional and practical. For example, many of us can understand wanting to annoy others just for the fun of it, and so can relate at least somewhat to the biker who revs up his motorcycle at midnight in a quiet neighborhood. Many of us can understand being opportunistic to the point of being willing to go to any extreme to win, and so can relate to the motivation of the lawyer who will say almost anything to get a guilty client off, and even to that of the contractor who offers to repair a home and then absconds with the down payment.

In mild psychopaths, slips of the tongue can sometimes reveal underlying secret fantasies. For example, an administrator accused of running his academic department in a scandalous manner is asked if he responded to the scandals by making changes. In a telling moment of truth, this administrator, who happens to be an ex-minister, replies, "My response has been *sinful.*" He then blushingly corrects himself by saying, "What I meant to say is that my response has been *simple.*"

However, just because we can understand the actions of the psychopath does not mean that we fully approve. More often we respond to their actions by thinking that it may be possible for us to explain their behavior, but that does not necessarily mean that it is desirable for us to excuse it.

POOR CONDITIONABILITY

Psychopaths appear to be unresponsive to both negative and positive conditioning—to both punishment and affirmation—so that we say "you cannot tell them anything," or "what's the sense of trying to be nice to them?" As H. J. Eysenck notes, "There is overwhelming evidence that antisocial and criminal people show relatively poor conditionablity compared with ordinary people."[3] Like the coffee shop owner mentioned throughout, they rarely acknowledge any power higher than their own, making them thoroughly immune to good advice coming from their family, friends, and therapists. This coffee shop owner was not paying her rent. When her landlord threatened to evict her for nonpayment, she responded not by improving her business practices so that she could increase her cash flow, but by fighting him in court. Her advisors all told her the same thing—that she was going out of business because she was not competitive. Her prices were high and her portions were small, and she opened so irregularly that one never knew when she was going to be there. But advice to her to increase her portion size and stay open on schedule went unheard and unheeded. Instead, she responded to her advisers by making one excuse after another: "The food is costly and

I need to make a profit, my dog needs to be walked more often, I refuse to go through life stuck in a routine, and anyway what is life all about when you can't have fun going to the beach during the day, at least a few times a week." As a result, she did not make positive course corrections. Instead she, like many psychopaths, disregarded feedback from people who knew better and allowed her status to deteriorate, as do many psychopaths, until it was too late to be rescued.

AFFECT

Anger

Anger is inherent in the psychopathic condition. As Millon suggests, these are "aggressively oriented personalities [who] tend to be argumentative and contentious . . . abrusive (sic), cruel, and malicious [who] often insist on being seen as faultless, invariably are dogmatic in their opinions, and rarely concede on any issue despite clear evidence negating the validity of their argument . . . [all] as if [their] 'softer' emotions [were] tinged with poison."[4]

Anger typically results when the psychopath feels crossed, or is cornered and runs out of excuses. He or she goes beyond rational argument in self-defense to become intimidating and threatening. An illustration of what can happen when a psychopath feels crossed is to be found in a letter to the editor written by a woman who personalized what she took to be an insult to all women. She met a measured inquiry into whether women in the entertainment industry needed to maintain a certain look about them with an unfair, manipulative, intimidating, bullying ad hominem rant that bypassed rational argument and instead resorted to intimidation by name-calling and character assassination. One part of her reply to the writer of the column in question serves as an illustration: "You are a crybaby bitch . . . you are a disgusting example of a man . . . I might be homely, but I can still kick your ass."[5]

A writer tells me that a reviewer wrote a mixed review of her book, saying that something was not in it when it was. When she pointed out that the reviewer obviously only read enough of the book to make herself mad, then acted on it, the reviewer got even angrier, to the point that she wrote a two-page diatribe defending her response.

Impoverishment of Affect

Cleckley speaks of a "general poverty in major affective reactions"[6] and a "far reaching, profound, and final . . . diminution of emotional range."[7] Generally speaking, psychopaths cannot cry, or at least they cannot cry real tears. This is partly because they lack ordinary sensibilities, have little or no capacity for deep object love, and fear allowing tender feelings to "seep through." Also, their blaming tendencies make them unable to look into their soul long and hard enough to sense, experience, and deeply feel what is going on inside.

Hypomania

At times fantastic behavioral flights can make the psychopath appear to be suffering from an affective disorder with hypomanic features. A differential point between the two disorders is that hypomanic individuals seem to become euphoric over a happy cause, while psychopaths seem to become euphoric over negative things, such as having effectively gotten revenge on someone they count as being one of their enemies.

THOUGHT

The image in the extant literature of the psychopath as an individual who thinks clearly but acts irrationally is, strictly speaking, imperfect. While the psychopath's thinking is not as disorganized as the thinking of the schizophrenic, psychopathic irrationality of a sort clearly does exist. Millon identifies a "pathological process of [cognitive] distortion"[8] as the basis of the formation of personality, and presumably, therefore, as the basis of some of the personality problems in psychopaths, and I believe that the irrational thinking I go on to describe is characteristic of the condition. This psychopathic irrationality may range from overt to extremely subtle, and when subtle may not even be perceived as psychopathic in origin. But I believe that it is pathognomonic to the point that I suggest only making a definitive diagnosis when the characteristic disordered behavior *and* the characteristic thinking that I go on to analyze are present together, and the observed psychopathic behavior is the product of the disordered thinking. Conversely, the diagnosis may not be valid if the disordered thinking is not there and/or the behavior under consideration is not the product of the specific disordered thinking but is, for example, the product of pure calculation, making it less a madness than a badness.

In psychopaths, the disorder of thinking consists of both thought *content* and thought *process* disorders.

Thought Content Disorder

In a disorder like schizophrenia, to a great extent thought process disorder forms the basis of thought content disorder. For example, predicative thinking, the most familiar example of which is "I am a virgin, the Virgin Mary is a virgin, therefore I am the Virgin Mary" forms the basis of many grandiose delusions. In psychopathy, the reverse process often predominates. Here characteristic thought content disorder creates, in part by facilitating and justifying, thought process disorder. For example, "I want what I want and am entitled to get exactly that" inspires the shifty sly self-justifications and casuistic rationalizations that enable the psychopath to "go for it" without guilt. Very typically, hunger for power originating in resolute competitiveness, grandiose wishes originating in narcissistic entitlement, and resolute rebelliousness originating in anti-establishmentarianism (all thought content) generate to a great extent the characteristic shifty or sophistical thinking (thought process) characteristic of the typical psychopathic con job.

Here are some key elements in the disordered thought content of psychopaths.

Hypocritical thinking.   For psychopaths what is sauce for the goose is not sauce for the gander. Hypocrisy is a reason a boss on the same time clock as her workers comes and goes as she pleases and then cracks down on her subordinates for coming in late. It is also the reason why a commentator can unfairly favor not letting a rapist use a victim's past sexual history in his self-defense, yet advocate convicting an alleged child molester simply on the basis of hearsay about his past sexual behavior.

Blame shifting.   We are all familiar with the quack practitioner the FDA is trying to put out of business. He defends his advocacy of a worthless nostrum by blaming the FDA for unfairly prosecuting him and contends that the agency is in cahoots with drug companies that fear his natural cures will put *them* out of business. A neighbor piles boxes in the lobby of his apartment building. When brought up short for not taking them to the recycling center, as is the accepted procedure, his retort is that "They should have known that I was moving and made some provision to dispose of my boxes for me." Just recently in the news was the probation hearing of a man accused of vehicular homicide. At the hearing his sorrow and grief were abject and his apologies seemed sincere. However, when the ruling went against him all that washed away and he lashed out at the probation officers and at his attorney along the lines of, "So if I am not going to be let go, why did everybody waste my time and put me through all this in the first place?" He did not acknowledge that he had done something unforgivable, but instead accused others of acting in an unacceptable fashion. The psychopath who is unfaithful to his wife regularly protests that his wife does not have what it takes to keep his interest. Psychopaths who do not improve when hospitalized often say that their case was mismanaged, and psychopaths who get arrested often claim that they did nothing wrong, and that the problem was not with them but with the ineptness and brutality of the police. To quote a fictional matron in a women's prison: "Honey, I don't know of no guy a lady shot who didn't ask for it."

In short, everything psychopaths do is second strike (provoked), not first strike (initiated), explainable not by who they are but by what they experienced in the past (e.g., in the form of child abuse) or by what they experience in the present (e.g., in the form of physical or mental illness, or social unfairness).

Psychopaths typically facilitate their blame shifting by using ambiguity. For example, psychopaths use simple gestures or words that can have different meanings depending on inflection (e.g., "Really!" can mean "Is it true?" while "Really?" can mean "I don't believe it."). In doing so, they deliberately set others up and steer them wrong so that they can go on to win big by attacking their victims for misreading them.

Psychopathic blame-shifting characteristically has as its basis the *narcissistic* view of the self as flawless and the *paranoid* view of the self as victim. In the realm of the paranoid, we hear "I am not a liar; others are unfairly calling me one" and the paranoid childish defense of tu quoque ("you are one too") along the lines of "I am not 'black'; you are the pot calling me names." It is my opinion that Ward Churchill, the professor who claimed that the victims of the World Trade Center 9/11 catastrophe "were the equivalent of 'little Eichmanns,'"[9] may not have been a full psychopath personally, but his assertion looked psychopathic in the sense that it was not only inhumane, departing as it did from the common and consensually validated national view of the incident as a tragedy for us all, but also heavily depended in its formulation upon the use of the manipulative childish illogic of the tu quoque defensive accusation. Thus, in effect he said that those in the World Trade Center towers were not victims but perpetrators—not themselves terrorized but terrorists themselves. Then, to ice the cake, he implied that the United States deserved what it got, for it too was not victim but victimizer. (Also psychopathic, at least in spirit, was his clever attempt to change others' outrage at what he said into guilt about defaming his character, as well as his ability to blame-shift the discussion away from the unsustainable assertions he made onto the media's presumed distortions of what he actually said, and how attempts were being made to abrogate his right to speak his mind freely in a free country.) (More later on this topic.)

The coffee-shop owner mentioned throughout was also playing the blame game when she blamed the landlord for demanding that she pay the rent, calling him "impatient" and "unsympathetic," instead of admitting that she had run her business into the ground. I went along with her view of the situation and felt sorry for her until one day I was in her shop chatting with her. The sign on her door read "open," but to her, conceptually, she was closed. Three people tried to get in to have lunch, and even though she had plenty of food, she decided that she just did not want to be bothered by the demanding public. So she told them: "Go away, I'm closed."

Psychopathic couples play the blame game when each falsely attributes all his or her marital difficulties to the other partner, so that as far as each member of the couple is concerned, it takes not two but one to make for all marital difficulties. In a typical scenario, a wife complained that her husband was a lazy so-and-so because he would not help around the house and instead wanted to sit on the sofa, rest, evade his responsibilities, and then make a thousand excuses for himself. He retorted: "I am not the lazy so-and-so my wife says I am. I am just a man hiding out from a difficult controlling woman like her. She expects too much of me. She should look instead to her tendency to evade *her* responsibilities, and stop trying to make herself feel less guilty by blaming me for evading mine."

Rationalization (spin).   Psychopaths are particularly adept at concocting alternate, more acceptable explanations for their behavior in order to hide the truly negative nature of their actions from the public and to enhance their self-image.

Psychopaths often rationalize their immorality by *minimizing* its significance. For example, a former SS guard at Auschwitz asserts that if he did anything wrong, he was at most guilty of violating some trivial human rights. Psychopaths also make excuses for themselves by *claiming altruistic motives*—justifying their criminal actions by citing the fundamental selflessness of their intent. A familiar example is "I don't do this because I am selfish, and for gain, but because I am a socially aware person acting out of a concern for the common good." In Chapter 7 I discuss an individual who exemplified this process when she hid her real motive—protecting her view—beneath the rationalization that she was protecting an historic district from being overbuilt. An example familiar to us all is the contention that bombing abortion clinics is justified as long as the bombings are motivated by the notion that human life is sacred.

Psychopaths typically rationalize their self-centered behavior on the grounds of entitlement. They argue that since art belongs to the masses, to all of us, great art is the property of the common man. Therefore, all artistic production ought to be freely available to all, say, on the Internet for them to download free of charge. They also argue that they are entitled to say and do whatever they please in this, a free country. According to Tim Murphy and Loriann Oberlin, a cynical, vindictive avenging music critic who apparently feels that he is entitled to speak his mind no matter how hurtful his commentary, uses "his column to pan the local artist's music, while lobbing low blows at his reputation, all under the guise of 'opinion' and 'free press' . . . ."[10] Psychopaths often invoke the entitlement that presumably comes from consensual validation along the lines of "Everybody is doing it, so why should I be any different?" Or they base their feelings of entitlement on the conditions actions have to meet before they become unacceptable, as in "after all, no one got hurt," or "mine is a victimless crime: Bill Gates has all the money he needs, so what difference does it make if I steal just a few of his computer programs?"

Entitlement rationalization easily morphs into grandiose self-serving morality based on personal decisions about what are higher and lower moral planes. For example, a con artist was fanatic about protecting his civil right to tout a worthless cure-all product. This "civil right" was deemed to be on a higher plane than the rights of his victims to not be mistreated by being fleeced financially and damaged medically by being steered away from timely and effective medical treatment.

As a corollary, rationalizing psychopaths often begin to think that they can get away with almost anything. They believe that their admirable motivation makes it possible, for them at least, to significantly break the rules without consequences. However, amorality and self-justification alone do not explain their fixation on this belief. The idea has irrational qualities as their self-exculpation takes on a dereistic (unrealistic) caste, having gone from a lie to themselves to an idea of delusional proportions— after crossing a boundary that is very tenuous, if indeed there is such a boundary.

Blurring the differences between right and wrong.   Psychopaths blur the differences between right and wrong according to one of three faulty premises:

Premise 1: Right and wrong are irrelevant abstractions. Self-interest, however disguised, is the essence of all motivation, and those who profess otherwise are fools or hypocrites.

Not surprisingly, psychopaths who operate according to this premise do not appear to reflect excessively on the morality of their actions.

Premise 2: Right and wrong are entirely valid considerations, and I am always right (and you are always wrong).

Without repudiating principles, these individuals change facts selectively to give themselves the answers they want and so conclude that they and they alone are justified and absolutely correct. Thus an individual who wants to drive after three cocktails convinces others that "Phobics like me can actually drive better when they are a little high." (This example also illustrates how psychopaths are likely to be victims of the same cunning distortions that they practice on others.)

The director of training for a psychiatric residency program wanted the students to double up on the services they performed: twice the work for the same amount of pay. He did not care that they would be performing so many services that they would have little time or energy left over for learning. To his end, he claimed that he was right to assert that training and service were so intimately related that they were one and the same, and that therefore "the more service, the better the training." With the connivance of the department head, a teaching program was drawn up to satisfy and impress evaluating agencies, but it was left unimplemented. Complaints by the students that they were getting little or no training were met with evasions and compromises, and the students were warned not to go to the outside authorities, a warning reinforced with secret recordings of conversations and an elaborate spy network.

Individuals who think they are always right will predictably blame-shift to others rather than accept blame themselves when things go wrong. There is a self-assured narcissistic component to this blaming that can help distinguish it from the "not me but you" projective blaming of paranoia. Consider the gay man mentioned throughout who basically said to someone he had possibly just infected with AIDS through intercourse, "It's not my fault for infecting you; it's your fault for believing that you were safe in a sex club." This man was not so much attributing his own forbidden internal impulses projectively to a hapless innocent victim, but proclaiming his belief that, since he could do no wrong, the other person must be the one who had not gotten it right.

Premise 3: If I am wrong it is only because I messed up, and I can and will soon fix things and make them right.

When these individuals fail—and they may fail repeatedly—they are sometimes perfectly willing to blame themselves (as much as to blame others or bad luck) for their being wrong. However, the blame they accept is not for acting on a morally unsound premise, but for having made a tactical error—one they will not repeat the next time.

Defensiveness. Psychopaths use a number of defenses to lull themselves into believing that they are okay and to convince others of the same thing. These are discussed in some detail in Chapter 10. To anticipate, psychopaths characteristically use repression to "forget" so that they can claim ignorance of their true motivation. For example, a former SS murderer was asked if he was aware that what he was doing was wrong. He replied that he did have a flash of such awareness, but that it was brief and quickly suppressed. One of Hitler's managers, a man who was in constant close contact with the Führer, supposedly claimed (and even seems to have believed his own assertion) that he knew nothing at all about the way Jews were being slaughtered in concentration camps.

In conclusion, psychopaths typically eviscerate reality in order to convince themselves and others that they are not criminals or that, if criminals, they commit their crime for good, not for evil. They believe that if they are adjudged to be criminals, the problem resides not with them but with those who judge them.

Thought Process Disorder

Psychopaths employ a pathognomonic set of cognitive distortions that form the basis of characteristic psychopathic cognitive errors, which in turn underlie equally characteristic psychopathic behaviors. The cognitive errors they make are at once purposeful and timely. They are *purposeful* in the sense that they are employed, consciously or unconsciously, for benefit, for example, in order to obtain an aggressively self-serving strategic advantage.

They also tend to be more *timely* than the cognitive errors other individuals make. For example, few depressives need to have fashionable symptoms. In contrast, many psychopaths make certain that they are challenging current beliefs, because doing so is part of their avowed attempt to challenge contemporary morality.

The following are some of the main cognitive errors psychopaths harness, consciously or unconsciously, for their manipulative self-serving ends:

Similar things are the same thing.   This thinking is central to psychopathic name-calling meant to attack, hurt, and defeat the opposition. Psychopaths regularly call their adversaries "Nazis" based on tenuous overlapping equivalencies. Thus the previously mentioned enraged college professor speaking of the victims of the World Trade Center 9/11 catastrophe said that "'technocrats of empire' working in the World Trade Center were the equivalent of 'little Eichmanns.'"[11] To arrive at this conclusion, he had to equate on some level the actions of a stockbroker trying to do a midlevel job in a large company with the actions of a man running concentration camps that killed millions of people. Though we might defend the professor's right to speak freely, we ought not to defend his right to speak immoderately. Hyperbole is wrong and is psychopathic-like in the sense that it plays loose with the facts to make what is to me an unsustainable point. (This professor also possibly used psychopathic-like "similar things are the same thing" equivalencies in order to shock the opposition: to hit them in the midriff, knocking the breath out of them in order to render them unable to think on their feet, well and fast enough to defend themselves properly. He was effectively stunning them so that they would find it hard to strike back in a timely and effective fashion.)

An owner of a cooperative apartment defended another owner, a woman who seriously altered the building by tearing a hole in its side so that she could have a window in her basement. He noted criticizing this woman harshly was not justified; as he reasoned, everybody in the building had altered their apartment in some way without getting permission. For example, he noted that one tenant had put up a ceiling fan and another a bathroom shelf. This man successfully cowed his victims by persuasively glossing over the really big differences between hanging a shelf on a wall and cutting a hole in the side of a building, while simultaneously intimidating them by reminding them of the biblical admonition (one that itself depends on confounding similar things with the same thing): "Let he who is without sin cast the first stone." (In character too was this man's attitude about selling his apartment. He fully intended to put it up for sale without full disclosure that the spectacular view—the apartment's main selling point—was about to be blocked by a building going up next door. Speaking of the rules of disclosure when selling property, he said, "Unless they specifically ask you about whether a new building is going up, you don't have to tell them that there is one being planned.")

In like manner, the assertion that "It's right to stop gays from getting married because marriage is by definition a sacred ritual between a man and a woman" fails on logical grounds because it glosses over the differences between two very dissimilar things: tradition and definition. While antiabortionists castigate abortionists for overlooking the similarities between abortion and murder, abortionists castigate antiabortionists for overlooking the differences.

"Similar things are the same thing" thinking is a central aspect of the thinking of victims of psychopaths. Psychopaths count on their victims thinking "clean-cut is reliable," or "smooth-talking is honest" or "friendly is safe" to make headway with the desired victimization of their marks.

Selective abstraction. There are two steps to the process of selective abstraction, or what Aaron T. Beck simply calls "selectivity."[12] The *first* step involves creation of a partial truth. The partial truth may be created by selective inattention, whereby the individual omits bits and pieces of the whole truth. For example, a salesman is not living up to an agreement. Calls to his office are not returned. When he is finally cornered he says, "I tried to return your call but the line was busy." This may be true. But it is only a part truth, for another, equally important, part truth is omitted— if he had really wanted to get through he would have called until the line was not busy.

In dissociation, one form of selective inattention, the individual maintains a separation (thus, dissociation) between ideas that in fact belong together. Activists who persuade by telling one side of the story and not the other may indulge in this kind of reasoning. For example, antivivisectionists have a point, but they make their point without simultaneously acknowledging another: that animal experimentation saves human lives. Therapists who advocate doing only affirmative therapy based on the belief that psychiatrists who make medical diagnoses and do conventional psychotherapy are supposedly "damning their patients with medical formulations and treatments" also have a point, but they forget at least one thing of equal importance: that medical diagnoses are established useful ways to conceptualize and convey information in a nutshell and to organize treatment methods; and that emotionally troubled patients can and often do benefit considerably from identifying their syndrome so that they can look it up and discover what the experts have to say about it.

The second step involves equating the part truth with the whole truth, so that speaking a part truth is tantamount to telling a lie. It is spiritually a lie to say that George Fredrick Handel was a composer of hemidemisemiquavers. One patient told an ethicist that he felt no one should demonstrate against his or her own country in a way and to an extent that it might demoralize troops active on the front. The ethicist disagreed and countered that only in totalitarian states is one prevented from speaking one's mind. He then reminded the complainer that a strong society depends on being free to say what is on one's mind. What he said was true, but only as far as it went, for while the ethicist's advocacy of speaking freely and debating openly was admirable, the absolute purity of the admirable quality to an extent depended on his overlooking another, equally valid, truth: that the well–being, strength, and morale of the soldiers depended to some degree on the support coming from back home, and that not giving them the support they longed for and needed could be interpreted as a lack of empathy similar to that found in and characteristic of the psychopath. My work with ex-soldiers at the VA taught me that soldiers, no less than writers, block when they get bad reviews, little support, and no love from those they are, to no apparent avail, trying so hard to please. I know from my direct patient care with veterans that it is precisely this kind of lack of public support that figures prominently in the development of a soldier's Posttraumatic Stress Disorder.

Many psychopaths escape punishment for their impulsivity by the following part-to-whole overgeneralization: "Because my impulses have an irresistible quality, they are completely irresistible." The blame-your-parents individual, who claims he or she suffered abuse as a child and then passes the past abuse off as a full explanation for present antisocial behavior, is also drawing an entire picture out of a few of its (admittedly significant causative) lines, while omitting key aspects of the whole, such as biological vulnerability, and the potential capacity that most adults have for getting beyond early trauma and making a free mature choice about what they want to respond to and how to behave based on latter-day mature consideration. The blame-your-genes psychopath in one sense belongs spiritually with the psychopath who overemphasizes environmental influences to the detriment of personal contribution. Instead of "I cannot help myself; I never had all the advantages other children had," we hear "I can't help myself; it's inborn."

Particularly psychopathic is the technique of being dishonest by covering a secret whole truth by being direct, upfront, and honest about a part truth. A patient suggested that it was perfectly okay to cheat on his wife as long as he did not lie about it. Here the whole truth, "It's not okay to cheat," fell victim to the part truth, "Since I am cheating on my wife it is better to be completely honest about it, instead of running the risk of getting caught at it."

A common form of selective abstraction involves leaving out the beginning of a story and instead starting in the middle. Psychopaths classically make themselves look like innocent victims by simply overlooking what they did to provoke their own victimization. In one possible sequence, criminal psychopaths first provoke the police and then, forgetting the provocation, claim police brutality. Recently a waitress was fired from a lucrative job with no notice. She blamed the proprietor for her firing. As she told it, she was fired "just because I was a little late in returning from an errand she sent me out on. I was using her car, and she accused me of using it for joyriding." Her story elicited the sympathy she wanted, but only after omitting one simple fact: that she was fired for using the proprietor's car to make a drug sale. Another common form of selective abstraction involves quoting out of context to be negative. Here again, a common variety of this method involves omitting qualifiers, particularly "some" and "often," to make the negative point. The statement "Some gay men have emotional problems" becomes in the hands of a chop-shop reviewer "This man said that 'gay men have emotional problems.'" A third example of selective abstraction involves the assertion that a person who focuses exclusively on one thing is motivated per se to devalue another. Raeleen D'Agostino Mautner, author of *The Sweet Life*, reports (personal communication, 2005) that "a woman from Venice came up to me after my talk last Thursday . . . to compliment me on my presentation (October is Italian Heritage Month, so I was invited to talk about what my heritage has meant to me). This Venetian woman after kissing my ass all night, decides to write me a three page email the next day, saying my talk was distasteful and that because I mentioned my grandmother's Southern Italian cuisine and did not give equal time to the North, I undid the entire Risorgimento (movement for Italian unity) and divided her country once again. Oh, and I also made the death of her grandfather be in vain (he fought with Garibaldi, a soldier of the Risorgimento)."

In reduction ad absurdum, a related process here involving selective *inattention*, psychopaths effectively attack an opponent by reducing him or her to ugly skin and bones. As children paint their parents as all black by overlooking their good points, psychopaths—for example, psychopathic politicians—paint their rivals and enemies as all black by overlooking anything at all about them that might elicit a favorable response.

Switching figure and ground (switching cause and effect).   This cognitive error is typified by an advertisement written by the group first mentioned in Chapter 2 trying to sell a procedure for treating nearsightedness without glasses. The advertisement notes that as people put on stronger and stronger glasses as they age, their vision gets worse. The implication, of course, is that strong glasses cause worsening vision. The truth is more that worsening vision "causes," i.e., "requires," stronger glasses. Along similar lines, an individual asked for psychiatric admission when he really needed a place to stay for the night. When refused admission he feigned suicide, saying, "You'll hear about my death in the morning." This individual changed "I am suicidal because you won't admit me" to "admit me because I am suicidal."

Guilt by association.   A psychopath seeking a large monetary settlement blamed all the members of a present generation for actions taken by a few of their ancestors, and then sued them even though they had nothing to do with the earlier events.

Minimization.   Psychopathic individuals use minimization, also discussed above, to rationalize and make excuses for their amoral or illegal behavior. Here they change big to little in order to trivialize their actions. For example, applying their very personal distortive colorimeter, they view a big lie as a "white lie." Such statements as "What does it matter?" or "Is it so important that . . . ?" are clues to the presence of minimization. So is the psychopathic justification of amoral behavior along the lines of "What I do is okay because it's not as bad as something else," a thing to which they make an instant gratuitous, and of course personally beneficial, comparison. For example, they say that having sex on the streets is okay because it is not as bad as mugging someone in an alleyway, as in the prostitutes' claim that they are entitled to hook Johns to their hearts' content, and have sex with them in the semi-shadows, because they are not actually doing anything violent. In like manner, the pornographer justifies his or her actions not by evaluating the thing on its own (as he or she ought to) but by comparing it to something else in order to note that depicting sex is far less amoral and destructive than depicting violence, which is not quite the point.

Dichotomous thinking.   Psychopaths think dichotomously in order to create a false and self-serving perception of personal injustice along the lines of "either they are for you or they are against you." They can view anything less than unconditional love as complete dislike and abandonment and then, seeing themselves as treated unjustly, use that as a jerry-built reason to conclude that "Someone like me has to take care of himself the best way, and any way, that he can, whatever that might involve."

Arbitrary inference (arbitrariness).   Here a self-serving premise is deemed proven even in the absence of sufficient evidence. The idea is, "I know it is so because I know it is so and you can't tell me otherwise, so you had better believe and go along with me." Quack medical theories and the questionable treatments based on them, especially when they form the basis for a lucrative medical practice or become the subject of a best-selling book, serve as familiar examples.

In *omniscience*, a process related to arbitrary inference, the psychopath shamelessly makes his own rules or, figuratively speaking, passes her own laws. (The Germans call the rough equivalent of arbitrary inference/ omniscience *rechthaberei*, which means thinking and behaving as if you know it all and no one else knows anything at all.) He or she simply states, "I do know" because "I know it all," in anticipation of saying "You, not I, are mistaken." I was working on a manuscript in a coffee shop when the proprietor came over and asked me what I was doing. I told him that I was writing. He told me that I could not do that in his place. This man apparently just knew that because I was writing, I planned to spend all day at his coffee counter, keeping others from being able to sit down. (He would have been wrong about that, because I had a train to catch in ten minutes.) Clearly, although I had only been there for a few minutes and nobody was actually waiting for my spot, he wanted me to drink up and get out so that he could have the seat at the counter available for the next person. I never actually checked the official rules of conduct for local coffee shops to find out if a proprietor is entitled to make such a rule or has to follow other, different rules laid down by the city, but I do know that he was doing what many psychopaths do—winning through omniscience, while counting on intimidation to back him up. Along similar lines was the laughable negative book review of one of my scientific offerings, in which the reviewer gave as her qualifications "an interest in the topic and future plans to study it in school." There is a website devoted to the philosophy of psychiatry, where self-styled philosophers, some without impressive (or any) relevant credentials, review books of psychology. They often, and somewhat narcissistically, congratulate themselves, as does Perring, along the lines of "it's a good thing we are around to keep those people in check."[13] (Specifically he says, speaking of Hare's book on psychopathy, "Here's a book that shows why philosophers need to be studying psychiatry.") I once inquired if one of the reviewers of a clinically based textbook had ever actually seen a patient, and was told that she had not (she was an English major)—but that that was okay because it is not necessary to have experience seeing patients in order to review books on clinical psychological matters, even those (like the one Perring was reviewing) about diagnosing and treating patients. There is no arguing with such an omnipotent, self-serving assertion. It simply puts forth the equivalent of the equally "unarguable" psychopathic-like self-serving "reasoning" W.S. Gilbert advances in his lyric in *H.M.S. Pinafore*, outlining with tongue firmly in cheek what it takes to hold a certain high position: "Stick close to your desks and never go to sea, and you all may be rulers of the Queen's Navee."[14]

Evasion. When all else fails, psychopaths put "I don't know" forward as a last manipulative resort. Just recently an important politician was asked, "Do you believe that being gay is a choice?" He answered, "I don't know," which of course was merely his sly way to duck the issue so that he could avoid taking a politically unpopular stand.

Finally, psychopaths are adept at knowing how to make it difficult for others to identify, and so to explode, their cognitive errors. They are often sophisticated, clever pseudologisticians whose illogic is so subtle and clever that it causes us to do a double take or escapes us completely. We sense that there is something wrong with their reasoning but we cannot exactly put our finger on it. We do that double take when told that a man who just killed his parents deserves leniency on the grounds that he is an orphan. Similarly, one (nonpsychopathic) son's ephemeral critique of his mother's salad dressing was cleverly, and impenetrably, sophistic, as well as unwarranted: "Bottled is better than your homemade, because they don't bottle and sell yours commercially, do they?" So was his complaint that his mother kept the door locked when she was home, forcing him to use his key to get in. "Why do you have to do that?" he whined. "So that no one breaks in on me," she patiently explained. "But," he retorted, "Isn't the whole purpose of breaking in to do it when nobody is home?"

INSIGHT

Therapists confronting severe psychopaths with their maladaptive behavior soon discover that they tend to respond by denying all shortcomings. Many are too grandiose to fully recognize how troubled they are. Instead they prefer to view themselves as flawless. As they see it, if they have any problem at all it is that they have difficulty in getting others to recognize their fine qualities—one of which is that they are free of all defects, making them, as one psychopath averred, "just too perfect for my own good."

In contrast, mild psychopaths are often insightful, at least to a degree. They do know, and can learn, some key things about themselves. Some are aware that they are unable to feel anxiety and guilt when appropriate. Some are also aware that they are too narcissistic to feel much empathy for others. But even the most insightful psychopaths have difficulty translating their insight into self-control and personal change. Whatever insight they have seems detached and separated by an emotional and intellectual wall from the mainstream of their thinking, and so from their awareness of how their basic personality is constructed and what needs to be done in the way of improvement.

In many cases their insight is defective not only atrophically but also hypertrophically. For example, some psychopaths consciously exaggerate insight for gain—so that they can get a favorable response from a parole board, be released from a psychiatric hospital, or stop psychotherapy because they find it too costly and time-consuming.

A special kind of understanding exists in those psychopaths who use remarkable skill to cultivate insight into others' psychology in order to con them more effectively. For example, many psychopaths, some realtors among them, pick up on how people tend to want most what they seem to have the least chance of getting. They then use that information to manipulate their clients—in the case of one realtor, making a property look hot by falsely claiming to have people lined up waiting to purchase it.

MEMORY AND ORIENTATION

Psychopathic individuals tend to have uneven memories. They often have good practical memories—that is, they remember what they need to remember to advance themselves. Typical is the response of an individual questioned about someone he and the questioner knew well. The individual had a poor recollection of many details that almost anyone who knew the person might be expected to know. However, when asked about quirks and shortcomings that made this acquaintance vulnerable, the individual showed himself to be a fount of information and anecdote. One example: "Play hard to get with him. When he finds out he can't have something, it makes him want it all the more."

Unfortunately for them, psychopaths also display a degree of "forget-fulness" that leads them to block out a great many important things that they need to keep in mind for their very survival. For example, they get into trouble because they forget why they got into trouble previously. An unreliable memory is an especially serious handicap for people engaged in tricky or shady activities, and psychopathic individuals are often undone by this very deficit.

As will also be mentioned in Chapter 7 on associated disorders, many psychopaths try to protect themselves in difficult situations by feigning partial or total memory failure (amnesia).

INTELLIGENCE

There exist a number of different "intelligences." Psychopaths possess some of these more than others. Psychopaths can be "intelligently calcu-lating" when it suits their immediate purposes and long–term goals. They may be "cleverly empathic," knowing just who will and will not fall for their schemes. Overall, however, they do not run their lives "brilliantly." In particular, it is not "smart" to be overly materialistic if that makes one in the long run an unloving individual without real friends and family, or a self-destructive individual who cannot sustain a positive adjustment without becoming his or her own worst spoilsport.

JUDGMENT

Successful psychopaths may be said to have good judgment when their level of performance vindicates—at least to a meaningful extent—their excessively high self-esteem and with it their excessively positive view of, and belief in, themselves. True, some tend to overestimate what they can get away with, and others pay a disproportionately high price for their gains. On the other hand, mild psychopaths do not get into trouble as often as we might think. We probably hear more about the ones who get into trouble and less about the ones who do not. When mild psychopaths do get into difficulty, they often succeed in getting out of it. They are par-ticularly good at manipulating others to sympathize with them and treat them kindly and nonpunitively.

However, judgment must be accounted defective in those individuals whose level of performance does not validate a too-high degree of self-love. Among these are the overconfident psychopaths who think that you can fool all of the people all of the time—forgetting that sooner or later most individuals, and the general public, catch on to what they are doing, resent being scammed, and retaliate by making yesterday's hero tomorrow's villain. Machiavelli may or may not have realized that politicians who reach the top using his methods have a history of going far at first, only to later become the targets of an increasingly sophisticated—and sadder and wiser—following. Realizing that they have been duped, those scammed latch on to Machiavellian methods on their own and use them to turn against their leaders.

Judgment is also deficient in those who are unproductively focused on reaching trivial goals that range from having and wearing the latest hot sneakers to getting a big house with beautiful furniture in a hot resort—all by whatever means they can, without regard for others, and to the detriment of achieving personally rewarding and deeply meaningful social and personal relationships. To some extent, even the lives of the most successful psychopaths epitomize bad judgment. Their pleasures are superficial, and they miss much of what makes life truly worthwhile, for few people really love them, at least for long, and many people hate them deeply, and forever.

Judgment deficit often lies as much with the victim as with the psychopath. This was the case for a patient of mine who had just, in all innocence, been done in by a psychopath. She responded to being scammed as follows: "I don't understand why my lover would run up all those charges on my credit cards if he were planning all along to leave me." Victim psychology is discussed further in Chapter 13.

CAPACITY FOR INTERPERSONAL RELATIONSHIPS

Failure of Empathy and Absence of Altruism/Sham-Enhanced Empathy and Sham-Enhanced Altruism

Many observers speak of the psychopath's inability to feel empathy. Even mild psychopaths lack a degree of empathy—both because they are selfish and because they are sadistic. They want to be as hurtful as possible, and they do not care whom they hurt, or how or how much they hurt them. The above-described psychopathic boss—the man who convinced himself that the resident's best teaching came from the most service—bought a building with several professional offices for rent. He then offered to rent the offices to all but one of the residents, whom he resented for speaking out against one of his (unfair) policies. Practically in tears, the resident told her boss how hurt she was that he did not invite her to share his office. To that outpouring the boss unfeelingly countered, "I can do what I want with the office; it is, after all, my place."

However, I believe that many mild psychopaths can feel empathy—but only selectively. They can certainly feel empathy when it is to their benefit. Some are natively empathic, while others, highly motivated to use psychology to understand people's weaknesses so that they can manipulate them most efficiently, acquire their empathy through a lifetime of practice. Psychopaths use their native or cultivated empathy to spot suckers when they see them and to discern, and effectively play on, their heartstrings in order to receive nutriment, gain control, seize power, and rise to the top, all with a minimum of effort. They may be said to have the equivalent of an emotional dousing rod that emits a positive signal when in the vicinity of others' vulnerabilities. For example, they know when others have rescue fantasies and sympathies for the underdog and use these as an opening to mount an effective pitch. They also know what people like, whom people admire, what moves them, and whom they pity. To illustrate, a subway beggar attributed much of his success to a simple ploy: apologizing for interrupting the riders and then promising to be brief in order to spare them from having to hear an unnecessarily prolonged spiel. Natively he seemed to know how productive it was to shift the focus from the unwelcome intrusion, which everyone hated, to its welcome brevity, which everyone appreciated. At Christmastime he knew he could put people in a giving mood by singing Christmas carols. After some months of therapy, he became a telemarketer whose success was largely attributable to his ability to act as if he were a widowed grandfather just trying to eke out a living in order to be able to keep his house out of foreclosure. He seemed to know intuitively who ached to be complimented, and would flatter them in order to "get them eating out of his hands." Likewise, he knew who ached to be abused, and would put them down, secure in the knowledge that they would do almost anything to turn things around to get into his good graces. He was particularly adept at uncovering the loneliness of old people and how their desire to please him in order to get at least a few drops of kindness left them unprotected. In short, like most psychopathic individuals, he did not so much feel *for* others as he felt his way *into* them.

Many observers have suggested that the psychopathic condition is characterized by a lack of altruism. This lack of altruism, present to some degree in even the mildest psychopaths, reflects a basic deficit of object love as manifest in impoverished, narcissistic, immature, self-oriented relationships. This deficit of object love creates a psychic void that psychopaths compensate for and fill up with self-serving activities and relationships marked by little or no feeling for their victims—to whom they promise everything only to give nothing. If these individuals do give, it is only in anticipation of getting. They remind us of Ponzi, who in the beginning paid his investors off handsomely to win their confidence. Ultimately, however, their true colors show. In a characteristic sequence, a psychopath knew how to appeal to potential employers by working hard during his period of trial employment. His goal was not to get the job done but to ingratiate himself to and gain the trust of his employers. As soon as he accomplished that, he started cooking the books so that he could stealthily steal cash from the business. Individuals like this may guiltlessly groom children and adolescents for sex by giving them trinkets, and shamelessly even fleece their own parents by promising to love them in order to blind them to the fact that they are about to rob them of everything they have.

A mild psychopath who knew how to appear highly altruistic became the politician who knew how to fake altruism by kissing babies for political advancement. He wanted to appear to love children because he knew that most people consider that quality to be a sign of good character and indisputable honesty, both of which presumably carry over into political ability. Of course all he was really doing was "kissing up" to the parents, and he was doing that strictly in order to get their vote.

Narcissism

Psychopaths are also *narcissistic* individuals. As Cleckley says, theirs is a "self-centeredness"[15] and an "incapacity for object-love."[16] If there is "concern for the other person [it is] only (or primarily) in so far as [it] enhances or seems to enhance the self."[17] This "lack in the psychopath makes it all but impossible for an adequate transference or rapport situation to arise in . . . treatment."[18] These narcissistic psychopaths want what they want, and they want it now. They typically complain loud and long when they do not get it, even pushing demands that are close to impossible to meet. To illustrate, there is a small subculture of career patients at a Veterans' Administration Clinic that bends a system established primarily to treat illness to serve their own selfish, personal, nontherapeutic ends. This small subgroup of individuals does not primarily attend clinic to obtain relief from suffering. Rather, their goals are to feed their addictions, get disability payments, or evade the consequences of prior and present aggressive or even criminal behavior. To get their way they might malinger, or really milk, a legitimate Posttraumatic Stress Disorder. In one case a patient, a Vietnam veteran, regularly beat up his wife and then in court got off without jail time by claiming that he mistook her for an enemy on the attack. One day he and his wife were standing on line in a resort area waiting to get in to see a show. Behind him were two Vietnamese men who were speaking in their native tongue, thinking my patient could not understand what they were saying. Unfortunately for them, during the war he had learned the language thoroughly and, equally unfortunately for them, they were saying that the patient's wife had a very fat ass. The patient turned and smashed one of the men in the face, severely fracturing his nose. The patient then claimed in court that the verbal attack on his wife had reminded him of being physically fired on by the Viet Cong. That was a good enough excuse for the judge to consider letting him off without exacting any punishment at all. (In most cases like this, it is extremely difficult to tell to what extent the individual is troubled versus to what extent he or she is exaggerating.)

Disloyalty is an important feature of psychopathic narcissism. If mild psychopaths are capable of a degree of loyalty at all, it is not beyond what is for the moment and for their convenience. In a typical scenario they have partners in crime, but if and when they get caught, they willingly turn against them and turn "states' evidence" to save their own skins.

Psychopathic narcissism is also characterized by a degree of interpersonal distancing. Even the most charming psychopaths (many unsuccessful psychopaths are too crude and aggressive to fall into that category) can be hard to really warm up to. Instead we get the sense that their charm is ersatz and based strictly on self-interest. So we walk away convinced that their skin-deep beauty covers an inherent basic, intrinsic, and very deep ugliness.

CHAPTER 7

Differential Diagnosis: Associated and Overlapping Disorders

Like most disorders of its kind, psychopathy tends to affiliate itself and overlap with other personality disorders. As a corollary, the more other personality disorders color and influence the psychopathic process, the more the patient can be considered to be less "bad" than "mad."

SUBSTANCE ABUSE

Both of the following statements are true: psychopaths tend toward substance abuse, and those who abuse substances tend towards being psychopaths. Certainly, substance abusers often act in a psychopathic fashion in order to get difficult-to-obtain drugs. However, perhaps as often, those who abuse drugs act psychopathically even when they can get their drugs relatively easily, and without having to lie and cheat to obtain them. Three possible explanations, which are not mutually exclusive, come to mind: drug abuse is one symptom of the psychopathic condition, for example, a way to relieve pervasive boredom; drugs enhance preexisting psychopathic tendencies; and drug ingestion can by itself create psychopathic behavior de novo, e.g., by causing drug toxicity.

HYPOMANIA

Both psychopathic and hypomanic individuals have a tendency to act in an irrepressible, irresponsible fashion as they indulge in what Cleckley calls "fantastic and uninviting behavior with drink and sometimes without."[1] As *DSM-IV* criteria suggest, they can "fail to sustain consistent work behavior or honor financial obligations."[2] Both believe that planning ahead is the devil's work, so both avoid making long-term plans and instead favor immediate gratification of needs, preferring to live for today over delaying gratification until tomorrow.

Both psychopathic and hypomanic individuals can become euphoric, in part because both freely use the defense of denial. As a result, both really seem to believe that their lucky stars will keep them out of harm's way or, if things go against them, bail them out of any and all troubles they might get themselves into.

Psychopathic lack of self-control bears a resemblance to hypomanic wildness. This was the case for a patient who signed a contract on a house that she could not afford to purchase. The owner of the house called her a crook and a con artist. In fact, she was suffering from an acute exacerbation of her affective disorder—an acute manic episode that required hospitalization.

Like hypomanics, psychopaths are often charming when they get their way, but turn ugly when crossed. For example, a psychopathic con-artist would act pleased and grateful and freely issue "God blesses" to those who gave her the dollar or two she begged for. But she would tell those who did not give her a handout to go to hell—in her typical sneering, unctuous "have-a-nice-day" way—one that meant exactly the opposite of what she was saying.

Both psychopathic and hypomanic individuals focus on having fun whatever the cost to themselves and others. For example, both like to play practical jokes on unsuspecting victims. However, the hypomanic individual tends to find impersonal practical jokes (like giving someone a hot-foot or pulling a chair out from under) satisfying enough, and on their own. In contrast, the psychopath requires more and is satisfied with nothing less than setting someone up to be belittled, humiliated, and brought down from his or her supposed "highfalutin perch." For example, a mildly psychopathic man told his wife with tongue in cheek that he liked recordings by a pop star generally out of favor with the cognoscenti. The wife, trying to please him, obliged and gave him all of the singers' pop records as a Christmas gift, at some cost and effort. Only later did she discover that her husband was planning all along to rope her in and then put her down by telling all their mutual friends of her poor taste, just to have them snigger at her behind her back for spending so much money on so many records by such a tacky singer.

Both hypomanics and psychopaths have a grandiose core to their natures. When a customer challenged a realtor who seemed to be overstating the square footage of a property he was trying to sell, the realtor, adept at evasion for financial gain, told his complaining customer to relax and take it easy. When the customer told this realtor that the way to get her to relax and take it easy was to prove to her that the measurements were accurate, not inflated, the realtor flew into a rage. Bluffing to intimidate her, he told her that he did not need to sell to someone like her—someone who gave him such a hard time—but that she needed to buy from someone like him—someone who was willing to make the awful compromises that would permit a muckety-muck like him to sell to a complete lowlife like her.

A difference between hypomanics and psychopaths is that while both set out to experience a steady euphoric state, only the hypomanic achieves anything resembling pure and true joy. Psychopaths have a hard time even conceiving of pure joy. They usually can do no better than try for, and experience, a temporary sense of coming alive.

Hypomania was also discussed in Chapter 6.

PARANOIA

Sometimes what looks like psychopathic behavior is really pseudopsychopathic behavior—that is, it is a response to delusional thinking or hallucinatory ideation. In such cases, we sometimes call the result "pseudopsychopathic schizophrenia."

The psychopathic tendency to lay the blame on others for all one's troubles has some basis in the paranoia-imbued tendency to project. Psychopaths and paranoid individuals alike project both defensively—to relieve anxiety and guilt—and in order to manipulate others into doing their bidding (I call the latter process "manipulative paranoia"). Like paranoids, psychopaths frequently claim victimization in order to disavow responsibility for their actions, attribute that responsibility to others, and then demand reparation for wrongs done to the person. Thus an abortion clinic bomber views his murderous actions not as first strike but as justified retribution; and a lawyer defends a culpable client by claiming that his client was framed, or defends someone who is clearly a lawbreaker by asserting that the laws broken were too irrational and strict for any sensible person to take seriously and follow. Both paranoids and psychopaths justify their own (to us) unacceptable actions by citing victim culpability along such lines as, "If he were an honest man, you could not cheat him." Thus psychopaths who cheat a victim out of money often justify their actions by blaming their victims for being cheats themselves. They might say, "I can freely steal Microsoft's programs because Microsoft charges too much for what they give you." Or they blame their victims for being carelessly and stupidly trusting, along the lines of "If he weren't so dumb he would have seen right through me," or "Lonely old people should learn not to put their faith in strangers." The man with AIDS discussed throughout accused his sex partner of being so stupid as to believe that he could have sex in a sex club with someone who was HIV negative. To quote him exactly, "When I met a 23-year-old guy at a sex club nine months ago, I didn't practice safe sex (as the bottom), and when we later emailed he wanted to be reassured I was 'disease free' (Dream on, and you met me at a SEX club?)."

Because both paranoids and psychopaths rarely take responsibility for themselves, they both become angry with anyone who even suggests that their life is the way it is because of the choices they have made. Not surprisingly, both rarely admit that they are wrong and that others are right. A psychopathic builder constructs a restaurant for an entrepreneur using shoddy material. The floor sags, and a leak destroys the kitchen. The restaurateur complains, only to have the builder respond that the problem is not with him but with the owner. As the builder puts it, "You didn't press hard enough to have me do a good job. And anyway you, not I, were the chief contractor on the project."

When caught committing crimes, both paranoids and psychopaths like to wriggle out from under by complaining that they were unfairly singled out, entrapped, and duped into confessing, and that a violation of their rights to privacy and freedom has occurred. In the news recently was the story of how a state and city were cracking down on people who bought tax-free cigarettes over the Internet. When caught, instead of owning up to their obvious disregard for the law, these individuals with one voice accused the state and city of behaving illegally by invading their privacy and limiting their freedom of commerce. A tenant who fails to pay the rent typically cites the landlord's failure to provide a habitable environment, very much as a man who shoots a cop typically justifies his actions as a response to police brutality.

Both psychopaths and paranoids have a tendency to use the same questionable cognitive/logical distortions in order to justify their attitudes and behavior both to themselves and to others. For example, both typically make a case for their innocence by selectively abstracting—acknowledging only the part of an incident that proves their contention of being misunderstood, put upon, and mistreated—by the police, by the judge, and by society as a whole. It is also common for both psychopaths and paranoids to switch the order of cause and effect for self-serving purposes. One man explained and excused his becoming a terrorist on the basis of his inability to find a job. In his case it was truer still that he could not find a job because he was a special sort of person: someone who had the personality to become a terrorist.

Both paranoid and psychopathic individuals show a tendency to identify with the aggressor as they turn tables in self-defense. Both, in order to sustain their self-esteem, get back by treating others just as badly as they believe others have treated them, and then justify their actions with such clichéd phrases as "What goes around comes around" or "Revenge is sweet."

When challenged, both have a tendency to issue warnings and threats. For example, both might threaten to "see you in court." Thus the woman first mentioned in Chapter 6 tried to block construction of a proposed new building opposite her apartment by embarking on a save-the-neighborhood campaign. Everyone knew that her real motive was to preserve her fine view of lower Manhattan that the new high-rise would cut off. But when anyone even hinted that her professed historical and esthetic concerns were a cover-up for her self-interest, she angrily threatened to sue them for slander. Note that in spite of the paranoid backlash, the woman was essentially psychopathic. Paranoia did not enter into her basic motivation. Motivated to protect her view, she did not see the advocates of the building as the same enemies, only in different guise, that she had been contending with all her life. Rather, she tried to promote an interest that was confined to her and a handful of others by a fraudulent appeal for support as victims. When she did not get the support she had hoped for from hundreds, or perhaps thousands, of people, she fought—really fought back—because she felt angry about having been hindered in her quest.

NARCISSISM

To a greater extent than with most mental disorders, the pathological significance of narcissism may lie in the other disorders to which it gives rise. These disorders may be presumed to be latent, with their development stimulated by the narcissistic condition. At the same time, none of them is inevitable in narcissistic individuals. Though the degree of apparent narcissism varies considerably between individual psychopaths, some authorities have theorized that all psychopathy is, to a great extent, narcissism gone underground and intensified.

In the literature, the term narcissism is used in at least three ways. It is used *descriptively* and *dynamically* to mean self-indulgence and self-love; *developmentally* to refer to a stage predating the stage of object love; and *diagnostically* to refer to a personality disorder in its own right or to an aspect of another disorder, such as schizophrenia, Borderline Personality Disorder, depression, or psychopathy.

A certain degree of narcissism is normal. It is inherent in self-awareness and in one's sense of self-worth. As always, but particularly here, it is important to distinguish between the narcissism characteristic of the unsuccessful and successful psychopath. *Unsuccessful* narcissistic psychopaths give themselves away, as others see right through their machinations, pick up on their selfishness, and respond accordingly. In contrast, *successful* narcissistic psychopaths are able to control their behavioral excesses to the point that they fool others into giving them what they want, exactly as they would like to have it.

Narcissists and psychopaths alike are *selfish* individuals. As such they take more than they give back. A psychopathic son, the doctor whose case was presented in Chapter 5, refused to help his father when the father was dying. The father had been good to his son and was trying before he died to finish writing a little paper on something he had discovered when he was a young man. Not being particularly skilled academically, the father asked the son, an English minor, to help him write the paper. But the son refused, saying that for the moment he was just too busy to be bothered with something so trivial—he had just met a new boyfriend and they were about to go off on a wonderful vacation together.

As selfish individuals, they are *spoiled* people full of inordinate self-interest and self-concern, what the layman perceives as simple egocentricity. Their "I care about me, not you" attitude leads them to go for any and all pleasurable experiences in life, regardless of consequences and effect, and to express whatever feelings they have, no matter who gets hurt in the process.

As *hedonistic* individuals, both narcissists and psychopaths are willing to do almost anything to get the gratification and excitement they seek and demand—in the shortest possible amount of time, and with the least possible effort. Easily bored, both look for distractions, but with wholesome outlets blocked their distractions often take the form of antisocial behavior. As hedonists, both also tend to stress the basely material and sensual over the deeper and more abstract rewards of life, such as those that come from giving rather than getting. Because love for them is deeply entwined with materialism, they love most those who give them exactly what they want. Also, and not surprisingly, love for both of these individuals is not something that you must earn but something that you can buy.

Both also tend to be basically *lazy* individuals who fondly wish for immediate, effortless gratification without having to put forth much effort in order to obtain it. Theirs is a desire to get something for nothing, and to capture spoils not only immediately but also effortlessly. As such, they favor get-rich-quick schemes over making money the old-fashioned way. Their fabled recklessness is due in part to their tendency to resist acknowledging the role that hard work so often plays in significant achievement.

As discussed throughout, both tend to be *unempathic* individuals who do not care about how others feel, and *insufficiently altruistic* individuals notable for their ungiving natures and their inability, or refusal, to put others before themselves and to make sacrifices for others. Both these dificiencies result partly from their egocentric view of situations—seeing everything from the vantage point of "What's in it for me?"—and partly from their "If it feels good do it" philosophy that omits any thought of how "it" might make "you" feel. Both actually go beyond thinking of themselves first and others second to not thinking of others at all. They simply use people as disposable objects and then drop them when they no longer need them. This is partly because they view others as inanimate objects put on earth for their gratification, as wholes that are only as good as their giving parts—like the mother's breast they willingly suckle as long as it gives milk, but angrily bite and abandon should it run dry.

Of course, empathic and altruistic gestures may be made for the sake of appearance. What appears to be a true feeling for others often turns out to be self-serving sham behavior that is subtly coercive. It is limited to identifying others' vulnerabilities in the search for an opening that allows for a move in for the kill. What appears to be real altruism is often just a clever ploy. An example of such sham altruism from everyday life is the advertisement that claims, "Save money, big sale." This rarely means "I will take less and give you more" but instead means "I will take more by virtue of appearing to take less. I am going to increase the price and then cut it so that you can think I am giving you a big bargain and be suckered into buying from me what I am trying to unload on you."

Narcissistic *feelings of centrality* lead patients with a Narcissistic Personality Disorder to believe that they are the center of everything and that everyone revolves around them. These feelings overlap with the psychopath's grandiose narcissistic belief that he or she is too special to be grouped in any way with the peasants of this world. A friend who ran the advertising department of a local newspaper told me that she had contacted the above-mentioned realtor to ask him to advertise in her paper. What he did instead was to hurt her feelings by bragging, "No, your paper isn't important enough for me to put my ad in. I would only consider putting an ad in *The New York Times*—and, by the way, that paper's advertising representative just happens to be waiting on the other phone to speak to me, and to beg me to take out a big ad in her paper."

The immense feeling of *narcissistic entitlement* found in both disorders makes the mottos of both psychopaths and paranoids "I am, therefore I deserve." As such, they come to believe that their needs are rights, and if in claiming their rights they abrogate those of others, then so be it. In demanding the gratification they expect, they favor actions such as nudging others off the tennis court before they have finished their game, and monopolizing exercise machines in the gym. They tend to be irresponsible individuals who buy trinkets before paying their bills, and buy cell phones first and medical insurance next. Theirs is a demand for immediate supplies obtained effortlessly, so that they find it perfectly acceptable to embezzle from a company they work for just because they happen to need the money. Theirs is a voracious "all-the-world's-my-caretaker" attitude, one that we all have when we are children, but which they transfer in their adult life to strangers whom they expect to be like the all-giving self-sacrificial mother who was, or should have been, available to them 24/7 without charge or obligation on their parts. A patient of mine, a therapist on call for mothers of young babies, frequently complained that when a prescription ran out during business hours, his mothers would wait until nighttime, when it was convenient for them, to call for a renewal. This made it much more difficult, if not impossible, to get the prescription refilled. I explained that some young mothers compete with their babies to be the ones cared for. They feel depleted by all the responsibility and therefore entitled to look to others, in this case to him as a mother/caregiver surrogate, to fill their emptiness by demanding that they do something palpable for them immediately, and whenever they have a need. Along similar lines, I well remember a patient who came to the emergency room at 3 a.m. with the following chief complaint: "I have had hemorrhoids for 37 years, and I cannot stand them for one minute longer." Clearly, when such feelings of narcissistic entitlement reach severe proportions, psychopaths can go from mere arrogance to complete foolhardiness and commit acts that arise from dangerous errors of judgment.

Not surprisingly, both narcissists and psychopaths tend to disregard rules and laws in the belief that they are made for others. They may smoke, spit, jump lines, speed, push subway doors open so that they do not miss the train, use counterfeit bills, walk through the streets with boom-boxes blasting, or even hustle and have sex right out in the open on city streets. Just recently I watched in amazement as a man pulled his personal truck up to a dumpster on a construction site and proceeded to unload three old, beat-up mattresses into it. Guilt, remorse, and fear of getting apprehended seemed very far from his mind.

Grandiosity, as noted throughout, is an integral part of both the narcissistic and the psychopathic personalities. In their grandiosity, believing themselves "God's gift to the world," they seek attention in the form of mass adoration and unconditional love. Not surprisingly, they see themselves as too special to even question their belief that they are completely justified in asking others to figuratively kneel down before them, and do obeisance.

Here are some composite examples that illustrate a few of the points made above.

A patient's behavior in a number of sectors of his life exemplified the actions of the psychopathic narcissist. As a construction worker he manifested his lack of concern for others' rights by blasting his boom box when working in a residential neighborhood, regardless of whether the noise might bother the neighbors. In character too was his selfish anger at anyone whose needs conflicted with his pleasures. Once, for example, he could do no better than complain when his girlfriend threw out her back. Because she had stupidly and carelessly lifted heavy objects, he would have to miss a square dance—and, as he put it, "square dancing is an important part of my life."

Particularly psychopathic was his knowingly infecting women with AIDS, just for the fun of it and to satisfy his own orgasmic pleasure. Though he knew that he had AIDS, he nevertheless continued to have unprotected sex with a string of prostitutes, virtually single-handedly started a mini-epidemic in his corner of the world. In character too was his attempt to convince me as his therapist to lie and say that his many girlfriends were emotionally disabled, just so that they could collect Social Security Disability benefits. What was in it for him? If they did not have to work, they could spend more time visiting him for sex.

At the gym, a psychopathic patient virtually adopted all the machines that she was using. She would do a set and walk away, all along claiming ownership of the machine in her mind. When she returned to discover that the machine was occupied, she would actually feel startled, and then annoyed, to find that someone had usurped her throne, and would either whine and complain that she had a few more sets to do or summarily order the intruder off in a transport of what she felt to be justified anger.

Just recently I was riding in a cab whose driver blew his horn to get a double-parked truck to move out of his way. The truck driver, though he was the one who was parked illegally, clearly felt that the cab driver should have been more patient—patient enough to sit there quietly until the truck driver was ready to move his vehicle. Shifting easily between objects, with no real attachment to any one object beyond its representation in his mind as "people in my way," he conveyed his displeasure to *me*—though I was just a passenger—by looking at me and giving me the finger, as if I had something to do with the horn blowing and was somehow in a position to make it go away.

Psychopathic narcissism involves a certain amount of *aggressiveness*, which in turn is often displayed in acts of attempted control, e.g., "I know what's right, so I do it, and who cares what you think or how you feel." An example of the aggressively controlling narcissistic psychopathic individual is the condominium commando who constantly checks on whether or not the neighbors are following the rules to a "T." Such aggressively controlling individuals often have difficulty cooperating with everybody—subordinates, whom they view as slaves; equals, whom they nevertheless view either as inferiors not to be taken seriously or as dangerous competitors to be on the lookout for; and those in authority, whom they view as misguided and irrational. They also make such aggressively outlandish demands on others and on society that they flirt with becoming criminals—like the individual who seemed to be speaking more than figuratively when he said he "would kill for" the expensive sneakers he could not afford to buy.

Not surprisingly, aggressive narcissistic psychopaths tend to react with rage and anger when their demands are not met. However, they tend not to direct their rage against themselves—which would produce a depression. Instead they tend to direct it against others or the world in general—which produces antisocial behavior. When I was covering the emergency room, an employee came to see me requesting a prescription for benzodiazepines. I asked her to please register first. She told me that the line was too long and that she was too busy to wait, and she demanded that I see her immediately. She continued to make that demand even after I patiently explained to her what the rules were: that if I did see her without her registering it would mean that I was not working for the hospital but for myself and therefore would not be covered for malpractice. I stood my ground, and she responded by reporting me to the authorities. She was so effective in spinning her tale of how I mistreated her that my boss called me down to explain my actions. Worse, she wrote letters reporting me to every higher-up she could think of, and to so many people that it took months for me to clear up matters and regain my reputation as an all-around caring and responsible person.

Many aggressively narcissistic psychopathic individuals go beyond being undaunted by danger to being actually attracted to it. In doing so, they actively provoke and seek trouble. Unfortunately for them, they characteristically display an emotional fragility that makes them acutely vulnerable to shocks and disappointments. This hypersensitivity makes minor reversals seem major, as the prideful sense of specialness that forms an integral aspect of their identity magnifies the impact of any reversal that might come their way.

SADOMASOCHISM

Like sadists, psychopaths are bullies who attempt to get their way by intimidating and controlling others. They rage when crossed and lash out when cornered. Also like sadists, they get their kicks from frustrating, hurting, and torturing people. Many find depriving others of something they want as satisfying as getting something they want for themselves. I have had one patient admit: "I love it when my family feels helpless to know what to do with me, just as I love it when you, as my therapist, feel frustrated and defeated by how I don't change in spite of all your efforts to get me better."

Some psychopaths accomplish their sadistic ends through verbal abuse. A patient flew into a rage at a technician testing her baby because of what she believed was his failure to inform her of possible "complications" of the test. She then wrote letters of complaint to different administrators, saying that he failed to "warn me that the baby might cry when picked up to be tested." Other psychopaths accomplish their sadistic ends through physical abuse. Sadistic psychopaths who abuse others physically are legion. Of course, physical abuse—of a child, a mate, or an elderly person—only suggests, but does not define, psychopathy. But as a general rule, especially applicable here, it can be helpful both conceptually and therapeutically to consider all abuse to be at least partly of psychopathic origin—until proven otherwise by ruling out the existence of other motivation, means, and method.

Psychopaths—especially, but not exclusively, those who are unsuccessful—are often as masochistic as they are sadistic. Indeed, psychopaths defeat themselves so often that we are forced to consider the possibility that inherent in the psychopathic condition is guilt so severe that it makes psychopaths reluctant to allow themselves unalloyed success. Many psychopaths appear to practically beg others to punish them. Some do this by pushing the establishment's buttons—provocatively and rebelliously spouting outlandish countercultural assertions geared to provoke shock and outrage in those of a conservative bent, those who have all the usual loyalties and sensibilities, and often the hold on the reins of power. Others do this by deliberately arranging to be impenetrably evasive, intolerably unpleasant, and aggressively argumentative. Still others do this by defeating the family, friends, and therapists who are trying to rescue them from themselves and the consequences of their own actions—defeating them by staying just as sick as they are—and making certain that there is nothing that anyone can do about it. (Technically, we call this having a "masochistic triumph.")

As might be expected, the masochistic psychopathic individual's failures go right to the heart of his or her aspirations. Thus the oral individual, who sets him- or herself up to fail by expecting something for nothing, typically loses everything; the anal individual, who sets him- or herself up to fail by being too dominating, typically ends up in jail, powerless and controlled; and the phallic individual, who sets him- or herself up to fail by no-holds-barred sexually tinged or openly sexual piratical behavior, ends up loveless and friendless, often retaining wealth or power that has lost its essential value. On the assumption that oversimplification—if not taken literally—can be useful, we might say that the masochistic psychopath is likely to be broke, convicted and jailed, and divorced, often several times over.

Psychopaths, however, differ from true masochists in several ways. True masochists tend to actively and single-mindedly court self-destruction, while true psychopaths tend to self-destruct if not exclusively then at least partly out of a failure to properly assess reality. For example, the true psychopath fails to recognize the inescapable fact of life that instant gratification is rarely the straightest path to long-term satisfaction. While the true masochist's self-destructiveness is almost always a way to satisfy the dictates of a punitive conscience, psychopathic self-destructiveness often results, at least in part, from an insufficiency of conscience—for we all need conscience to satisfactorily watch over, protect, and guide us safely down the road to success.

DEPRESSION

Both psychopaths and depressives experience feelings of low self-esteem as reflected in two opposing tendencies. On one hand, they try to *compensate* for feeling defective by seeking supplies, seizing control, and gaining power. On the other hand, they *act out* feeling defective by being self-destructive. A difference between psychopaths and depressives is that, while at least some depressed individuals set their goals at a reasonable level, many psychopaths set their goals at levels so high that they are predictably unattainable. Also, unlike depressed individuals, who tend to tout their failures, psychopaths tend to take pains to conceal them. While the depressed individual expects failure, the psychopath is often surprised by it, or at least by its extent. Psychopaths may anticipate the possibility of a scheme falling through on its own or because someone in authority moves in to stop them. But they rarely anticipate the possibility of being prosecuted criminally. Thus, after being convicted of being a traitor, an attorney who aided terrorists said, in effect, "I knew they would be furious, but who ever thought that they would try to put me away for twenty years?"

Like depressives, psychopaths can get depressed, or more depressed, when they fail. However, while depressives sometimes become truly suicidal after failing, psychopaths are more likely to make suicidal gestures for the sake of appearance and effect, e.g., to gain sympathy. This is always a dangerous gesture for anyone, but it is particularly dangerous for the psychopath, given the especially precarious state of his or her interpersonal relationships. More characteristic for psychopaths than for depressives is that when psychopaths fail they unwittingly and foolishly court disaster, and with a good probability of success, by disingenuously throwing themselves on the mercies of those they have wronged in an attempt to manipulate them.

SEXUAL DISORDERS

Psychopaths can be sexual predators. They are, however, not true sexual addicts in the sense that they are primarily and exclusively driven by insatiable sexual needs. Their sexuality often appears to be one of many manifestations of typical psychopathic desires. These include the need for immediate gratification, the desire to control their victims, and the need to compete with others by having a gun with more notches than those they are in competition with. Psychopathic desires also include the need to be shady and manipulative, so that sex is a prize not to be obtained in all the usual and acceptable ways but to be gotten by conning people out of it. They achieve this by lying about their true feelings ("I love you") and true intent ("I plan to marry you"), and by coming on as one thing ("your date") and then turning out to be quite another ("your rapist").

BORDERLINE PERSONALITY DISORDER

Like borderlines, psychopaths often form intense engulfing relationships with a sadomasochistic caste. Soon afterward, they predictably turn and withdraw affection and go on to the next person, seemingly with very little provocation or warning. However, while borderlines tend to drop people because they feel engulfed by too much closeness, psychopaths tend to drop people because they feel they have extracted from them all that they are ever going to get.

SCHIZOTYPAL PERSONALITY DISORDER

Both psychopaths and schizotypals have omnipotent wishes—they believe, for example, that they can cure a medical disorder by devoutly wishing it gone. Both then go on to form quack theories, particularly those of a medical nature, e.g., "think yourself well." Both also process information autistically—for example, both tend to perceive reality according to their inner dictates, along such lines as "the world *is* what I *would like it* to be."

However, while the schizotypal thinks and behaves out of an inner sense of conviction, and often stops short of demanding that others believe and reward him or her, the psychopath thinks and behaves more out of a need for palpable, immediate, personal gain—e.g., money, control, and competitive power. We might say that as a general rule, the schizotypal expects to be believed, but the psychopath expects to be paid.

HISTRIONIC PERSONALITY DISORDER

Many psychopaths resemble histrionic *femmes fatales* and *Don Juan characters* in their seductiveness and in their tendency to play sexual games—e.g., they manipulate people into giving in to them by playing "hard to get." Both use sex for gain—for example, both willingly lie on the casting couch if they feel that is what they have to do in order to advance their careers.

Both also believe truth to be a reflection of their inner reality, with the truth in each case evolving from the exaggerated emotionalism common to both disorders. However, in the histrionic's case the emotionalism is real, if overdone ("I was absolutely shattered when you told me that I didn't get that job"), while in the psychopath the emotionalism is primarily for effect and gain ("Look what you did to me. I am going to sue you for a billion dollars for ruining my life by making a verbal slur on my integrity.")

Like histrionics, psychopaths are *competitive* people who regularly turn inherently noncompetitive interactions into struggles to the death. Often they struggle over what they believe to be finite supplies, so that what you get comes at their expense (zero sum). Both psychopaths and histrionics are covetous people who envy and set out to devalue and defeat those who have more than they do—those in authority or higher up than they are on the social ladder. As a predictable corollary, both feel most comfortable with others they can perceive as one step down from them, and so both shift their focus away from defeating those who are struggling to get ahead and toward defeating those they perceive as already having made it. These people, in their opinion, "need to be taken down a peg or two—fixed for good, and once and for all." Both attempt to defeat their rivals by devaluing them, both to their faces and behind their backs, and by the use of subterfuge. In the realm of the latter, an opportunistic psychopathic medical student told everyone that she was not planning to study for a final exam just so that others would follow her lead and not study either. With a smirk on her face, she then closed her door, put out the lights, and crammed all night before the test by flashlight with the shades down—so that she could get the best grade and go to the top of her class. Both psychopaths and histrionics use people to get ahead in life. They are like the doctor who entertains colleagues not because he likes them but so that they will refer patients to him and further repay him by putting in a good word for him with the hospital's medical board when it comes time for promotion. But histrionics devalue and defeat others more for emotional than for practical reasons. According to one theory, competitive histrionics are caught up in a lifelong oedipal frenzy: A man goes through life seeing everyone as his rival father and attempting to destroy the father so that he can come out on top with (e.g., marry) his mother, and a woman goes through life seeing everyone as her rival mother and attempting to destroy the mother so that she can come out on top with (e.g., marry) her father. In contrast, psychopaths are competitive less for oedipal and more for practical reasons. For them, "I enjoy having something and how and why I get it doesn't matter so much" is more like it.

POSTTRAUMATIC STRESS DISORDER

Not all psychopaths are born psychopathic. A number of observers suggest that psychopathy can be reactive. Millon, in differentiating "long-standing clinical traits [from] those that arise in response to transient stresses,"[3] quotes Pritchard as describing a "morbid state of mind [that] has been the effect of . . . external and accidental cause."[4] This reactive form of the disorder can resemble the endogenous form in all ways except for beginning acutely after real-life conditions deteriorate. So one patient's psychopathy can begin early in life, without apparent reason, with the pathology seemingly generated by mysterious and unfathomable "primordial forces" instead of as the outcome of environmental events. But another patient can generate virtually the same set of symptoms as a reaction to an external, usually catastrophic, event. Such cases make it apparent that psychopathy, with its roots in an infrahuman past and evolutionarily refined, is a response available to all, a mechanism there for anyone to use when needed—conjured up after an unfortunate occurrence that calls for nothing less than a life-saving emergency measure. Images of otherwise honest, salt-of-the-earth people, and the police themselves, looting after a disastrous hurricane bring this process to mind. (I think it somewhat moot as to whether these individuals should be diagnosed as psychopaths or as patients suffering from a Posttraumatic Stress Disorder.)

Psychopathy that starts in childhood as a way to deal with parental abuse can continue into adulthood as a continuation and repetition of the early traumatic experiences. In such cases the adult psychopathic symptoms are aroused, really rearoused, by specific triggers we might call "parental," and the psychopathy is replayed with one parental surrogate after another. This form of psychopathy contains elements of an attempt to master anxiety not by deflecting it, avoiding it, or nipping it in the bud, but by actively repeating the early traumatic experience(s) that originally created it, along with the original psychopathic method chosen for coping with the trauma(ta)—adaptive for the child, but maladaptive for the adult.

For example, I saw a few patients whose countercultural fanaticism was less a product of free choice than a repetition of an early traumatic relationship with a father whose abusiveness triggered a defensive rebelliousness on the part of the child. These individuals came to see the image of their feared and hated father in all authority and found it soothingly reassuring to shoot these "fathers" down over and over again. Each time a father symbol came up in their lives, their resolute antiestablishmentarianism flared and led to an overblown and irrational response. Some traitors side with the enemy out of a recurrent need to destroy the unavailable rejecting father, as symbolized by the "fatherland."

At times the acute reactive form of the disorder shades over into the chronic form. In a common scenario, a previously nonpsychopathic individual who is jailed after being falsely convicted of committing a crime becomes a chronic psychopath, having discovered a useful mechanism that he or she goes on to find worthy of repetition. For example, a woman became acutely psychopathic, essentially for the first time in her life, after being falsely convicted and jailed for an offense she did not commit. She then went on to discover that the psychopathic mode suited her ongoing need to never forget how authority wronged her, and to get back at authority for what it did to her.

A man started cheating on his wife when she refused to have sex with him after only a year of marriage. His cheating was less a symptom of a chronic disorder than his way to cope and deal with a force he believed to be beyond his control, and to handle what to him seemed an irresolvable problem. Instead of saying "We need marital therapy" or "I get so depressed" or "I will leave," the patient decided to "fix her good." Unfortunately, what started as a maladaptive attempt to come to terms with an unalterable reality eventually developed a life of its own and became perversely and inappropriately widespread and repetitive until the patient, finding himself "getting into the spirit of things," developed a true psychopathic disorder. Like many reactive psychopaths, he could no longer count on being in control of a process that he had in the beginning "purposively" initiated, so that what began as a way to achieve temporary comfort effectively became a bad habit he could not break, even after his wife made considerable progress in therapy, and met his demands and exceeded all his needs.

Posttraumatic psychopaths should never be viewed as possessing simple and exclusive moral laxity. This is because these individuals truly suffered severely at the hands of others or because of circumstances at one time in their lives. Therefore, it is important that practitioners recognize the origins of the psychopaths plight and then, as they might do with any other patient suffering from a form of Posttraumatic Stress Disorder, help them find a better way to integrate their earlier traumata once and for all. Only then can psychopaths stop constantly trying to have to master traumata by repeating them, predictably and frustratingly, not to their benefit, but to our detriment.

CHAPTER 8

Social Issues

Three terms are conventionally employed to describe the sensed diagnostic entity that is the subject of this text. These terms are:

1. Antisocial Personality Disorder (*DSM-IV*);
2. Sociopathy; and
3. Psychopathy (Psychopathic Personality Disorder).

Each of these terms contributes something, and something different, to our understanding of the psychopath. For our present purposes, I note that the first two terms are more heavily imbued with social criteria than the third, as follows:

ANTISOCIAL PERSONALITY DISORDER

The first term, Antisocial Personality Disorder, emphasizes in its central criterion the role an individual's social behavior plays in the *manifestation* of his or her disorder. This central (*DSM-IV*) criterion is "[d]isregard for and violation of the rights of others [as manifest in a] failure to conform to social norms with respect to lawful behaviors as indicated by repeatedly performing acts that are grounds for arrest."[1]

There are two caveats to consider in applying this criterion. First, in making our diagnosis we should, as much as possible, seek fundamental rights to serve as our diagnostic standard-bearers. That in turn means identifying not rights that are unique to one society but rights that are the same from society to society. In the realm of rights that are unique to one society, rights that are a given in an individualistic society may not be rights in a collectivistic society. Second, we must correct for the conflicting rights that exist within a given society. For example, a worker, a young mother, called *her boss* a psychopath because she claimed that he was depriving her of her rights as a woman and as a mother by not letting her work at home so that she could take care of her children. But her boss called *her* a psychopath, claiming that she was demanding special consideration and treatment without comprehending that he was simply requesting the same performance from her that he expected from everyone else.

SOCIOPATHY

As its name suggests, the second term, *sociopathy,* emphasizes the role social criteria play in the *creation* of the disorder. While the term and concept of "Antisocial Personality Disorder" focus on the individual's disruptive effect on society, this term and concept focus on society's disruptive effect on the individual. The term implies that the individual's troubles are either the product of a faulty upbringing by or maladaptive identification with one's parents, or else the product of maladaptive identification with deviant members of a given society—often a "deviant" subsociety such as the Mafia. We might say that while those suffering from an Antisocial Personality Disorder operate immorally as they operate *against mainstream* society, sociopathic individuals operate morally as they operate *for* a *deviant* society.

While not everyone agrees that psychopathy is primarily the product of social influences, almost everyone agrees that social attitudes determine whether a psychopathic individual will be successful or unsuccessful—rich or poor, free or in jail. For one thing, our society, like most societies, has quirky and irrational laws. For example, in some segments of our society, those truly dangerous psychopaths who get caught driving drunk tend to fare better than the petty criminal psychopaths who get caught shoplifting, and in the more liberal segments of our society there are times when prostitutes who are heterosexual fare far worse with the law than prostitutes who are transsexual.

There are two caveats to be observed. First, we should not condone patients (and their defenders) by misusing the term and concept of "sociopathy" as an excuse for bad behavior as we extrapolate "I am not at all responsible for my bad behavior" from "I am a victim of circumstances." There are, after all, matters of individual variability and personal choice to be considered that do, or at least should, dilute the absolute—"society made me what I am"—with the more relativistic "How I could and ought to have mustered some personal strength and courage to be something better." Second, we must not equate being a sociopath with being a member of the underbelly of society. While sociopathy certainly exists in the lower classes, in part because it leads to downward social mobility, as much or even more exists in the middle and upper classes; however unfortunate and paradoxical, sociopathy can also lead to upward social mobility

PSYCHOPATHY

The term "psychopath" as I use it focuses more on the internal workings of the individual than on the individual's relationship to his or her society. In particular, the term as I use it emphasizes disordered intrapsychic processes such as the inability to feel guilty when appropriate; disordered cognitive processes (the making of cognitive errors)—casuistic thinking, for example; and troubled interpersonal relationships, in particular the lack of empathy and deficit of altruism that lurk behind the psychopath's apparent inability to feel for others and treat them honestly, fairly, and humanely.

SOCIAL CAUSATION OF PSYCHOPATHY

I begin this part of my discussion with yet another caveat. We must not overlook the role social factors play in causing and enhancing any personality disorder, and especially psychopathy. However, it is important to neither overemphasize nor oversimplify these factors. We must not overemphasize the role violence on TV and in video games plays in the disorder's creation and maintenance. It is the rare individual who becomes a psychopath simply because he or she has decided to become like the superheroes on TV, in the movies, and in video games—people who get what they want through force and intimidation, solve all problems by blasting anything in their way to smithereens, and maim and kill others if they feel that is what they have to do to win. Individual vulnerability and variability are important determinants of how such input influences output. Besides, in my opinion, violent video games do not cause psychopathy so much as the individual's predilection to be violent and psychopathic (if only in fantasy) causes him or her to pick and play these games. The same is true of peer group identification. What looks like a one-way process ("gangs make psychopaths") is often just one way on a two-way street: People who are already neighborhood gangster types seem to find each other and manage to form associations.

This said, there are two broadly valid sociological theories about the cause of psychopathy, each of which makes a worthwhile, although different, point of its own. (It is not easy to integrate both viewpoints, however.) These are:

1. A society that is too liberal and too permissive creates psychopathy.
2. A society that is too conservative and too repressive creates psychopathy.

A Too-Liberal and Too-Permissive Society Creates Psychopathy

The prevalent belief is that a society that is too liberal and too permissive creates psychopathy. In an exaggeration of this view, a liberal permissive society not only lets but also encourages people to run amok by offering boundless freedom for all without consequences for any. By implication, the remedy would be to open more jails and institute harsher penalties for crimes committed. Otherwise, as Hare suggests, "Society [will continue to move] in the direction of permitting, reinforcing, and in some instances actually valuing some of the traits listed [for psychopaths] such as impulsivity, irresponsibility, [and] lack of remorse [as we become] not only fascinated [by] but increasingly tolerant of the psychopathic personality."[2]

Benjamin B. Wolman, a psychologist whose view of the causes of and cures for psychopathy reveals a conservative bent, also suggests that psychopathy is caused to an extent by social permissiveness. He specifically blames a "flimsy, inconsistent, overpermissive, and procrastinating judicial system"[3] for creating "a social climate conducive to sociopathic, antisocial acts."[4] Focusing on the problem of unlimited freedom, he insists that "[d]emocracy does not mean unlimited freedom to organize self-righteous sociopathic gangs."[5] He then suggests (in text he italicizes for emphasis) that *"democracy means the same freedom for all, [not as the] dictators and terrorists practice [it] all freedom for some."*[6]

H. J. Eysenck, another theorist with a conservative bent, argues that being criminal is normal, for "babies and young children [after all] take whatever [they] need. . . ."[7] He then suggests that the question to ask is not what makes people psychopaths but "why do most of us behave in a socially desirable fashion?"[8] He answers the question by saying, "we behave . . . well because our consciences would trouble us if we did not"[9] and concludes that psychopathy is the product of faulty conscience development. To Eysenck, "[c]onscience . . . is a conditioned response,"[10] and problems occur when health-giving "conditioning experiences are missing"[11] or when "the wrong experiences are reinforced."[12] In effect, Eysenck concludes that treatment that does not focus on conditioning, or really on reconditioning, is likely to be ineffective, so that "[t]raditional psychodynamic and nondirective client-centered therapies are to be avoided within general samples of offenders."[13]

Speaking more specifically of the kind of conditioning he favors, Eysenck asserts that in order to counter psychopathic criminality it is necessary to get serious about punishing crime. He notes that "[c]aution should be given on the occasion of the first offense . . . serious punishment should follow the next offense,"[14] and that punishment should consist of "the restricted use . . . of prison [as] rehabilitation."[15]

All of us can see with our own eyes how an everyday degree of social laxness can create a degree of psychopathy. We can also appreciate how some of us participate in creating and fostering this development. On

Christopher Street in New York City's Greenwich Village, it is not hard to spot the development of psychopathy in action. This area is fast becoming a place where institutions with an antisocial bent, such as tattoo parlors, porno shops and S and M costume shops, are rapidly replacing the more wholesome coffee shops, chocolate shops, haberdasheries, and small independent theatres. A few voices complain that a mini sin city is arising out of the ashes of the old place, but they appear to have been drowned out by the voices of those who fear being labeled repressive totalitarian bigots and do nothing to put a stop to the deterioration. They instead choose to look the other way when people openly sell drugs out in the streets or when prostitutes have sex on the sidewalks. These individuals turn away using this type of rationale: "The presence of transsexual prostitutes having sex out in the open is acceptable, for they were here first (before gentrification), and besides we feel for them. After all, given that they cannot get hired in traditional jobs, there is no other way for them to obtain the money they need to buy their hormone shots and pay for their sex-change operations." To some people's way of thinking, society's enabling transsexual prostitutes to have sex out in the open is not much different from patients enabling crooked practitioners to cheat the insurance company by remaining silent when these practitioners report that the sexual massage they gave was in fact "massage therapy" and so as such should be reimbursed by the patient's major medical insurance.

An important caveat here is that it is helpful to distinguish overpermissiveness from charitableness based on simply humanity. Each individual has to draw his or her own comfortable line between the two.

A Too-Conservative and Repressive Society Creates Psychopathy

There are flaws in the hypothesis that overpermissiveness is the root of all psychopathy, that cracking down is always a remedy, and that Eysenck's "build[ing] up a conscience through appropriate punishment"[16] is the only and perfect way to stop the present social epidemic of psychopathic acting out. A main flaw in the hypothesis is that becoming more conservative and less liberal (e.g., cracking down) often provokes retaliative rebellion. Many of my patients became and remained psychopaths in part to get revenge on an establishment they felt had, and indeed sometimes actually had, repressed them. As an example, it is probably correct to say that crackdowns on potential terrorists, however necessary they may be, are one possible cause of terrorism.

Overly conservative approaches also tend, so to speak, to catch dolphins in nets meant for tuna. Tightening the bankruptcy laws may prevent bad tenants from running up big rent bills and then escaping responsibility for paying them by declaring bankruptcy, secure in the knowledge that as bankrupts they can stay put throughout the duration of the lengthy eviction procedure. But the tight bankruptcy laws also penalize families whose breadwinners get sick, accrue big medical bills through no fault of their own, and then, on top of that, lose both their jobs and their medical insurance. A society that jails fathers for not providing child support can in fact create a psychopathic father who provides even less child support. A jailed father cannot work at an honest job for an honest living to pay the bills, and a father who is released from jail is likely to discover that the only way an ex-con can find the job he needs to have to obey the law is to become someone who breaks that law. Finally, sending people to jail can have the effect of sending them to a training camp for psychopaths. Sending adolescents to reform school for psychopathic criminality often backfires when, instead of reforming, the individual learns even more psychopathic ropes.

(I am not implying that all psychopathic rebellion is rebellion against a conservative society. Rebelliousness is politically neutral. A person can rebel in psychopathic fashion against the *liberal* establishment too—for example, by protesting a large corporation's giving gays and lesbians equal rights by joining hands with similarly minded homophobes and starting a countrywide boycott against the company.)

A SERIOUS PROBLEM WITH ALL SOCIAL THEORIES

A serious problem with all social theories (as with most or all developmental theories) is that suggested by Eysenck: Since psychopaths show relatively "poor conditionability,"[17] they will not respond to any kind of social input, liberal or conservative. This means that they will not become psychopathic either because the liberals overdo telling them to hang loose, or because the conservatives overdo telling them to exercise self-control. As one patient said about himself, "I reflexively become like the dog that pulls right through its choke collar to be able to continue as before, testing all limits even though I know how unpleasant or dangerous the consequences of my actions are likely to be."

A POSSIBLE REMEDY: AVOIDING ENABLING PSYCHOPATHY

Perhaps prevention is the best way to stop the current epidemic of spreading psychopathy. Prevention in great measure involves not enabling psychopathy in the first place. In our society, we as individuals too often not only *tolerate* but also actively *encourage* individual psychopathy, and we do so for a number of reasons, and in ways that originate in both liberalism and conservatism.

The enabling that comes from the *liberal* side comes from those elements of an individualistic (as opposed to collectivistic) society that resolutely ("no flexibility, no exceptions!") advocates the sanctity of my rights over yours, and over the rights of society as a whole. Those in authority consciously or unconsciously give psychopaths a free hand based on one or more fanatical convictions that roughly equate to the phrase "It would be repressive to stop someone from falsely shouting 'fire' in a crowded movie theatre."

Also originating in our liberal side is the tendency to get others to act out our own distressing tendency to be frustrated psychopaths ourselves. We secretly want to act psychopathically, but laudable self-restraint keeps us in check. What we do instead is provoke others to do our bidding. This we do both actively, by egging psychopaths on, and passively, by hesitating or refusing to condemn psychopathic behavior where we find it. For example, writing about street vendors selling fakes, Tracie Rozhon and Rachel Thorner, two *New York Times* reporters, asked someone buying from the vendors "[Does] the fact that selling . . . fakes might not be legal matter to [you]?"[18] The revealing and all-too-typical dismissive response was: "Whatever . . . I'm not the one who's going to get into trouble."[19]

Excessively liberal psychotherapists can, in the guise of trying to be helpful and corrective, enable psychopathic behavior simply by failing to consider unintended consequences of their more permissive therapeutic attitudes and actions. For example, in their focus on the health-giving attributes of freely expressing anger to get it out of the system, they fail to recognize that it might be a bad idea to encourage people to feel good by making others feel bad—selfishly being "free" and "me," regardless of how that might affect "you." Worse, some therapists set a bad personal example by self-serving actions; thus, since being a psychopath appears okay for the therapist, the goose, it must be okay for everyone else, the ganders. As Alan A. Stone notes when speaking of forensic psychiatrists, "[i]n the glare of the public spotlight and the pressures of the adversarial system, forensic experts seem to become more dogmatic and more convinced about their own clinical judgments; direct contradiction by the forensic experts for the other side only seems to strengthen their certitude. . . . The ethical guidelines developed for forensic psychiatrists that emphasize honesty will not protect trained practitioners from the pitfall of their own hubris."[20] Certainly, therapists set a bad example for society when they give corrupt testimony in court while acting in an expert capacity. They set even worse examples when they cheat on Medicare, or tout idiosyncratic therapy based on ill-considered theories that cross over a very low barrier into the realm of quackery.

In contrast, some of our enabling comes from our *conservative* side. In particular, many of us tend to have a competitive sadistic streak inside, prompting an appetite for enjoying the suffering of others (Schadenfreude). To satisfy that appetite, we psychopathically stand by and watch with glee as the true psychopaths among us crush our rivals. We get secret "sinful" pleasure from seeing our enemies brought down, and from being able to say to ourselves, "They deserved it" and "I am smart, not like those idiots. I would not fall for that line, or be sold that bill of goods."

Therapists enable psychopathy when they swing from liberal to conservative views to avoid representing a too-liberal society they believe is entirely to blame for the world's psychopathy. They enable psychopathy when they unthinkingly cast aside their traditional liberal biases of caring, concern, affirmation, and permissiveness. As a result, they become punitive, critical practitioners who renounce sympathetic understanding in favor of uncomprehending condemning, warning, and disciplining in the misguided belief that this is the best and only way to avoid becoming enablers. Mostly what they accomplish is dehumanizing the patient and either driving him or her out of therapy or inspiring him or her to greater heights of antiestablishment rebellion.

On a personal level, all of us, not only therapists, need to help our children, our parents, our neighbors, and our coworkers/superiors/underlings on the job become healthy, balanced people. We can do that by modeling healthy behaviors for them. We need to set a good example by being moderates—individuals who tread the fine line between excessively overpermissive and excessively punitive enabling. We can all become more empathic and less dehumanizing by acknowledging the other person's point of view, understanding others' motivations even or especially when their actions are not to our liking, and treating other people whenever we can as intelligent, sentient beings with simple human desires—people whom we ought to respect and, whenever reasonable and possible, gratify, instead of treating them as unloved objects to be pushed around, used, toyed with, bled indiscriminately, or controlled like chess pieces on a board. It may not be possible to treat psychopathy once developed with the tincture of tolerance, kindness, and reserve, but it certainly may be possible to prevent it from developing in the first place.

We can and should also use what personal and professional influence and political clout we have to inject rationality and fairness into a world where too often passion (Murphy and Oberlin's "feelthink")[21] replaces perspective, where dishonesty triumphs over honesty, and where getting away with anything and everything replaces accountability. For example, we should all speak out against social hypocrisy. In particular, we should all work toward a society that does not send mixed messages that are the product of, and in turn create, severe crises of morality. We must in particular avoid saying "Do as I say" on one hand and saying "Do as you wish" on the other. It strikes me as maladaptive and counterproductive that we condemn drunk driving yet build bars on the highway, or condemn computer hacking but fail to pursue and punish hackers or, pursuing and finding them, let them off easy and reward them with jobs working for us as consultants, side by side as allies in the fight against computer crime. (In a recent case a judge let the creator of a major virus that caused millions of dollars worth of personal and industrial damage off with a suspended sentence.) To me, common sense says that there is something wrong in the world when a company that sells programs to search and destroy computer spyware and adware advertises these programs—using spyware and adware. Certainly a society that condemns spyware and adware for clogging computers and stealing personal information and catches but fails to punish those who write the programs needs to do one of two things, and to do neither of them half-way. It needs to either change its attitudes and ways, or it needs to just accept the fact that sooner or later psychopaths, both mild and severe, will be in the majority, and that psychopathy will come to constitute not an emotional disorder that needs to be prevented and cured, but a standard of normalcy that needs to be accepted.

As I see it, today's most important social question is whether we are on the way to being unable to be sure of the answer to Dr. Raeleen Mautner's perceptive and troubling question (personal communication, 2005): "Is psychopathy abnormal? Or is it normal to be a psychopath?"

CHAPTER 9

Successful Psychopaths

On the whole, psychopathic individuals—and mild psychopaths especially—do not fail as frequently or as predictably as we might, and even prefer to, believe. Undoubtedly many make out very well professionally and personally, and some do better than the rest of us. The belief that they regularly fail is based in part on an artifact. Many successful psychopaths live their lives if not quietly or unnoticed then at least unremarked both by the general public and by the psychiatric clinician. In contrast, those who are unsuccessful get most of the publicity. They are the ones who tend to attract the attention of the general public through stories in the media. They are also the ones whom clinicians study and report on, for much of the extant literature about psychopathy is based on observations of psychopaths in places where failed psychopathy is the rule rather than the exception: in forensic settings, or in the psychiatric clinic or hospital.

As previously noted, Millon (1981) uses the term "aggressive personality"[1] to describe psychopathy and isolates two varieties: "nonantisocial and antisocial types."[2] Millon's term "nonantisocial aggressive"[3] is close to my term "successful psychopath." According to Millon, nonantisocial aggressives have "essentially similar 'basic' personalities"[4] as do antisocial aggressives, only they "fit into the mainstream of society, displaying their characteristic traits through socially acceptable avenues [not coming] into conflict with the law [and instead] find[ing] themselves commended and reinforced in our competitive society [and] find[ing] a socially valued niche"[5] as they "participate in the ordinary affairs of everyday life."[6]

To a great extent, psychopaths become successful due to their ability to process their negative tendencies—their hostile instincts, for example—into positive creative-interpersonal-social presentation, however much the result retains some of the original psychopathic characteristics. In this effort at socioculturization, the defense of positive sublimation is typically joined by the defense of positive reaction formation.

Positive sublimation *channels* aggressivity. It may channel it into creativity. Dadaists might be said to positively sublimate their antiestablishment rascality into great art, as evident in Marcel Duchamp's satirical sculpture of a urinal. Positive sublimation may also channel personal vendettas into sacred trusts. Psychopaths may say that they are not out to crush a personal enemy, but to defeat an enemy of society. Thus a politician runs on a third-party ticket to hurt the chances of the current leader of the race, someone he personally dislikes, by taking votes away from him. However, he denies his real motivation and instead avers that he is out to offer the public the opportunity to have a real choice.

Positive reaction formation *converts* hostility into refined admirable social activity. Anger is turned into an excess of love and sinfulness into excessive saintliness. Both the love and the saintliness tend to be of the all-encompassing, flower-child kind that can, in the wrong hands, take on a narcissistic "look at me—how caring and loving I am" quality that is too indiscriminate to ring true.

Psychopaths also become successful to the extent that they figure out how to operate within the gray area of the law. Some get rich by selling worthless nostrums after making unfulfillable promises. They make sure, however, to use escape clauses to protect themselves in case of legal challenge: instead of saying "this product will change your life," they use "this product will *help* change your life." Others learn exactly how to cheat on their taxes in ways that fly under the radar of the IRS, using their accountants first as a sword and then as a shield.

Some psychopaths do not do what is illegal, just what is immoral. It is immoral, though not illegal, for shyster ad writers to sell stereo racks using false advertising that hides the stereo equipment wires so that the picture of the finished product looks neater than it could ever be in real life. The same may be said of the behavior of the entrepreneur who announces a limited-time sale and then says he is extending the sale beyond the cutoff date due to an overwhelming response, when in fact he is extending it because he has not sold much of anything the first time around. No less immoral, but still legal, is the behavior of the big company that enhances profits by offering rebates that most customers will not claim because they make the paperwork too difficult for almost anyone to complete.

Psychopaths also become successful to the extent that they use sophistic reasoning effectively. The editorial page of a well-known newspaper justifies its own selective advocacy of lawlessness by saying it is right to break the law when one deems the law to be wrong. In support of this view, the editorial staff cites the admirable motives of those who participated in the Boston Tea Party—an event that can always be cited to justify unlawful behavior as being right so long as it is deemed to be for an ultimate good.

Psychopaths also become successful by finding ways to misrepresent themselves. For example, an unscrupulous reporter created powerful news stories by acting like a psychotherapist in order to gain the confidence of someone she was interviewing so that he or she would open up and expose all secrets. By lending her interviewees a sympathetic ear ("Tell me, where is the pain in your heart?"), she would get them to think they were confiding in someone who understood and cared about them. All she was doing was leading them on while secretly setting traps for them and guiding them right inside. She would then betray them by printing the emotional asides and confidences that came tumbling out, although these were told to her as personal confessions never meant to see the journalistic light.

Psychopaths become successful to the extent that they discover how to do good by being bad. They streak in order to convince the world to be freer and more spontaneous, or they use such passive resistance as hunger strikes to advance currently unpopular but ultimately desirable political agendas. Some Germans saved Jews not so much because they cared about Jews or thought that the Nazi policies were bad but because they were motivated in part by a desire to rebel against the establishment and in part because their resentment of anyone interfering prompted them to ignore official policy.

Psychopaths also become successful to the extent that when brought up short they know exactly what to do to smooth things over and wriggle out from under. For example, a successful psychopath in one town knew how to avoid a traffic ticket simply by claiming to be a friend of a certain powerful local who, having his own issues with the police, freely allowed his name to be used by anyone who wanted to get off easy after breaking the law.

In short, when selective and controlled, psychopathy can be a way to succeed and even reach the highest echelons of the business, political, and professional worlds—higher than some uncompromising moderates could ever go due to their admirable but stifling morality. Certainly, the *inability* to think and act like a psychopath can work to one's disadvantage. We all need to be able to tell a little white lie now and then when we are cornered, and those of us who cannot do so often fail, however much we fail for all the right reasons. The doctor who is too morally constrained to be able to prescribe placebos to a patient whose illness has a considerable emotional overlay will be an honest healer. But in practice he may not be providing his patients with the best medical care available, and so while he will be a healer who is very honest, he may not be a healer who is terribly effective.

CHAPTER 10

Cause

I view psychopathy as a disorder that has biological, psychological, and social roots, with each individual's psychopathy a unique blend of innate and acquired characteristics. Hare put it this way: "An individual with a mix of psychopathic personality traits who grows up in a stable family and has access to positive social and educational resources might become a con artist or white-collar criminal, or perhaps a somewhat shady entrepreneur, politician, or professional. Another individual, with much the same personality traits but from a deprived and disturbed background, might become a drifter, mercenary, or violent criminal."[1]

BIOLOGICAL FACTORS

Instinct Theories

Some observers believe that psychopaths are the victims of aggressive and sexual appetites that are simply too strong for them to control effectively. Other observers, however, believe that psychopaths have weak instincts that meet an even weaker resistance. Theoretically at least, instinctual weakness can account for the typical psychopathic:

1. Diminished or selective capacity for positive interpersonal arousal.
2. Poor conditionability, which may be, as Eysenck suggests, due to innate "low arousal [so that] conditioning [is] less likely to occur."[2] This may help explain the typical psychopathic slow response to others' attempts to correct behavior through positive means (cajolery) or negative methods (punishment), as well as their inability to learn from experience. However, as mentioned throughout,

I believe that most psychopaths are not *poorly* but *selectively* conditionable. They often respond to reward more than to punishment, as they freely seek pleasure while simultaneously disregarding the potential for negative consequences.

3. Constant need to seek thrills and high excitement in order to feel less bored and more real and alive. Willie Sutton said, "Why did I rob banks? Because I enjoyed it. I loved it. I was more alive when I was inside a bank, robbing it, than at any other time in my life. I enjoyed everything about it so much that one or two weeks later I'd be out looking for the next job. But to me the money was the chips, that's all."[3]

Theories of "Regression"

Some observers view psychopaths as resembling in some ways overage children. They note the descriptive overlap between adult psychopathic behavior and the behavior of "normal" children, many of whom are selfish—to the point that, incapable of feeling much empathy or of displaying altruism, they just reach for and take what they want. Certainly some psychopaths appear to have never grown up. They favor developmentally primitive survival methods such as lying and stealing. They also remind us in some ways of rebellious adolescents who deliberately take defiant antiestablishment stands, either because they do not care what society thinks or precisely in order to develop a distinct and separate identity from peers and elders. Like these adolescents, psychopaths try to distinguish themselves from the rest by being bad boys and girls who, so to speak, skateboard their way along the sidewalks of life, scrawl graffiti on society's face, defiantly moon the world, and shockingly streak the establishment in its most hallowed places. They are rebellious rascals who—like overage fraternity and sorority members—have the most fun when they are being the most unmanageable. As a hapless psychiatrist treating one such patient, I felt more than frustrated when I suggested that he not insert a device into his earlobes to stretch them into a doughnut shape, only to be told, "You don't understand me and what I am about." Then, when it appeared as if gangrene of his earlobes were about to set in, he got angry, claiming that "You should have stopped me, but apparently you didn't care enough about me to try to save me from myself."

Animal Models

Psychopaths may be said to resemble animals in that, speaking generally, both psychopaths and animals suffer from an inappropriately clear conscience. Some observers compare the psychopath to the sneaky dog that rummages through the garbage when it thinks no one is watching, or to the sneaky cat that behaves well only when someone is looking (if then). One man compared one of his psychopathic friends to one of his devilishly clever cats. This man tried a little experiment. He put food in a Havaheart trap and watched to see what happened. All but one of his cats went right in to grab the food, only to have the trap door shut on them. There was, however, one cat that did not fall for that ruse. This cat, after watching all the other cats lose their freedom, refused to be scammed like the others. So it entered the trap and stood near but outside of the trap mechanism. Without springing the mechanism, it reached in with a paw and rolled the food over and out. Then it did something unique. Rather triumphantly and defiantly, almost as if it were a smirking, crowing human psychopath telling the world to go to hell, it selected its owner's best oriental rug, and urinated all over it.

I view the psychopath as being in some respects like the cuckoo bird. According to legend, the cuckoo manipulates other birds into raising its offspring—entering their nests, throwing out their eggs, and replacing them with eggs of its own, thus tricking the owner of the nest into hatching the interloper's eggs and nourishing the newborns to maturity. I also see a rough comparison between the way psychopaths manipulate people and the way animals manipulate their predators, like the cat that arches its back when cornered to make itself look bigger, the blowfish that cons other fish into thinking it is larger and more intimidating than it is by blowing up its belly, and the fish with a fake face depicted on its tail in order to fool a predator whose method of attack is to bite off the heads of its prey.

Organic Causation

Many observers view psychopaths as somehow organically damaged. Some suggest that psychopaths are in effect wired incorrectly from birth—in the vernacular, "with certain chips missing." Others cite prenatal damage resulting in a fetal alcohol syndrome or its equivalent coming about when the mother's alcohol, drug, or even tobacco usage damages the fetus in utero. Still others cite postnatal brain damage that results from an accident (dropping) or physical abuse (shaking).

Some observers believe that psychopaths suffer from a frontal lobe syndrome characterized by inappropriate euphoria that blends into impulsivity and a lack of concern for the consequences of their actions, paralleled by a lack of concern for the sensibilities of others. Still others cite temporal lobe damage and note how it can help account for prolonged episodes of violent antisocial behavior that resemble temporal lobe seizures in their timing, duration, and content. While "abnormal" EEG findings, such as slow waves detectable in the temporal lobe, are said to have been found in psychopaths, some observers suggest that such phenomena are consistent not with brain damage but with simple disinterest.

Cleckley compares psychopathy to an organic aphasia.[4] W. A. Newman Dorland's *The American Illustrated Medical Dictionary* defines aphasia as a "defect or loss of the power of expression by speech, writing, or signs, or of comprehending spoken or written language, due to injury or disease of the brain centers."[5] There are certainly descriptive parallels between aphasia and the psychopath's apparent inability to put into action what he or she promises—agreeing to do one thing but actually doing another—and the psychopath's apparent difficulty in learning social skills that require aligning external input (like criticism) with internal input (like information from one's conscience and one's affects).

Some observers hypothesize that these individuals function more with their right than with their left brain, thus generating motivation, action, and reaction spontaneously and wordlessly, seemingly without knowing what they are about. As a result, they produce psychopathy, much like— as the composer Charles Camille Saint-Saëns said when speaking of his compositional skills—an "apple tree produces apples."[6]

Theories of sociobiology that focus on the evolutionary advantages of social behavior suggest that the wild, fantastic sexual behaviors of psychopaths are little more than a strategy for passing on their gene pool via promiscuity. This theory can help account for and explain such psychopathic behavior as a father's lack of loyalty to any one mother and child, resulting in the broken homes that psychopaths often come from, and then go on to create.

DEVELOPMENTAL THEORIES

A number of developmental theories have been postulated to account for psychopathy. While they all contribute something to our understanding of the final picture, no one theory can adequately explain and fully account for everything about the disorder. Psychopathy may only become severe when multiple developmental patterns and events have occurred. In turn, many of the developmental patterns and events that some consider to be pathognomonic for psychopathy are also to be found in the upbringing and lives of individuals with no discernable, or no important, psychopathology.

Upbringing

Many observers believe that a child's upbringing plays an important role in inducing and maintaining psychopathy. Thus Millon notes that two types of psychopath have been described—the indulged and the deprived,[7]—while Wolman cites along similar lines the triple determinants of parental "overpermissiveness,"[8] "deprivation,"[9] and "rejection."[10]

The *indulged* psychopath may have had excessively permissive, overly accepting parents to account for his or her poor self-control and in turn his or her characteristic irresponsibility and unpredictability. Cleckley's cases contain a high proportion of individuals whose parents rescued them from the consequences of their actions, either with money or by taking them in when perhaps they should have sent them away for residential treatment.[11]

Indulging parents can enable psychopathy either overtly or covertly. They might enable psychopathy overtly by actually egging the child on. In such cases the child who turns out to be the black sheep of the family is the one whom the parents incited to do their acting out for them—by provoking and encouraging the child to behave in the antisocial way the parent always wanted to, but could not actually bring themselves to, behave. As Wolman notes, some overindulgent parents actively "encourage ... their child to be dishonest as long as the dishonesty [is] successful."[12]

Or parents might enable psychopathy covertly. They might do this by spoiling their children, sending them the message that they deserve to have anything they want because of who and what they are, with the result that the child grows up believing that all the world is a good, giving parent and that all demands are to be gratified, no questions asked. They may ignore their mandate to put a stop to psychopathic-like behavior—accepting the behavior and even viewing it as a form of desirable self-expression. Or they simply may react positively to the manipulative lying, conning, and cheating as if these are charming and amusing character traits that are more of an asset than a liability.

In another view, it is excessively harsh *depriving* parenting that can account for such aspects of psychopathy as psychopathic rebelliousness and contrariness. Certainly there are cases where excessively guilty moralistic parents have provoked one or more of their children to counteridentify with them, and to decide to go through life being, as one patient put it, "as exact an opposite of a creepy solid citizen as I could possibly become."

Wolman also states that the homes of some psychopaths have been notable for a relative or complete "lack of parental affection."[13] Some parents so starve the child for affection that he or she vows to go through life getting what he or she wants and when he or she wants it, which is, predictably, right now. Wolman also emphasizes the role played by lack of guidance or misguidance "on the part of the parents,"[14] with the lack of parental supervision leading to the formation of a "teenage 'culture.'"[15] Sometimes the damage occurs because the father is absent and the mother is working to support the family, an especially devastating combination when there is also an absence of "stable social relationships in childhood"[16] outside the home.

Wolman notes that severe abuse and rejection can produce "feelings of mistrust [in the child] that can lead to sociopathic justification of hostile behavior."[17] Severe abuse and rejection can also lead to a failure to "identify with the parent and...to internalize the parents' values."[18] Furthermore, as Wolman suggests, violence between parents is highly conducive to violent behavior in children.[19] Parental emotional and physical abuse of the child often also occurs. The child may cower and then become psychopathic as a way to cope with feeling passive, or rage and become psychopathic as a way to retaliate.

I suggest two more, overlapping, possibilities. First, psychopathy can arise in the setting of parental *unpredictability*. Unpredictable parents provide irrational guidance/feedback that can lead the child to disregard authority simply because he or she does not know what authority expects, wants, and demands. Second, psychopathic parents or other family members can serve as malignant identification figures for the child, providing the child with models of antisocial behavior. Along these lines, Wolman cites unhealthy identification leading to formation of an "inadequate superego [as the reason why psychopathic individuals] appear to experience very little anxiety."[20]

This said, an intriguing theory states that psychopaths are born that way, and are therefore immune from birth on to parental or any other sort of feedback, so that it hardly matters at all what the parents say or do. This helps explain why no clear, if any, connection between adult psychopathy and the type and nature of early parenting has to date been definitely determined. So often the psychopathic condition must be regarded as sui generis, with the disorder arising under circumstances that not only are not conducive but are actually inimical to it. It often happens that healthy parents recognize the symptoms of abnormality in a child and make intelligent and even heroic efforts, sometimes with professional assistance, to correct it, but everything that all concerned do is absolutely to no avail.

BEHAVIORAL CONSTRUCTS

Learning

Some learning theorists view psychopathy as an acquired skill—an adaptive if seminormal mechanism that provides the individual with a way to avoid danger or to get out of danger once in it. In this view, psychopathy is less a compulsive and automatic problem than a considered and purposeful mechanism, less like a true unplanned personality disorder and more like a "disorder" of convenience—a method there for all to use when they feel that their circumstances warrant a form of behavior, no matter how extreme, that allows them to survive and prosper even if to do so they must take advantage of another person, and of the world.

Machiavelli's *The Prince* is, in effect, a teaching manual on how to become a psychopath. Today it might be titled *So You Want to be a Psychopath: How to Use Psychopathic Methods to Triumph and Win Big.*

Machiavelli in essence advocates that those who want to make it big politically should develop a compendium of psychopathic traits, including evilness, disloyalty, shrewdness, aggressiveness, deceitful manipulativeness, single-minded goal direction, corruptness, the assumption of blamelessness, hyperalertness to danger, and self-reliance.

Machiavelli advocates:

- *evilness* when he says that it is necessary to "[b]e able to do evil if constrained."[21]

- *disloyalty* when he says, "Astuteness to confuse men's brains ... ultimately overcome[s] those who have made loyalty their foundation."[22]

- *shrewdness* when he says, "Imitate the fox and the lion, for the lion cannot protect himself from traps, and the fox cannot defend himself from wolves."[23]

- *aggressiveness* when he says, you "will always have good friends [if you] have good arms."[24]

- *deceitful manipulativeness* when he says, "One who deceives will always find those who allow themselves to be deceived,"[25] and adds that it is not "[n]ecessary for a prince to have all [these] good qualities, but it is very necessary to seem to have them . . . . [to] have a mind [disposed] to adapt itself according to the wind"[26] in order to "satisfy the populace and keep it contented."[27]

- *single-minded goal direction* when he says, "The end justifies the means."[28]

- *corruptness* when he says, "Princes [cannot] avoid being hated by some one"[29] "so [whomever] you consider necessary to you for keeping your position...is corrupt, you must follow [their] humour and satisfy [them]."[30]

- *assumption of blamelessness* via the mechanism of blaming others (or arranging to have them blamed) when he says, "Let the carrying out of unpopular duties devolve on others."[31]

- *hyperalertness to danger* when he says, "It is a common fault of men not to reckon on storms in fair weather."[32]

- *self-reliance* when he says, "Only those defences are good, certain and durable, which depend on yourself alone and your own ability."[33]

In medical circles it is well known that malingering can be taught by word of mouth. It is a fact of life that many individuals teach each other what to say and do to work the medical system. When I trained in Boston, patients learned the symptoms of what was then called alcohol hallucinosis (flagrant delusions and hallucinations due to the heavy use of or withdrawal from alcohol) in order to gain hospital admission, and so a warm bed for the night. Some dishonest veterans learn how to convince a doctor that they are suffering from a compensable Posttraumatic Stress Disorder in order to get a pension, or a larger pension. Patients with Ganser's Syndrome (*DSM-IV* "Factitious Disorder With Predominantly Psychological Signs and Symptoms,"),[34] Munchausen's Syndrome

(*DSM-IV* "Factitious Disorder With Predominantly Physical Signs and Symptoms,"),[35] and compensation disorder have in great measure learned how to dissimulate, although undoubtedly unconscious reasons also exist for their having chosen this route.

Today people can learn how to be psychopathic by logging on to Web sites that instruct them how to devalue, beat, and even destroy the system. For example, there is a Web site that calls for disrupting a talent show by voting for the worst rather than the best candidates. It is possible to learn from the Web how to manipulate reality, in order to make oneself look not bad but victimized. Activists teach their followers how to agitate socially to maximum effect in order to bring the crowd around to their way of thinking. For example, they teach each other how to pique a group's curiosity and then, with persuasive illogic, to induce the members of the group to suspend their judgment and enter that hypnoid-like condition peculiar to influenced crowds—an almost tumescent anticipation that sets the stage to accept a newly self-proclaimed omnipotent leader as guru, the rescuer who gains power in exchange for offering wisdom.

Unsuccessful psychopaths often fail due to an *inability* to learn. For one thing, they have difficulty associating their maladaptive behavior with its negative consequences, making it hard for them to change course, and harder still for their therapists to effectively point out ways that they can behave more adaptively.

CONSIDERATIONS OF ID, EGO, AND SUPEREGO

Some observers suggest that it is a waste of time to try to understand psychopathy dynamically from the perspective of instincts that press for release, ideals that press to be achieved, conscience that presses to control and criticize, and an ego that attempts to manage all these disparate forces and forge a reasonable healthy compromise out of them. For example, Hansen (1998) suggests that the psychologist's "tendency to focus on drives and conflicts"[36] is inappropriate in these cases because psychopaths are profitably viewed as individuals with "defects"[37]—that is, theirs is a problem of absences, resulting in a condition where the afflicted individuals truly do not know what they do.

However, I believe that we can profitably attempt to understand the mild psychopath the same way we can attempt to understand any patient with an emotional disorder. Though the hypotheses I am about to advance are somewhat speculative, I believe that they still offer valuable insights that are at least occasionally and somewhat applicable to treating mild psychopaths, as well as potentially helpful for those who are in the psychopath's orbit and looking to find ways to cope with and manage these difficult people.

The Id (Instincts and Impulsivity)

Unsuccessful psychopaths are more "id-oriented," and so more instinctually oriented and impulsive, than psychopaths who are successful. While successful psychopaths calculate and carefully plan for the future by forgoing present satisfaction in favor of a later reward, unsuccessful psychopaths resolutely seek gratification of the moment while giving little or no thought to the future. They seek fun and excitement with little or no regard for the consequences—to themselves or others. This said, even mild and successful psychopaths can show an appalling tendency to be "neophiles"—easily bored thrill-seekers who make mischief just to stir the pot and live on the edge. They do not, can not, or will not control their hedonism—in part because their impulses are so strong that they cannot effectively manage them, in part because they lack guilt and remorse, and in part because they have no real wish to counter their Epicurean desires with Spartan restraint, and so have every reason to make their mantra "to eat, and to drink, and to be merry, (for tomorrow we die)."[38] Favoring the short-term over the long-term perspective, they allow their appetitive pressures to lead them to disregard social norms with little or no concern for their own good or for the good of society as a whole. So they act out without reflecting on or trying to control their instincts, saying anything that comes to mind and doing what they want to do without caring about truth or consequences, promising anything with no intent of keeping their word, and being as aggressive as they like to get what they want, without caring about how others might feel or react.

The Superego (The Conscience)

The literature suggests that psychopaths are less able to experience guilt than the rest of us. Mild psychopaths are not, however, as completely guilt free as much of the extant literature would have us believe. They at least seem to have a rudimentary superego, or conscience, which from time to time acts up and sends them messages about what is good and what is bad, what is right and what is wrong, what they should versus what they do, aspire to. However, even mild psychopaths can fail to hear these messages from conscience, or if they hear them fail to heed them. They talk back to them, arguing with them in order to justify their maladaptive behavior. They do what they like and rarely admit to being wrong—preferring instead to blame others for their own actions while expressing pride where others would only feel shame. They become especially adept at minimizing guilt and shame by accepting their past transgressions with the cry, "What I did wasn't so bad," and by rationalizing present or potential maladaptive actions as they proclaim, "What I plan to do is okay because everyone else is doing it too."

However paradoxical it may seem, they become not only hedonists but also masochists who fail frequently and persistently. On the one hand, they do not respond to punishment from others, while on the other hand they appear to long for it, and seem to ask for it, and even mete it out to themselves. As criminals they might have gotten away with murder if only they had not returned to the scene of the crime. Through the hedonistic self-indulgences for which they are famous, they assure not their well-being but its neglect, often because they create figuratively or literally fatal conflicts with others who recognize and protest that they are simply milking the system. In a typical, almost Faustian, denouement, they ultimately slip up after getting away with lying or cheating for a long time because they regard themselves as invulnerable. Forgetting the basic rules of self-preservation, they let down their guard and get either caught or into trouble.

A comfortable analogy to explain this paradoxicality is that their superego/conscience is full of holes, or "lacunae," clinically manifest as inconsistency and unpredictability. Indeed some observers, thinking concretely and then speaking figuratively, will compare their superego, and with it their morality, to Swiss cheese.

The Ego

The management functions of the ego.   The ego is a theoretical construct that in large measure represents a short-hand way to refer to the management functions of the psyche, consisting of dealing with the drives (impulses) in order to keep impulsivity in check; dealing with affects (feelings) in order to reign in emotions and keep them under control; and staying in touch with reality, e.g., responding to external (interpersonal) events, particularly feedback.

The management functions of the ego are seriously compromised in unsuccessful psychopaths. These individuals do not modify their impulses to develop a direction in life or to show regard for others. In fact, they often deliberately set out to hurt, torture, and maim people just to satisfy some momentary whim or need of their own.

In contrast, successful psychopaths are not so lacking in the ability to manage themselves that they become completely erratic, thoroughly unpredictable, and totally disregardful of others. They can and do plan their rise to the top, and they know how to accomplish their goals without letting their appetites and feelings seriously interfere. Acting less for fun and more for profit, they go about their business consciously and calculatedly, for discernable individual, interpersonal, and social gain, in their usual manipulative and dishonest manner.

Anxiety and psychopathy.   The literature, essentially with one voice, suggests that psychopaths are completely unable to experience anxiety.

In (simplified) psychodynamic terms, anxiety exists in the ego as a signal that a conflict between instincts and conscience is brewing. For example, in the obsessive-compulsive individual a wish to dirty, or smear, causes anxiety because it runs afoul of the philosophical ideal—of being clean—and of the guilt about being dirty. The individual then deals with the resultant anxiety-laden conflict by creating a compromise formation, the obsessive-compulsive symptom, that simultaneously expresses the unacceptable or forbidden wish, the guilt about the wish, the anxiety that results when the wish and guilt clash, and the methods chosen for making sense of, coping with, and bringing order out of the internal chaos—that is, the defenses, typically in such cases the defenses of doing and undoing, isolation of affect, and reaction-formation.

A patient develops a bathroom ritual. He is unable to get out of the men's room in less than fifteen minutes because he first washes his hands, then touches the door handle, then thinks that he has dirtied his hands again, then goes back to wash his hands one more time, and so on. This man's symptoms simultaneously express his wish to dirty, his disgust over being dirty and his fear of being embarrassed and punished for dirtying, and his attempt to deal with the opposing forces in his psyche. In the realm of the latter, he employs two defenses. The first, doing and undoing, involves alternating between dirtying and cleaning up, in effect compromising by being "all things to all men." The second, isolation of affect, involves going about his business coolly and calmly, saying to himself, "I have these urges, but I do not feel them strongly, or at all, so why not just go ahead and act on them?"—which he goes on to do, and does so dispassionately. Many obsessionals also use the defense of reaction formation, suppressing one side of a conflict and taking the other side to its ultimate conclusion, in effect deciding which is the lesser of two evils and casting one's fate with that, and with that only. These are the obsessionals who are scrupulously clean, unctuously nonhostile, or who make an obsession out of not being obsessed by anything at all.

A passive-aggressive individual was an angry person who nevertheless needed to avoid the anxiety/guilt associated with expressing anger directly. To this end, she allowed herself to express anger, but only indirectly—in the symptom of passive-aggressive foot-dragging that at one and the same time expressed her anger and took it back. She felt satisfied (that she was able to get angry) and less guilty (over having gotten angry). However, there was a price to pay: Her relationships with others were at a minimum strained and were sometimes deeply damaged.

Much of the extant literature tells us that this is not at all what happens in psychopaths. We hear that because psychopaths have a weak conscience they feel little or no guilt, and therefore little or no anxiety. That would make psychopathy a unique creation: a nondefensive disorder that in some respects is so unlike a neurosis that it is virtually its obverse. What we hear is that psychopathy, is not primarily a disorder of excessive, maladaptive, and poorly handled anxiety and fear. Rather, if it is a disorder at all, it is, unlike the neuroses, one characterized by an absence of anxiety and fear, so that the psychopath can freely be as immoral as he or she might like, and be that way entirely without compunction.

Certainly other disorders do have immoral consequences, but they are secondary. That the obsessive-compulsive seems unconcerned that he or she is driving others to distraction, that the passive-aggressive impresses others as a complete reprobate who is totally oblivious to others' feelings, that the schizophrenic injures others because of voices, or that the euphoric manic signs contracts on which he or she cannot deliver, is of lesser concern and is rather incidental to the defensive maneuvering. In these cases the immoral consequences are mainly troublesome by-products of an illness created for other "defensive" purposes—that is, to reduce anxiety.

In contrast, much of the extant literature tells us that psychopathy is *primarily* an amoral disorder—one marked by absence of anxious conflict, which in turn is due to the absence of appropriate feelings of shame and fear of being punished, along with an inability to register social approbation and to fully appreciate the consequences to others of one's negative actions. We are told that instead of hearing from their conscience, or the protests of others in their world, they continue to act out, selfishly, hurtfully, and free from anxiety, without caring about what they do and its negative impact. From them we hear, "If it feels good, I do it," "My way or the highway," "What counts is what is in it for me, not what's in it for you," "I don't care about you, only about me," and other statements that reveal their attraction to the fun and gratification of immorality and destructiveness for the havoc these create, and sometimes for their own sake. As a result, we read that the psychopathic disorder is less a solution, however imperfect, to a problem, than the outcome of one—the outcome of an amorality that is the flower of inconsistency, moral deficiency, or even "degeneracy," making psychopathy less a useful mechanism than a rather troublesome, or, in the case of successful psychopaths, a rather useful handicap.

If all this were absolutely true, we could not treat psychopaths by helping them resolve their emotional conflicts. We could only offer to lend them some of our ego—showing them how we manage to cope and then encouraging them to do the same—and some of our superego—tagging everything they do as right versus wrong in the hope that they will listen and become as socialized as we are.

But I believe that some psychopaths, and mild psychopaths in particular, do retain at least some ability to experience inner conflict and feel anxiety. As I see it, the maladaptive behavior of psychopaths is not purely the product of lack of guilt and does not entirely represent conflict-free acting out. Rather, the maladaptive behavior represents to an extent the psychopath's attempt to cope with and manage his or her anxiety-laden inner feelings, wishes, and fears. For example, conning may not be the purely manipulative behavior it at first seems to be but a way for the psychopath afraid of closeness to relate and not relate simultaneously—socializing and holding back, acting human yet retaining a fundamental inhumanity that reassures the psychopath, "I keep my distance; see, I am just dealing with people in order to take advantage of them." That makes their apparent lack of anxiety (and guilt) more apparent than real, less due to an absence than to a presence, which is often of one or more of the following defenses:

1. Reaction formation. Psychopaths may deal with their severe anxiety about behaving maladaptively by giving themselves permission to do *anything* and *everything* they please—which is often whatever they think they can get away with. Psychopaths who become successful may achieve their success by turning socially maladaptive behavior "on its head" to become socially adaptive behavior, e.g., the fire setter becomes the fireman. (Conversely, when reaction formation fails, the fireman becomes the fire setter, or the police commissioner becomes a law breaker who takes bribes, hires domestic help off the books so that he does not have to pay their social security benefits, and keeps a mistress in a luxury apartment paid for by the taxpayers.)

2. Denial. Some psychopaths who appear to lack empathy are simply denying what they consider to be fearful urges to get close to and resonate with another human being. The familiar psychopathic inability to tell right from wrong may be due less to an inherent inability to discriminate between the two extremes and more a way to deny feeling bad about having done something they know they ought not to have.

    Often the psychopath's so-called nonanxious behavior is a way to deny feeling another, greater anxiety in another, related situation. This anxiety is often about loss. For example, leaving his patients uncovered, the doctor whose case was presented in Chapter 5 walked off duty, apparently free from anxiety and guilt, and went to a party. He did not seem to care at all about what he was doing or what the consequences might be. But that was not because he was completely incapable of experiencing anxiety. It was because the most important thing to him at the time was that he was anxious about something else. He was afraid of losing a lover who would be at that party, someone he (rightly) felt needed watching.

3. Repression. In a statement that reveals how some psychopaths repress, or "forget," when it is reassuring for them to do so, a former SS guard asked how he felt about murdering so many people described flashes of recognition that what he was doing was wrong, followed, however, in quick succession by an actual awareness that he was suppressing all knowledge of his cruelty.

4. Displacement. The antiauthoritarian stance of many psychopaths is partly the product of their attempt to deal with anxiety-laden feelings over abusive past parental mistreatment by displacing these early feelings onto present-day society, and then fighting back against their parents by fighting the society in which they now live. A patient of mine became an advocate for civil rights less because he despised civil wrongs and more because as a child he feared and hated his father. As an adult he dealt with his fear of and hatred for being

controlled by his father by becoming an irrational advocate of unlimited social freedom—living his own life completely without constraints, and advocating that others do so as well. (Later on in life he became an activist judge, the type whom *The New York Times*, in another context, stated "use[d] the Constitution as a cloak for [his own] desires to remake society in the mold of [his] own [personal] preferences."[39])

5. Dissociation or splitting. Psychopaths who dissociate avoid anxiety by deliberately keeping their left hand from knowing, or caring, what their right hand is doing. They think one thing and say another, and say one thing and do another, blissfully unaware of how hypocritical they are being. A possible example is that of an entrepreneur who shamelessly mounts a television show on how to be a successful businessperson while his own businesses are teetering on the edge of bankruptcy.

   Psychopaths often deal with anxiety by splitting what they know about cause and what they know about effect, so that when caught up in the appetitive rush of the moment they can overlook how they might get caught and go to jail if they do something wrong. They fearlessly dissociate social insight away so that they *can* fail to recognize the negative implications and consequences of their actions, so that they *can* act as antisocially as they want to. Some plagiarists are in dissociation. In what is an almost altered state of consciousness, they conveniently "forget" that they are stealing and that stealing is wrong, and go on to crib anyway. In a kind of dissociation are members of minority groups with a double standard that enables them to tell the same ethnic and racist jokes about themselves that they condemn outsiders for repeating. Here too belong hypocrites like psychopathic bosses who dissociate away the significance of their actions by preaching honesty and hard work for others while they steal from their own companies, as well as the proselytizing strict vegetarian who feeds her dog pig's ears and chicken giblets (meat was all the dog would eat) on the sly and then reassures herself that what she was doing was okay because the pigs and chickens are already dead, so it's only, and indeed especially, humane not to waste their byproducts. In therapy, psychopaths who develop deep insight often wall it off in order to make certain that it does not scare them straight. They often do the same thing in their personal lives. For example, a psychopath much in demand socially often cancelled dinner invitations at the last minute and then excused her behavior as due to a compulsive avoidance of feared closeness, something she went on to insist she was completely helpless to control.

6. Identification/identification with the aggressor. Niels Peter Rygaard, in speaking of identification in psychopaths, refers to their "extreme field dependency."[40] Many of their identifications are with the aggressor, as they "screw" people to avoid being, or to get back for having been, "screwed" by them—a way to deal with their own underlying fear of others by becoming someone whom others fear.

7. Rationalization. Psychopathic rationalizers often deal with their low self-esteem by telling themselves the same kinds of untruths that they tell others. Thieves typically rationalize their predation by claiming that their victims can afford to lose what they, the psychopaths, take from them. People who use

other people typically rationalize that behavior by claiming it is for the person's own good. For example, a psychopathic administrator told his medical residents that they needed to stay up all night and throughout the next day not to provide the hospital with cheap service (as was his real motivation), but because the only way to learn all there was to know about a disease process was to study its natural course over time. (He failed to mention that some diseases take a very long time to develop, and in the meantime the students would certainly need some sleep.) Like any demagogue, he also convinced himself that his was the one and only truth, that he was thinking clearly and not responding emotionally, and that he was not leaving out important facts in order to make an otherwise unsustainable point.

8. Projection. As noted throughout, psychopaths regularly project to avoid the anxiety associated with accepting blame. They are past masters at attributing the responsibility for their actions to others. Viewing themselves not as victimizers but as victims, they claim that their antisocial behavior is merely an expected and natural response to others' provocation. A rapist blames the woman he rapes for being sexually provocative, much as a man who bombs an abortion clinic proudly justifies his behavior by asserting that they deserved it. Authority is often the object of this projective blame. Psychopaths frequently falsely accuse the police of brutality in order to excuse and justify their own true and substantial brutality toward the police (and other authority). Of course there are psychopathic policemen too, who blame a compliant victim for provoking beatings that were strictly initiated by the police themselves.

Ego-Ideal Factors

In psychopaths, self-pride is excessive and originates in mostly negative sources. These individuals are, as Millon says, proud of being rebellious and "contemptuous toward authority, tradition, sentimentality and humanistic concerns."[41] They are proud of their disregard for social norms, and of how they goof on authority and the sacred established beliefs of the majority. They favor delinquent, disobedient behavior as their way of achieving their ideal self as rebel and outcast. Sick practical jokes appeal to them a great deal. For example, a doctor I once worked with congratulated himself for being funny. He thought it highly amusing to repeat a disturbed brain-damaged patient's hate-filled words to all the people the patient said he hated. Psychopaths believe that loyalty is for suckers, with disloyalty the order of their day, just the ticket for clever knaves and rogues like themselves. They idealize becoming advocates for people society despises, typically claiming that they are for the underdog when in fact their desire is to incite the underdog to rise up and overthrow the alpha dog. If they act altruistically it is not because they want to help the weak but because they idealize defeating the strong. For them, narcissism is not a problem but a goal. They want to act like primitives or animals and to do so by defying social norms and conventions. For example, an angry, defiant manager of an apartment complex that abutted on a row of nice, well-kept houses thought it a good idea to deliberately put her garbage out not in back where code dictated she should have stored it but in front where everyone could see it—just to spite the elitist people who were buying houses and fixing them up. In like manner, an owner of a gas station, intent on smearing and soiling symbols of authority, deliberately filled his property with old scraps of metal and then refused to clean up his mess, no matter what the town said or did to try to enforce compliance. He even willingly squandered large sums of his own money to pay for the court costs involved in fighting the town. As he put it, "I hate the town elders so much that I am even willing to hurt myself just to get at them." Not surprisingly, some such individuals think it is a great idea to become sexually wild just to shock and defeat the bourgeoisie. They find it thrilling and amusing to act like the decorticate cats in a film I saw in medical school, animals whose brain lesions led them to have nonstop sexual intercourse. A particularly unfortunate outcome occurs when sexual perversity fuses with psychopathic aggressiveness: the psychopath goes on to develop a new ego-ideal that leads him or her on to gloat over being a dangerous sadistic sexual predator.

CHAPTER 11

Course and Prognosis

Most observers view psychopathy as a long-standing problem that creates an ongoing disruptive influence in the lives of all concerned—sufferers, families, and society. According to the *DSM-IV*, psychopathy is a disorder that by definition starts in adolescence and continues into adulthood. In effect, the *DSM-IV* suggests that while not all so-called "bad adolescents" become psychopaths, all psychopaths start off as so-called "bad adolescents." That is, they start off as individuals with a conduct disorder characterized by specific disobedient and unconventional actions, in one of four *DSM-IV* categories: Aggression to people and animals, Destruction of property, Deceitfulness or theft, and Serious violation of rules.[1] Along similar lines, the title of Joseph J. Michaels' book *Disorders of Character: Persistent Eneuresis, Juvenile Delinquency, and Psychopathic Personality* sets forth two early behaviors that Michaels believes to be forerunners of the adult disorder.[2]

A caveat is that, as with any other emotional disorder, one's view of its early antecedents can be retrospectively colored by one's determination of the adult diagnosis. This is particularly so here because if we look back on the lives of nonpsychopathic adults, we often discover that many of them as adolescents displayed at least some signs of an early conduct disorder. As an example, a large number of adolescents, many of them quite healthy emotionally, guiltlessly defied their parents and used their home to give a big wild party with underage drinking and even drugs when the parents went away on vacation.

Conversely, I have seen some psychopathic adults who at least did not appear to have been "bad children." In these individuals the adult disorder seems to have developed de novo without having first been formed and become initially manifest in adolescence. As previously discussed in Chapter 7, sometimes psychopathy is in effect "posttraumatic psychopathy"—that is, it is by definition acute rather than chronic, starting as it does relatively late in life and as a response to traumatic life circumstances. I have treated a number of veterans whose chronic psychopathy seems to have first begun acutely on the battlefield as a kind of "offense is the best defense" and "get them before they get you and any way you can" response to being in the trenches. I have also treated a number of individuals who were essentially nonpsychopathic until they were sent to jail for purely opportunistic crimes. It was their legal troubles that seem to have created their psychopathy, more than the other way around.

There are mixed cases in which symptoms of a conduct disorder existed but would possibly not have led to adult psychopathy were it not for specific harsh, later precipitating events. A doctor, who resembles in some ways the doctor whose case I presented in Chapter 5, had relatively mild early symptoms of a conduct disorder and did not become discernibly psychopathic until he entered medical school, where he felt lonely because he was far away from home and hated what he was doing because of the harshness of the medical school rites of passage. He then entered an internship where he had to do what he considered disgusting things, such as going from refrigerator to refrigerator testing particularly ripe stool specimens for blood, an especially daunting task in the summertime in a hospital without air-conditioning.

The administration was apparently inspired by the psychopathic maxim "no good deed goes unpunished," and the young doctor's reward (or comeuppance) was to be treated not only like a peon but also like a big nobody. After working him to the point of exhaustion with crushingly routine dirty work, and giving him no personal training to speak of, the administration refused to write letters of recommendation so that he could apply for residency. They refused to do so on the grounds that they "hardly knew him well enough for that because they had so little personal contact with him." Pressures like this led to his acting out sexually, frequently calling out sick claiming chronic fatigue, coming to work so tired after staying up all night cruising for sex that all he could manage to do was disappear to take a nap, and acting with his patients as if he did not really care if they lived or died just so long as they left him alone.

I believe that his and other similar cases illustrate how psychopathy can be a defensive, self-protective response to stress, ranging from job stress to the stress of being incarcerated. In other words, psychopathy can be a way to get through life—a resort, and sometimes a last resort, for individuals who are just trying to survive. (The *DSM-IV* notes that "personality changes [can] emerge and persist after an individual has been exposed to extreme stress."[3] However, in such cases it suggests that a diagnosis not of personality disorder but of "Posttraumatic Stress Disorder should be considered."[4])

This does not necessarily mean that if stress is the precipitant then the personality changes that result from the stress will subside once the initial stress is over. Many times a stress disorder is not reversible. Even mild trauma can produce negative effects long after the fact, and even for a lifetime.

Most observers believe that psychopathic behavior tends to subside in the patient's middle years. But they do not necessarily believe that this observation means their patient's underlying personality structure has changed significantly. What has happened, these observers say, is that psychopaths do not really get better. They just learn how to be better psychopaths. They learn to con more subtly, more powerfully, and more effectively.

However, I have seen cases of mild psychopathy in which not only does the psychopathic behavior remit but also the underlying personality improves to the point that the individual truly becomes a former and healed psychopath; as the old saying might go, the young sinner basically becomes an old saint. These psychopaths seem to have achieved a permanent reform. There is no shortage of examples in our society of individuals who start off as party boys who burn down the fraternity house and then grow up to be effective, honest, creative CEO's, or who go from lawyer to attorney, politician to statesman, charlatan to healer, saw-bones to doctor, and manipulator of to leader of the masses. Their hormones and neurotransmitters diminish and subside. Their residual guilt and shame emerge and intensify. Their general philosophy of life deepens and broadens as they belatedly start to reflect about the meaning of their existence. Additionally, they finally learn from experience all about the disastrous consequences of business as usual. Luck can also make for a positive outcome, so that a favorable environment can create a milder disorder and even completely interrupt a disorder already in progress. An understanding wife, a permissive therapist, a large inheritance, and even a positively inclined parole board can make as much difference here as the natural course of the illness.

In the most favorable outcome, a conversion or "epiphany" takes hold. In the psychopath this is often associated with a special sense of moral exaltation that appears "from out of the blue," without obvious antecedents. The individual becomes a great person with that proverbial cluttered history, that great statesman who in his younger years consulted with astrologists, had mistresses, and smoked and drank heavily, or that equally great statesman who in his younger years used opium and had a history of having been removed from office.

Clearly it is unjust, unfair, and unrealistic to embarrass our great leaders with their juvenilia and long-ago secret peccadilloes, as if these necessarily diminish their present status and sully their later good works.

A good president can have been a dishonorable adolescent who cheated on examinations and lied about his army service. A senator can, at least theoretically, still become a statesman, even if as a young man he belonged to an arch-conservative or an exceedingly liberal organization. A spokesman of minorities can still be worth listening to today, even though yesterday he made his reputation antisocially by defending psychopathic-like false accusations of rape at the hands of the police. In my opinion, it is less psychopathic to ingest forbidden substances when one is young than to corner someone when he or she is older and demand a confession of usage as a way to defeat him or her. Indeed, so many great men and women have only become great after overcoming and mastering their personal psychopathy that it sometimes appears as if psychopathy early in life is a precondition of, a prerequisite for, or at the very least a step in the right direction on the way to their later greatness.

CHAPTER 12

Therapy of the Mild Psychopath

Many observers believe that psychopaths are untreatable using either traditional methods or nontraditional approaches. For example, Cleckley states that "I do not have any dogmatic advice as to a final or even a satisfactory way of successfully rehabilitating psychopaths,"[1] while Hare says that "[with] few exceptions, the traditional forms of psychotherapy . . . have proved ineffective in the treatment of psychopathy. Nor have the biological therapies, including . . . the use of various drugs, fared much better."[2] Hare has even suggested that psychotherapy can sometimes actually make psychopaths worse.[3]

In a dissenting view, Otto F. Kernberg states his overall belief that not only are psychopaths treatable, but they are treatable essentially just like everyone else. Kernberg suggests treating these individuals psychoanalytically and implies that one can expect a good result. A cornerstone of his psychoanalytic method involves "systematic interpretation of the psychopathic transference [to] gradually resolve it and transform it into a predominantly paranoid transference [which] may then be explored in the same way that one analyzes the severe paranoid regressions in nonantisocial narcissistic personalities."[4] Black offers us a sensible, nonpsychoanalytically oriented treatment approach that presumably works. He suggests focusing not on "why behaviors developed"[5] but on "how they can be eliminated"[6] and recommends cognitive therapy that focuses on exposing and challenging "cognitive distortions,"[7] such as my "desires are adequate grounds for [my] actions."[8]

I view mild psychopathy as a maladaptive strategy comprehensible and analyzable in human terms. Therefore my goal is to find ways to employ traditional therapeutic techniques to help the patient resolve the underlying problems that are keeping him or her from achieving a healthier adaptation. Of course, certain modifications of traditional therapeutic approaches need to be made, e.g., individual psychodynamically oriented psychotherapeutic approaches may have to be combined with behavioral and milieu therapies. Also, sometimes our goals for these individuals have to be kept modest. Particularly when psychopathy is severe, often the best we can do is to help the psychopath become a better psychopath.

GENERAL PRINCIPLES

I believe that while severe psychopathy can be very difficult at best to treat with any form of therapy, mild psychopathy can be effectively treated using traditional approaches specifically adapted for dealing with the special problems these patients present.

That does not mean that even the mildest of psychopaths are easy to treat. Mild psychopaths tend to be uninsightful individuals who deny their illness. What awareness they have of the nature, depth, and extent of their disorder tends to be dim at best. They might say, "I am not sick," or "If I am sick it's because of what the world did to me." Many also have an aggressive side that puts some therapists off, as well as a narcissistic character structure that leads them to believe that they do not have to change because they are just fine the way they are. Many are reluctant to do the hard work that effective therapy entails, and few willingly relinquish the pleasures, rewards, and excitement they obtain from frantic acting out, especially the fun they get from defeating authority as they sadistically watch their do-gooder therapists fail in their crusades to help them live a better, more socialized life.

However, the outlook improves somewhat when:

- Unsuccessful by chance or self-destructive by design, they find themselves in trouble with society or the law and are ordered to attend, and expected to show progress in, therapy.
- They retain a modicum of guilt and self-loathing.
- They are lonely because material gain has come at the expense of the loss of friends and family—those fleeced, and those critical of the individual's antisocial behavior.
- They finally become aware of the inefficiency involved in attempting to get "something for nothing."
- They finally become aware of how they have failed to meet their potential and want to rise up from being a subpar "social misfit" to become a "pillar of society."
- They have been coping psychopathically with unfavorable circumstances beyond their control, and these unfavorable circumstances have been resolved and are behind them.

In my experience, mild psychopaths often benefit from an *eclectic* form of individual treatment that emphasizes both early and here-and-now issues, and employs a combination of psychodynamic, cognitive-behavioral, and interpersonal approaches—simultaneously resolving unconscious conflicts; recognizing and correcting cognitive distortions; correcting behavior by both positive and negative enforcement, that is, with both encouragement and admonition; and working through interpersonal difficulties, particularly those that are products of narcissism and hostility. Specific techniques that I have found most helpful with individual patients include controlled abreaction of anger; identifying and resolving conflicts about closeness, control, and competition; and identifying and analyzing acting out both as a defense and as a resistance to treatment.

A General Rule

As a general rule, it is important to be open and honest with psychopathic patients. Liars themselves, they know when they are being lied to, and they particularly dislike being treated in the same cavalier and shady ways that they treat others.

Opening Salvos

I often start treatment of psychopaths with a frank discussion about what psychopathy is and what it means to be a psychopath. I often state my belief that psychopathy as a lifestyle seriously and adversely affects not only the individual but also those around him or her. I often note that psychopathy is one of those "disorders" that is subject to at least a degree of self-control. As such, it is more like "obesity" than pneumonia, and therefore somewhere in between a madness and a badness.

At the start I inform the patient what can and what cannot be expected from therapy. Psychopaths (and their families) need to be told not to expect the impossible, belittle the possible, and then use the inevitable disappointment that sets in when things go less than perfectly to avoid or stop therapy. I will be honest that this disorder is difficult to treat, and note that improvement can take a long time, sometimes years, and that in the meantime a valid, doable goal might be a very limited one: just trying to stay out of trouble until the disorder burns itself out, as it often does on its own, even without therapy.

I will point out at the start some serious downsides of therapy. I will note that therapy for psychopaths can be a long, difficult, and even painful process, and for it to succeed the patient will no doubt have to experience the inevitable discomfort associated with abandoning favored utilitarian psychopathic manipulations and such comforting narcissistic beliefs as "I am the center of things," "I am better than you," "I am perfect," and "I am the cleverest one of all, who must always triumph." Patients will have to relinquish their protective paranoia, especially their defensive tendency to blame others for everything, and accept the newly emerging sense of the imperfect self that comes from that, and other, defenses going down. I believe that, warned of these things in advance, the individual will be less likely to feel "I am getting worse" and "Treatment is bad for making me feel this way," be less likely to blame the therapist for his or her fate instead of blaming the disorder, and be less likely to quit treatment prematurely and instead be more likely to see therapy through to the end.

I often forewarn the patient about anticipated resistances. Most psychopaths will resist therapy by attributing responsibility for their problems and failures to everyone but themselves; by demanding special treatment that is not in their best interests; by demanding a cure without having to expend any effort to get it; and by disregarding the therapist's basic needs, so that the patient might come late to appointments and then demand that the therapist give him or her full session time—one of those forms of unconditional love that psychopaths believe they should get without having to earn it.

I often attempt to undercut resistances by informing the patient that my fate does not depend on his or her improving. I make it a rule to simply point out that I am trying to do the best job I can, and that lack of improvement is more often due to noncompliance than to bad therapy. This approach is particularly effective in undercutting the psychopath's need for a masochistic triumph where the patient gets worse to spite, goof on, and defeat the therapist-as-symbol of the hated establishment. As importantly, such an attitude enhances the therapist's comfort by reducing any feelings of guilt he or she might have about not being able to offer the patient a quick, complete, and permanent cure.

All psychopathic patients should be discouraged from acting out in their relationship with the therapist (acting out the transference). For example, they should be discouraged from repeating their antiestablishment tendencies with the therapist-as-authority, say by hiding unrepentant calculation beneath the cloak of professed though false motivation, and doing that throughout the entire course of therapy.

Early in treatment, I attempt to deal with the inadequate motivation that plagues many psychopaths. It is unusual for psychopaths to apply for treatment on their own, at least for treatment of their psychopathy. Psychopaths usually do not apply for therapy, but instead are forced into it. That often happens when someone, or some institution, can no longer condone or tolerate their maladaptive behavior. Those psychopaths who do apply for treatment on their own tend to seek therapy for an associated disorder such as a reactive depression, especially the kind that comes on after they fail miserably in life. They also tend to have an ulterior motive (besides cure) in seeking treatment. They might wish to con the therapist into taking their side in a difficult and costly divorce; or they might be looking for an advocate to keep them from going to jail or to help them get a lighter sentence or, if already in jail, to move someone in authority to get them transferred to the less restrictive psychiatric hospital.

I treat the inadequate motivation that these patients commonly show as I would treat any other symptom—analyzing it, treating it cognitively, behaviorally, and interpersonally, and being affirmative in the hope that the patient will become "hooked on the transference." In the realm of offering a transference hook, I often nourish a positive relationship with the patient so that the patient likes me and wants to improve for me. This might not work well for the renegade psychopath who has few if any feelings for anyone but (or including) him- or herself, but it might work for the individual whose psychopathy is mild and partial enough to allow him or her to retain a degree of object love.

A fact of life is that it can prove futile to unilaterally cajole or force patients who do not want to be in therapy to start or continue in treatment. Here is an example of what can happen: I once made some appointments for a psychopathic patient, not with the patient himself but at the request of a relative, only to become a pawn in a game between the relative and the patient. The relative who made the appointments said to the potential patient: "I have this appointment with a psychiatrist for you; you had better come to it." Over and over the patient agreed to keep the appointment but then did not show up, leaving me with time unfilled. Another patient agreed to accept the court's mandate that she go for private treatment, but retaliated by selecting both a form of treatment that, and a person to treat her who, would be unlikely to be helpful—in this case a therapist manifestly psychopathic himself, a man who used primal scream group therapy because it was trendy and therefore lucrative.

Another fact of life is that even when the therapeutic process seems to be going smoothly, often nothing of any real substance is actually happening. Some of the "most successful" therapeutic interactions have consisted of little more than an old con in a new situation, with the patient's apparent motivation to explore him- or herself in depth a sham and part of a ruse. The patient lies to enlist the therapist's aid in getting out of trouble now, so that he or she can be free to get back into it later.

Dealing with Specific Psychopathic Psychopathology

Conscience problems.   As discussed throughout, one's conscience may be said to have two parts: the *ego-ideal*, which inspires, and the *superego*, which observes and critiques.

The *ego-ideal,* unlike the superego—that punitive part of the conscience that condemns the individual by making him or her feel guilty and remorseful—may:

- impel the individual onward and upward to greater and greater heights,
- suggest maintaining the status quo, or
- impel the individual to self-sabotage and self-destruct.

In many psychopaths, the self-ideal is overly grandiose and the self-esteem too high. It follows that with many psychopaths a therapeutic task involves encouraging the patient to expect less of him- or herself in order to ultimately get more. This often involves becoming more realistic about what he or she can and cannot accomplish, and learning to be satisfied with less instead of always striving to reach life's highest pinnacles, which, as life would sometimes have it, can only be scaled by cheating one's way to the top.

Therapists can influence the patient's ego-ideal not only by what they say—that is, interpretively—but also by what they do—that is, by encouraging the patient to identify with the therapist. With other patients it can be a good idea for the therapist to avoid revealing too much about him- or herself. However, many psychopaths present an exception to this rule. They can benefit from hearing about how the therapist lives the moral and loving life, one that the patient might do well to emulate.

To a great extent, the *superego* is the product of the internalization of parental attitudes and social norms. As emphasized throughout, the superego in psychopaths is paradoxical. Psychopaths appear to show both a lack of and an apparent excess of remorse, shame, and guilt. As a result they seem to be simultaneously:

- unconcerned about the rights of others and so unable to meet the dictates of social norms (the overly lax superego), and
- at odds with their own antisocial actions, to the point that they seem almost eager to be "punished for their sins," imagined or real (the overly harsh superego).

In the realm of the *lax* superego, some psychopaths permit themselves to act as if they have never grown up or have become like children once again. Like children, they put a positive spin on (rationalize) their maladaptive actions by blaming others for their own misdeeds, and have an insufficiently self-critical, excessively self-enamored, or even grandiose self view. As such, they practically beg to be asked, "Who do you think you are in the first place?" and to be told: "After all, you are not the only one who counts around here" and "Your expectations of people and life are excessive and inappropriate." I often find myself telling psychopaths that they appear to like themselves a bit too much, so that what they need is to stop the self-congratulating and start realistically assessing their real-world accomplishments in preparation for developing a more modest self-view, which in turn might lead to an awareness that the rules that apply to the rest of us *also* apply to them.

In the realm of the *overly harsh* superego, many psychopaths have had excessively and rigidly moral parents. These parents remind me of the parents of a teen-ager who wore his hair wild and a little long, but whose hairstyle was within acceptable limits and even attractive. Still, the first thing his father said on introducing his son to me was, "He's going into the army to get a new haircut." Children with a background like this often grow up to become rebellious. They can often benefit therapeutically from being helped to reassert their own individuality instead of letting a "compliant rebelliousness" against the parents take over completely to determine who they are personally and what kind of life they want to live.

Id and ego problems. As mentioned throughout, some psychopaths act out because their sexual and aggressive instincts are weak but their resistance to them is even weaker. Other psychopaths act out because their sexual and aggressive instincts are too strong to be adequately handled and contained by such healthy defenses as repression and sublimation. In the latter case, pharmacotherapy can play an adjunctive role by reducing instinctual pressures in the hope of allowing the ego to regroup its forces and function in a more adequate, effective, and healthy fashion. It must be admitted, however, that in the real world pharmacotherapy often does this ineffectively, and in many cases it may not work at all.

THE DIFFERENT THERAPIES

Established Individual Approaches

Next let us examine some established treatment modalities one by one to see if, how, and when they apply here. Since this text is not a primer on how to do psychotherapy, the following discussion does not go into detailed descriptions of the therapeutic processes themselves.

Supportive therapy. For therapists using a supportive approach, a cornerstone of therapy involves building a positive long-term therapeutic relationship that will at a minimum tide these individuals over the rough spots in their lives—keeping them alive and out of trouble while all concerned wait for the disorder to spontaneously remit.

Supportive therapists may settle for a transference cure, e.g., one where the psychopath improves by developing a new and healthier identification with the therapist that helps undo unhealthy identifications with others, especially with the psychopath's parents. The new identification works in part by influencing the psychopath's ego-ideal and superego for the better. However, in my experience, new healthier identifications can be transitory, with backsliding often occurring for little or no apparent reason. Once, for example, I saw a somewhat paranoid psychopathic patient who did well for a long time, in part because he identified with his therapist. All, however, was lost when the patient spied his therapist wearing a leather jacket—which to him meant that the therapist must be gay. So he fired his therapist and had a relapse, virtually just to get back at his therapist by becoming as much unlike him as possible.

Supportive therapists help reactive psychopaths cope with and resolve external difficulties that determine or worsen the disorder—for example, professional problems or personal loss. Psychopaths who somehow manage to straighten out the difficulties they are having in their personal lives can sometimes, on that account alone, go on to become honest, hardworking, related, loving individuals. Such was the case for a man who stopped acting out psychopathically after he managed to replace the wife he lost through death with someone also, if not equally, loved; to get a new job that was better than the old one; and to decide once and for all to ignore his parents' demands that he go to law school and to instead decide to go through with his plans to become an electrical engineer.

Affirmative therapy.   Just because psychopaths can be personally difficult and socially unappealing does not mean that they appreciate being treated inhumanely and disrespectfully—that is, unaffirmatively—by impatient and angry therapists. Therapists who do that can only cause the patient to act out even more.

Affirmative therapists strongly believe that a core of humanity remains in mild psychopaths so that they respond like anyone else, albeit perhaps slowly and incompletely, to expressions of confidence, demonstrations of empathy and understanding, and attempts to rescue them from themselves. A rule these therapists follow is that while positivity may or may not help, negativity most certainly will harm. This is their philosophy: By being affirmative I can, at a minimum, avoid provoking the patient unnecessarily, and in favorable circumstances actually support him or her through difficult times by offering him or her at least one reliable ally in an otherwise remote and hostile world.

Affirmative therapists focus on giving the patient as much positive feedback as they can possibly give, along with special incentives for doing well. They might promise him or her a day pass from the hospital to go shopping; award chits or tokens that can be exchanged for food and money as a reward for sticking with, learning from, and getting something out of occupational therapy; or offer to issue a favorable report if warranted to an enquiring potential employer. Many therapists have learned that psychopaths who respond negatively to punishment often respond positively to reward.

Affirmative therapists also take special care to respond in a health-giving way to those relapses that inevitably occur during the course of treatment of virtually all psychopaths. They do not reply to the inevitable flare-ups of symptoms with such negative behavioral correctives as "You'll be discharged from (i.e., 'thrown out of') therapy if you continue this way." Rather, they view relapses as an integral part of, not an unfortunate complication of, treatment—part of the process, and therefore requiring not undue pessimism or punitive action, but further treatment.

However, it must be admitted that affirmation and positivity are not especially helpful for those individuals whose psychopathy is so severe that they remain totally unmoved by another's humanity, view the humane therapist as a sucker, and turn therapeutic affirmation into a tool for manipulating the therapist into offering them support when they are figuratively (or literally) trying to get away with murder.

A caveat is that therapists should not affirm patients by taking their side under any and all circumstances. They should not tolerate unlimited rule-breaking, should resolutely refuse to respond, even when sorely provoked, in any way that can be considered to be at all punitive, and should not attempt to rescue patients indiscriminately and inappropriately, no matter what. Psychopaths want, provoke, and expect a degree of negativity on the part of others. They virtually beg authority to set limits on them. Conversely, they tend to view therapists who are too kind and too permissive as patsies, lose respect for them, and provoke them even more—just for the fun of it, i.e., for the good feeling they obtain from getting under the therapist's skin.

This said, some therapists deliberately and determinedly set out to be *nonaffirmative*. Some therapists have noted that mild psychopaths often become less psychopathic when they get depressed, say after getting into trouble with other people in their lives, or with the law. These therapists set out to convert psychopathy into depression and then to use the depression that results as an impetus for change and a focus of treatment. One therapist, actively attempting to induce a depression by treating her patient nonaffirmatively, undermined the patient's narcissistic defenses by asking him such confrontational questions as "Who do you think you are that you are entitled to get something for nothing?" or an even harsher "What makes you feel that you are really a special somebody, not a big nobody"—all to challenge and undermine the patient's high self-esteem and excessive grandiosity. However, this is a dangerous maneuver, since depression is a serious illness, and because depressed patients tend to leave therapy prematurely, convinced that they are hopeless and that there is no point in continuing.

Educational therapy/coaching. Some therapists, under the assumption that the psychopathic condition involves, at least in part, simply not knowing how to do better, have had a degree of success teaching, or coaching, the patient on how to live less maladaptively. These therapists might model morally and socially acceptable behavior for their patients. They might give their patients lessons on how to tell right from wrong. They might teach them what behavior is and is not acceptable and what the consequences of unacceptable behavior might be. For example, they remind the patient that since most people sooner or later realize that they have been conned and retaliate for that, often devastatingly, it is best in the long run to stop trying to get something for nothing and instead use a "pay as you go" approach that consists of making a living, and a life, the honest, old-fashioned way. They might exhort the plagiarizing journalist, the schlock lawyer, or the dishonest salesman to stop misusing the professional talents they have and to instead start practicing their profession in a more honest, more upright manner—to, in the vernacular, "straighten up and fly right." Some refer the patient out to an individual or institution that specializes in teaching professional skills, e.g., they refer them for occupational therapy. I often work on helping the patient substitute intellect for impulsivity—so that the patient thinks more about what he or she plans to do before he or she actually does it. I might also work on teaching the patient what emotions a situation calls for, and what sensibilities are normal to have, so that the patient can at least start to act as if he or she is appropriately anxious, truly guilty, personally empathic, or admirably altruistic.

In a few cases, when all else has failed, I might teach patients how to be better, that is, more successful, psychopaths. I might help them tone down their psychopathy so that they learn to demand and accept a little less if only in order to get a little more. In some cases, if that is the best we can do, we work on how they can walk through legal loopholes in order to continue to do business and stay out of jail. (This approach may not be helpful for those individuals who can ultimately benefit from a little jail time.) The patient whose morality is unlikely to improve can sometimes benefit from being steered away from professions where a degree of immorality is a liability and instead be encouraged to enter one of the professions where a little dishonesty is an asset, such as politics ("When I am elected you *will* see a 30 percent decrease in your property taxes"), the law ("As soon as the facts become known, my client will *certainly* be *proved completely* innocent of all charges"), or the construction business ("Your house will be ready next July, and probably even sooner, so it's time now for the balloon payment we agreed on.")

Psychoanalytically oriented psychotherapy. Psychoanalytically oriented therapists avoid addressing only the symptoms of psychopathy while failing to address their cause—avoiding speaking to the secondary gain of the disorder, like getting something for nothing, but not to its primary gain—the relief of anxiety and depression.

The psychoanalytically oriented therapist attempts to identify and break down the pathological defenses psychopaths use. Four in particular can be profitably challenged: (semiconscious and unconscious) *denial*, such as "I didn't know that my underlings were cooking the books"; *projective blaming*, such as "I am not the problem; the police in this town are, for they don't deserve my respect and cooperation"; *self-justification,* along the lines of "I only sell drugs because drugs are the only thing that sell"; and *removal* or *avoidance,* which consists of a defensive insensitivity to others' feelings that in milder psychopaths is less like the deficit it at first appears to be and more like an active process put into place to create and maintain desirable distancing in the form of antisocial behavior.

The psychoanalytically oriented therapist also focuses on dealing therapeutically with resistances to therapy that in the psychopath arise from the patient's pleasure orientation, need for excitement, irresponsibility, and narcissistic refusal to care how others, including the therapist, feel or think. A good starting point is a frank and open discussion of the negative aspects of the psychopath's relationship with the therapist. This can both facilitate therapy and be corrective by itself—as when working through the negative transference spills back and helps the psychopath relate more positively to people in the world outside.

Family, Inpatient, Milieu, and Group Therapy

Family Therapy. The family therapist's goal is twofold: to help the family of the psychopath directly, and to help the patient indirectly by involving the family in the patient's treatment. In the realm of helping the family directly, Black emphasizes the importance of being of assistance to those "who [every day] live with ASP . . . in someone they love."[9] The therapist helps the family recognize, learn about, and accept the diagnosis of psychopathy, and gives the family useful advice on how to deal with the psychopath—including advice on how family members can protect themselves from, cope with, and manage the psychopath's abusive verbal, emotional, physical, and financial assaults. The therapist can also help the family plan for a situation that does not improve. For example, the therapist might advise the family that it can be a bad idea to leave a psychopathic child an inheritance outright, and a much better idea to provide him or her with an annuity.

In the realm of helping the patient indirectly through working with the family, the therapist can gain a better understanding of the patient by double-checking what the patient says with what the family sees and hears. It is especially important to enlist the family's help in monitoring the patient's progress with a view to making certain that the patient is not continuing to behave badly and then covering up.

The therapist can also urge the family to take the appropriate corrective stand in relationship to the patient's antisocial behavior. This often involves helping the family to strike a healthy balance between being too permissive and being too punitive. Overly permissive parents need to strongly and unambivalently set limits that discourage children from acting out antisocially. They should avoid treating their children like infant kings and queens, bringing them up to believe that their parents, and hence the whole world, "owe them a living." As examples, parents should discourage their children from faking being sick in order to stay out of school, try to keep their children from associating with bad companions, and make certain that their children are not hiding drugs or bomb-making equipment in their bedrooms. To avoid having children grow up believing that they can get away with just about anything, their parents should stop reflexively rescuing them each time they get into trouble and instead allow them early on to get at least a controlled taste of the negative consequences of their antisocial actions.

However, parents should not go to the opposite extreme and deprive their children unduly. Parents who do that run the risk of turning their children into adults chiefly or only concerned with making up for previous lacks in any and all possible ways. I have seen cases where children become rebellious adults as a way of coping with ongoing negative feelings about their excessively controlling, punitive parents. Such children come to parentalize society and then behave antisocially to get back at their parents through such antisocial acts as keying cars, destroying neighbors' lawn ornaments, egging neighbors' houses, defacing property with graffiti, or driving through gay neighborhoods shouting anti-gay epithets out of car windows.

Clearly I do not fully buy into Black's suggestion that a central therapeutic task here is to always help families "[r]ecognize that it's not [their] fault"[10] if a loved one is psychopathic. I strongly believe that parents, other family, and friends frequently enable psychopathy by encouraging acting out, often doing so subtly, as did the mother who wished for a bouquet of flowers within earshot of her child each time the family passed a neighbor's garden. They often do this as a way of solving their own problems or of getting what they want indirectly. I have worked with spouses who subtly enabled psychopathy in their mates because they feared getting too close to them; because they were cheating themselves and so wanted the patient in jail and out of the way; because, fearing being dominated, they wanted the spouse weakened through alcoholism or drug usage; or because, being crooks at heart themselves, they enjoyed and profited from having a thief in the family. I worked with a mother who took her child out of school in order to begin home schooling. Her real motive was not the stated one: to provide the child with a better education. It was to avoid having her unruly child (whose behavior she admired as "spunky") properly disciplined by the authorities.

Such families need to stop enabling and to start setting firm limits and strictly enforcing rules. They need to stop rewarding psychopathic behavior and to instead start responding in a constructive way to family members who lie, cheat, steal, and otherwise behave psychopathically. When applicable, they need to stop undermining the therapist in order to defeat therapy just so the patient can continue or resume pathological ways that serve the family's dynamic needs and practical purposes. Enabling is discussed at greater length throughout this text.

Inpatient treatment.   Many observers suggest that whenever possible, psychopaths should not be hospitalized. It is true that as inpatients psychopaths can become so disruptive that they make it difficult for the unit they are on to function smoothly and effectively. For one thing, they often create trouble for the staff and for the other patients by undermining their own and everyone else's treatment. They may do this directly, by forging antimanagement coalitions with the other patients, or indirectly, by getting their, or someone else's, malignant family to do the undermining for them. I once treated a well-known artist who suffered from a prolonged, difficult-to-diagnose toxic-organic reaction that was so severe that he required constant monitoring in an open seclusion room. The patient's illness did not improve—until I stopped his immediate family from visiting him. As I suspected, it turned out that his family was prolonging his illness by slipping him drugs.

Of course, psychopaths certainly should not be hospitalized for punitive reasons—just because their family or society wants them out of the way, or purely out of a sense of desperation that tempts us to put them into an asylum even though they are not genuinely insane.

However, there are times when hospitalization is the best idea—e.g., to interrupt escalating acting-out—or absolutely necessary, as when the patient is in flight or aggressive to self and others. Though hospitalization may not provide definitive treatment, the patient may still benefit from intermittent short-term environmental holding as a form of crisis intervention meant to, at the least, keep the patient alive and out of big trouble until he or she grows older and his or her psychopathy burns out. Whenever possible, it might be wise to consider a day hospital over full in-patient treatment. A well-run day hospital can provide psychopaths with the inpatient facilities they need and can use, yet they go home at night before they can create complete chaos with the other patients and the staff.

Hospitalized psychopaths can often be managed and helped most effectively if their treatment is split between an administrator and a therapist. The administrator handles day-to-day organizational and disciplinary matters. In the realm of organizational matters, he or she decides on such issues as who is to visit and for how long, and what is to be the duration of the patient's stay in the hospital. When discipline is necessary, he or she might decide to reduce the patient's privileges or suggest an outright, even punitive, discharge. A potential benefit of this arrangement is that the therapist can maintain at least a semblance of therapeutic neutrality by leaving any and all required disciplinary actions up to the administrator, freeing the therapist up to focus on interpretative work without the distraction of constantly having to crack down on the patient's "bad" behavior—with all the transference negativity that comes from doing that.

Milieu therapy/group therapy. Briget Dolan, while holding out little hope for individual therapy, feels more sanguine about milieu therapy. As she notes, the "democratic TC [therapeutic community] approach . . . offers great hope for the treatment of individuals with severe PDs (Personality Disorders)."[11] Milieu therapy involves immersing the patient in a therapeutic environment that de-emphasizes hierarchy. Patients are treated not only by various mental health professionals but also by their own peers. All concerned make a contribution to and have an essentially equal say in the patient's therapy. There is a team, but the leader of the team is not necessarily, and probably will not be, the person with the most degrees. Rather the team leader may be, and often is, someone who comes from a background similar to that of the patient—even an individual whose main qualification is that he or she is a "recovered" psychopath. There is a governing body, but it is not made up exclusively of psychiatrists, psychologists, doctors, nurses, and social workers. The patients, under staff supervision, take over a great part of this responsibility, in effect assuming a form of self-government, and one that includes doing much of the discipline for their unruly peers.

An important theoretical basis of the nonhierarchical approach is the belief that psychopaths can respond better to being "told what to do" (as they often see it) by their peers than to being "told what to do" by those in authority. "Recovered" psychopaths know from experience what currently active psychopathic individuals are up to, and how to get through to them. They can often effectively show the patient the path that they themselves followed toward recovery.

A downside of therapy of the psychopath by those who have "recovered" from their own psychopathy is the tendency of some "recovered" psychopathic patients to act out the countertransference. They know the ropes, and are not averse to teaching others how to use them. Also, some psychopathic patients only respect those who have been highly trained formally, so they only listen, if to anyone at all, to the spiritual or even actual equivalent of a full professor.

For milieu therapy to be effective, all members of the treatment team have to work together. This means that the members of the team have to constantly check in with each other to be certain that the patient is not dividing in order to conquer—splitting the transference, making one member of the team all good and the other all bad in order to undercut one team member by favoring the other. Psychopathic patients like to induce intramural competitiveness between members of the staff. They play one staff member off against the other as part of their attempt to manipulate the entire system. In particular, patients should never be allowed to fire one therapist and transfer to another without first discussing what is going on with both therapists and with the entire team, giving all concerned an opportunity to explore the patient's exact motivation for making the change and to assess whether switching will or will not be therapeutic.

Group therapy, a cornerstone of the milieu approach, offers the isolated patient a degree of social enrichment. Role-playing in the group can be especially therapeutic. For example, the psychopath might be assigned the role of victim in an attempt to teach him or her what it feels like to be taken in by a psychopath. A downside of group therapy is that sometimes psychopaths see the group as an opportunity to be more highly disruptive than they could be if they were merely defeating a lone therapist. As with any approach that involves teamwork, the group can have the most success bringing a psychopath into line if all concerned speak with one voice. Different group members sending contradictory messages is a royal road to handing the patient a new and countertherapeutic opportunity to divide and conquer the staff.

Additional Approaches

Anger management.   Anger management approaches can be useful for dealing directly with the psychopath's hostility and so his or her potential to be hurtful, or actually violent. The therapist helps psychopaths better integrate their feelings of disdain and lack of respect for others. The therapist also helps psychopaths stop projecting their anger—blaming others for their own maladaptive behavior along such lines as,"I only lie, cheat, and steal because of the way they mistreated my ancestors." The therapist might also set out to help minimize the psychopathic narcissism that leads to ready rage when things do not go the patient's way, as was the case for the patient who smashed up the clinic's furniture in order to express his anger about not getting bigger welfare checks (which, not incidentally, he called, "my paychecks").

Cognitive therapy.   Cognitive therapists explore how the patient's thought processes create his or her maladaptive personality traits, maladaptive behaviors, and such pathological affects as extreme, inappropriate, and retaliatory anger. The therapist might focus on and attempt to correct the cognitive errors I describe in Chapter 6.

Behavioral therapy.   One reason therapists like to do behavioral therapy with psychopaths is that they feel it puts them, not the patient, in control of the situation. In an oversimplified view of behavioral therapy, the behavioral therapist treats psychopaths using negative and positive reinforcement. *Negative* reinforcement consists of direct warnings and prohibitions and limit-setting meant to help control psychopathic behavior. Court-ordered punishment, when appropriately used and judiciously applied, is one form of negative behavioral modification that can be employed to good effect with those psychopaths who are poorly motivated to accept or otherwise incapable of benefiting from other forms of intervention. *Positive* reinforcement involves asking the patient to do better, and then rewarding him or her when that happens. However, while psychopaths generally respond more favorably to reward than to punishment, those who are not conditionable tend to respond to neither.

Analytically inclined therapists use negative reinforcement less for its own purpose than to diminish acting out with the goal of fostering fantasy and making it more available for the purpose of developing insight. For example, a therapist once asked a psychopath to not be psychopathic for 48 hours. The patient complied. During this period, instead of acting out, the patient began to have revealing dreams that told a good part of the story of the origin and development of his disorder—material that had previously been totally unavailable for therapeutic scrutiny.

Expressive therapy. Psychopaths who suffer from affective numbness as a consequence of having been emotionally brutalized as children can sometimes benefit from controlled abreaction meant to help them get in touch, or back in touch, with their legitimate feelings. However, patients encouraged to express raw feelings may get worse if all that happens is they become openly angry with everyone and start acting out sexually.

Pastoral counseling and therapy. Some psychopaths have more respect for a minister, rabbi, or priest than they do for a psychotherapist. Some pastoral counselors have been able to play an important role in helping psychopathic patients progress from the proverbial old sinner to new saint by putting "the fear of God" into them.

Paradoxical therapy. Jay Haley, in personal communication in 1960, speaks of a form of therapy he calls paradoxical therapy, in which he attempts to elicit behavioral compliance by using reverse psychology. In a case he presented, previously discussed in Chapter 3, Haley, in effect anticipating that the patient would do exactly the opposite of what he was told, encouraged the patient to go ahead and turn off the alarm clock and snooze. The case illustrates a possible approach to treating psychopathic patients. Because psychopaths tend to lose interest in becoming oppositional when they see that it does not have the anticipated desired unsettling effect, paradoxical approaches, if not full therapy, can sometimes help reduce the psychopath's tendency to push limits in order to shock, appall, and defeat others, including, or especially, their therapists. But this therapeutic approach should only be used for those patients whose potential for acting out is minimal and whose capacity for destructiveness is quite limited. Needless to say, it should not be tried with the vast majority of psychopaths who are apt to take paradoxicality as a form of encouragement—if the approach backfires, if will have the exact opposite effect of the one intended.

GOALS OF TREATMENT

Therapists can justifiably have more ambitious goals for those psychopaths who can experience positive relationships on some level than for those psychopaths whose object love has failed to develop in the first place, leaving them with little or no innate capacity or potential for forming empathic and altruistic relationships. For these latter individuals, improvement would require that they develop a previously nonexistent interpersonal skill. For them, palliation—the goal of which would be reducing or eliminating the disorder's most maladaptive and destructive sequellae—would be a much more reasonable and attainable goal.

In contrast, mild psychopaths who know object love, only to abandon it and retreat after real or imagined disappointments in an effort to be free of vulnerability to all emotional hurt, can sometimes be helped to develop healthy, altruistic, empathic relationships. The therapist can help these individuals discover that while retreating from whole relationships with others achieves some immediate desired relief from disappointment, and some immunity to further disappointment, this solution as a long-term remedy is worse than the problem. Not only is the resulting deficit in object relationships itself disabling, but the patient also becomes more susceptible to further disappointment—the predictable consequence of having hurt those significant others who remain in his or her life.

With reactive psychopaths, the treatment goal may be a calming, healing transference response meant to tide the patient over rough times. In favorable cases, a positive transference can help keep patients from acting out dangerously if patients "clean up their act" just to please the therapist. That can keep them out of trouble until they learn to cope with and manage their bad experience, or until their troublesome reality improves on its own.

MASTERING ONE'S NEGATIVE COUNTERTRANSFERENCE

General Principles

Therapists have to be especially careful to avoid acting out their negative countertransferential feelings toward psychopaths. Too many therapists respond to a psychopath's maladaptive behavior by abandoning their neutral stance and liberal views and handling the psychopathy not at all as a madness but completely as a badness. They let the moral outrage that the psychopath's antisocial behavior provokes in them shatter their compassion and humanity. They then make matters worse by viewing their negative feelings about the psychopath not as countertransferential but as provoked, and therefore as entirely realistic, justified, and actionable.

Many therapists take a dislike to the psychopath's characteristic stubborn intransigence. It runs counter to their need to see progress, be in control, and feel loved, not rejected by a patient who refuses to listen and mind. Too often the therapist finds him- or herself drawn into the psychopath's sado-masochistic game. He or she gets annoyed and frustrated, feels put upon, and then gets back by criticizing the patient, by unnecessarily and punitively hospitalizing the patient, by offering drugs that the patient will not likely respond positively to, or by acting as if the patient is untreatable—declaring

the patient a complete reprobate and then interrupting therapy. Such therapists need to remember that the countertransference is something to be used
therapeutically to help the therapist learn about the patient's dynamics and,
if indicated, about the therapist's technical deficiencies. It is not to be used
countertherapeutically by being acted upon in a nihilistic and retaliative
fashion that can, often as much as the patient's illness, interfere with the
progress of therapy and worsen the patient's prognosis. Kernberg put it this
way: The therapist should "recognize a patient-induced impulse to action as
material to be interpreted and contained rather than acted on."[12] (Patients
can also profitably apply his advice to themselves.) In short, therapists
should respond to their countertransference feelings in one way only: by
using them in the service of offering the patient the same nonparental, non-
critical dispassionate clarifications and interpretations that they might, or
should, offer any other patient.

Some Insight into How I Respond to These Patients

My negative countertransference.   I do not like some psychopaths. I tend
to disapprove of people who seriously con people. I did not much like a
patient, a contractor, who had charges pending against him for gypping
people by taking their deposits and then running off with them. I even
refused to give him a prescription for benzodiazepines for anxiety
because his behavior outside of therapy (detailed in the local newspapers)
made me suspect that with me he was only claiming to be anxious in
order to get the drugs to which he was addicted. While I was correct in
key aspects of my assessment of him, I was still making moral judgments
that I should perhaps have not seriously entertained.

I tend to dislike those psychopaths who challenge my authority by cop-
ping their typical uncooperative and disruptive antiestablishment stances.
I prefer patients to be passive and submissive enough to at least, on some
level, accept and participate in treatment, over patients who constantly
rebel and who become demanding and controlling in order to be able to
fully dictate the terms of their medical care. Like most therapists, I prefer to
work with patients who seem more interested in undergoing long-term
change than in gratifying short-term appetites for money (e.g., disability
payments) or for medicine (e.g., Oxycontin), particularly when they
attempt to accomplish their goal by skewing, i.e., lying about, their medical
histories—falsely claiming, for example, to be suffering from anxiety
attacks in order to get benzodiazepines, or exaggerating or completely falsifying back pain in order to get opiates.

I find it hard to like the off-putting simmering and sometimes open
anger of some psychopaths. I particularly dislike it when they angrily
threaten to retaliate when I do not give them exactly what they want. For
example, a patient reported me to my boss for not fully reinstituting her
maintenance dose of an antidepressant after she went off her medication.

When I suggested restarting the medication gradually, she complained to the authorities about my ineptness—simply because she did not want to come in for the regular visits that gradually increasing the dose would have entailed. I feel particularly negatively about patients who try to get me to bend to their will by threatening to quit therapy entirely or to switch therapists (of course, to a more passive therapist who will let them effectively "run the whole show"). I feel threatened when patients lead antiestablishment groups meant to defeat me for being uncooperative, doing so by spreading disturbing and demeaning rumors that are meant to smear me and to stir up the other patients and the administration against me.

Like anyone else, I of course feel uncomfortable when patients actually threaten to harm me physically. But I feel almost as uncomfortable when patients become physically seductive toward me in the belief that that will be somehow to their advantage,

I particularly dislike it when patients take their stances from the strong but, in a given case, untenable position of the disenfranchised. For example, a patient, a veteran well familiar with guerilla tactics, once threatened me physically if I did not prescribe the Valium he wanted, and backed up his threats by warning me that if he did not get his prescription he would report me to the authorities for being prejudiced against people like him.

I certainly have problems treating individuals who are too unpredictable and selfish to keep appointments on time, and instead cancel ad lib or disrespectfully show up when it is convenient for them to do so and then insist that they be seen immediately no matter what. I once had a patient who, just to get my goat, deliberately and routinely came in when I was just leaving for lunch, claiming an emergency and demanding to be seen immediately. I once shared an office with another psychiatrist. She had the office in the morning and I had it in the afternoon. One late afternoon a psychopathic morning patient of hers appeared five hours late for his appointment. Then, guiltlessly disrupting my session, he demanded that I find a way to make his own psychiatrist come in to see him, and to do so on the spot.

Looking within, I do try to understand that some of these individuals act the way they do not because they are sinful and hate-filled reprobates, but because they are troubled individuals. Many are hypersensitive people just too easily hurt and angered to the point that they perceive minor rejection when there is none and then respond accordingly: by acting as if no therapist on earth can be relied on, ever, so it is better not to get involved in the first place or, failing that, to push away anyone trying to help before too much closeness threatens.

I also try to remember that I respond the way I do in good measure because I feel these individuals are rejecting me personally. For example, I often take it personally when I see these patients outside of a clinic and they do not return my pleasant hellos or do not even seem to recognize me. I still react personally even though I know that they are responding this way not necessarily because they dislike me as an individual but due to a combination of their inability to form close reciprocal relationships with me or with anyone else, and due to their (not always irrational) desire not to be seen publicly talking to me, which would raise the distinct possibility that they are being treated by a psychiatrist they are ashamed of seeing, for an illness that they are ashamed of having.

These insights into what I am feeling and experiencing help me avoid having my negative countertransference feelings seriously interfere with my ability to treat these patients. Insights like these help me keep my feelings under control and avoid acting on them to the extent that they affect my therapy. Of course, mere insight into negative countertransference issues does not make them go away. What is important is to keep all negative countertransference responses in good control by keeping feelings of anger, humiliation, weakness, helplessness, and foolishness foremost in one's field of recognition—e.g., spotting trends in the therapist that could potentially contaminate treatment, and quarantining them so as to not allow them into therapy.

In short, it is possible to have negative feelings about psychopaths without letting these feelings undermine treatment. Sidelining them can be enough to enable the therapist to respond to the patient, if not in a fully positive way then at least in an entirely professional way.

My positive countertransference. Paradoxically, I find some psychopaths more likeable than perhaps I should. I, like many other therapists, have a weakness for charming, handsome, and pretty psychopaths, especially the ones who flatter me. I have a soft spot for those patients who have risen from the bottom to the top by stealth and subterfuge—as long as they did not seriously damage others along the way. For example, I admire restaurateurs who manipulate their patrons into coming back for more by insulting them in order to play to their innate masochism, and politicians who are so focused on manipulating others to vote for them that they are able to harden themselves to what others think until they become insensitive enough to let all the insults roll off their backs and are able to dismiss them as "politics as usual."

Sometimes I deal with the helpless feelings these individuals arouse in me by becoming overly ambitious with them, trying a whole range of techniques that I know will simply not work. For example, sometimes I fool myself into thinking that psychopaths respond so well to affirmation that they can be cured if only I am sufficiently positive toward them. So, instead of saying anything at all that I perceive to be negatively judgmental, I go to the opposite extreme and become too nice, and too permissive, for the patient's ultimate benefit. However, I always stop short of falling for the pitying or "bleeding heart" response that these patients typically and inappropriately elicit in some therapists. I never have anything that even resembles a nonprofessional relationship with them. I never grant them special favors or privileges, and I never give them money in the form of a big loan, or sign off on an entitlement that they are not fully entitled to receive. Also, and of course, I avoid doing something really therapeutically distractive with them, such as taking them home and giving them a job around the house, or, even worse, although not necessarily unheard of, proposing marriage.

In conclusion, if a therapist is having serious countertransference problems that are at all like mine, or are in any other way too negative or too positive, I recommend that he or she talk about them with an understanding colleague or supervisor in order to make the transference-countertransference struggle a joint one. The goal is to avoid either brutalizing or seducing the patient, and to instead maintain if not one's therapeutic neutrality than at least one's therapeutic aplomb.

THERAPEUTIC ERRORS

Therapists should not automatically assume that these patients' prognosis is poor and then refuse to work with them on that account alone. They should always attempt to distinguish between mild psychopaths who can be helped and serious psychopaths who are difficult to influence in any way, let alone cure.

Therapists should avoid overgratifying their patients. Too often the bureaucracies involved in treating these patients enable their psychopathy by letting them have anything they want and request. Medically speaking, special privileges can harm more than they can help. Holding hands with a psychopathic patient allows misplaced humanity on the part of the treatment team to combine with selfish ambition on the part of the patient to completely deprive the patient of good medical care.

Therapists should not be psychopathic themselves. The psychopathic therapist fails to be a role model of integrity and honesty. He or she can do no better than to tell the patient, "Do what I say, not what I do"—not an effective way to treat patients with the same problem. A therapist who is having sex with a psychopathic patient is in no position to treat a psychopathic patient who is conning people for sex.

Therapists must never lie directly to any patient, but especially to psychopathic patients. Nor should lies contaminate any aspect of the extratherapeutic process. The therapist who gives tainted testimony in court, who promises to cure the patient simply to keep the patient coming and to use him or her as an annuity or solely to get material for a book, or the therapist who cheats the insurance company by overreporting the time spent with the patient, seeing the patient for ten minutes and then charging the insurance company for a fifty-minute hour, will probably not cure the patient of his or her psychopathy, but will instead participate in the antisocial process, showing the patient not how to get well but how to be a bigger, if not a better, psychopath.

Therapists should take special care not to fall for their patients' transference cons. Psychopaths know how to play into a therapist's rescue fantasies. They know how to act sick when they are well (to stay in the hospital) and well when they are still sick (to get out of the hospital). It is particularly destructive to effective therapy when therapists fall en masse for community cons and allow a whole group of individuals to manipulate a cadre of therapists. When I was working in Boston, a community of patients suffering from alcoholism would check on a regular basis to see who was on duty what night, and would then decide whether and when to come to the emergency room after hours to apply for admission—not to get treatment but to get free food, drink, and substances originally meant to heal but which they used to get high. In New York, I often said that it was not a good idea to give former heroin addicts methadone, sit idly by as they sold it on the street right in front of the clinic, and then, without even challenging their assertions, give them a second bottle just on their word that they lost the first one. This testimonial to complete therapeutic naiveté had the patients laughing behind our backs, and failing in therapy to our faces.

One of the worst therapeutic errors involves therapeutic impatience. Treatment of psychopaths is often a lifetime affair. Therapy with psychopaths has not necessarily failed just because it takes years to work. Sometimes the real reason patients get better "with age" is not because of diminishing hormones and neurotransmitters accompanied by the increasing reflective powers that come with the years (as often stated), but because after all this time their therapy has finally kicked in and helped them see the light. It follows that whenever possible, continuity should be a cornerstone of treatment of psychopathy. Ideally, the patient should have if not one therapist for the duration, then at least one institution to which he or she can turn for the long spell of what usually is an ongoing chronic illness with an unpredictable course. If all concerned hold fast, a favorable long-term outcome, better than the extant literature tends to suggest, is entirely within the grasp of both the patient and his or her therapist.

CHAPTER 13

Coping with the Psychopaths of Everyday Life

This chapter suggests a six-step method for helping victims cope with the psychopaths of everyday life. These steps are:

1. Learn all you can about psychopathy
2. Identify the psychopaths of everyday life in your life
3. Learn to spot the psychopath's cons
4. Identify the nature of your personal vulnerability to being victimized by psychopaths
5. Self-immunize against psychopaths
6. Avoid enabling psychopaths and their psychopathy

Step 1: Learn All You Can About Psychopathy

A good start might be to review one or more of the chapters in this book, and possibly read some of the entries in my lists of references. I particularly recommend Cleckley's *Mask of Sanity*, although it has sections that are dated and a few that go beyond being embarrassing to being completely unacceptable according to present day standards.

Step 2: Identify the Psychopaths of Everyday Life in Your Life

The following checklist of alerting (but not necessarily definitive) behavioral characteristics may help.

- In-your-face charm.
- Smooth, stylish, sweet-talking spiels meant to extract sex or money, attain complete control, or gain personal power. Example: A small town politician reveals,

"When I was younger I always told the girls I loved them; otherwise they wouldn't put out for me."

- A tendency to claim omniscience in order to intimidate, control, and buffalo others into giving forth, e.g., into buying into proffered scams.
- A penchant for excessive displays of high class, e.g., of expensive cars and flashy clothes.
- A partial or complete disinterest in obtaining life's substantial pleasures and rewards, particularly those that come from true loving relationships.
- A sexual franticness and wildness, especially involving resolute joyless sexual promiscuity.
- A propensity for covertness, e.g., cheating on a spouse who has been led to expect a monogamous relationship, especially when done less for the sex than for the cloak-and-dagger intrigue involved.
- A penchant for shady or illegal dealings. Example: selling real estate by downplaying or otherwise glossing over its flaws, e.g., touting a piece of land without mentioning that it happens to be unbuildable.
- A preoccupying interest in and constant pursuit of (honest or dishonest) get-rich schemes.
- An undue narcissism (self-absorption) associated with a lack of empathy for others in turn associated with few if any altruistic, caring impulses—what the layman perceives as simple selfishness, self-centeredness, and egocentricity.
- A fondness for name-calling that bullies and devalues others who do not agree, yield, permit, and cooperate, with two names especially predominating: "Nazi" and "racist."
- A savior identity, especially when associated with smug proselytizing.
- A highly developed skill at eliciting pity to get others to feel sorry.
- A resolute unyieldingly ambitiousness in search of high position and unlimited power, particularly in a competitive setting.
- A tendency to blame others entirely for one's own actions and failures along the lines of "You did it first," "You are one too," or "You made me do it."
- A tendency to appropriate the letter but not the spirit of the law, especially using the Constitution as a free pass for facilitating and permitting one's own narcissistic, selfish, and hurtful machinations, e.g., "This is a free country where I can do anything at all that I please."
- A marked tendency to self-promote, e.g., "Why would you want to buy a condominium here up north when you can buy one [of the ones I am putting up] on the water in Florida?"
- A covetousness—especially one that involves putting others' valid achievements down in order to enhance one's self-image. Example: A colleague asks a writer of self-help books if such books have ever helped anyone. Example: The same colleague asks me, "What possible use can there be for a book on psychopaths?"
- An unreliability, e.g., not keeping promises, such as canceling important dates at the last minute, more than once, and always with what appear to be iron-clad

excuses that leave others at the minimum faintly uneasy about how true the excuses happen to be.

- An immaturity and impulsiveness. Example: equating having a good time with getting high and screaming as loudly as one can in a closed space, oblivious to the fact that one happens to be seriously annoying to others.
- A tendency to mistreat pets. Example: beating dogs in the name of disciplining them.
- A tendency to mistreat children. Example: taking newborns out to restaurants late at night for one's personal convenience, e.g., to save money on a baby-sitter.

Step 3: Recognize the Most Familiar Cons

Some of these are:

- Too-good-to-be-true cons. Examples: Increase your penis size; eat all you want and still lose weight.
- Easy money cons. Example: Ponzi schemes, where an entrepreneurial type offers to pay very high interest on money, which interest he obtains from tapping the principle coming in from new money.
- Salvation cons. Example: I can learn all about you, predict your future, and change your life for the better by knowing your birth sign and reading your palm. Example: Your money is cursed; let me hang on to it for a while and I will remove the curse from it for you.
- Appeals to pity cons. Example: "I lost my wallet and need some money to get home"; "I am hungry and homeless" (when the evidence suggests otherwise, as when there is something "fishy" about the story, e.g., the individual appears to be high on drugs).
- Cons through aggressive promotions of products that are ordinary or of questionable merit. Examples: "No medicine is faster than the one that I am selling" (which really means "all medicines in this class of medication are equally fast," i.e., just as good, and probably cheaper); or "My aspirin contains the dose of aspirin you need to help you when you are having a heart attack; the more you know, the more you trust my aspirin" (which is merely a testimonial to the general usefulness of aspirin and not, as implied, to the superiority of my particular brand over all others). Example: promotion of high colonics/purges to increase body health (a television pitchman tells his audience that purging is life-saving, saying, "After all, the doctor who was there when the actor John Wayne was autopsied suggested that he would not have died if only he had had a cleaner colon.").
- Drop-that-name cons: Examples: I have friends in high places; I come from a fine, wealthy, highly connected family.
- Promised reciprocation cons. Example: Give me the name of your bank account and I will deposit millions in it for you to hang onto while I straighten out a few legal technicalities. Then I will give you your cut.

Here is a typical example of that kind of con, obtained from a missile that once made the rounds on the Internet:

From: <u>Saint Ubaji</u>

Sent: Friday, December 10, 2004 3:30 PM

Subject: An opportunity for us

ATTN,
FROM THE DESK OF SAINT UBAJI,
CHAIRMAN CONTRACT REVIEW COMMITTEE
OF NATIONAL ELECTRIC POWER AUTHORITY
(NEPA) NIGERIA.

DEAR FRIEND,

I am Saint Ubaji the Chairman Contract Review Committee of National Electric Power Authority (NEPA). Although this proposal might come to you as a surprise since it is coming from someone you do not know or ever seen before, I decided to contact you based on Intuition.

We are soliciting for your humble and confidential assistance to take custody of fifty Million, Five Hundred Thousand United States Dollars. {US$50,500,000.00}. This sum (US$50.5M) is an over invoice contract sum which is currently in an off-shore payment account of the Central Bank of Nigeria as an unclaimed contract entitlement which can easily be withdrawn or drafted or pay to any recommended beneficiary by my committee.

As a civil servant I am not permmitted to have a foriegn accounts due to the civil service code of conduct and I therefore need a trust worthy partner abroad to co-operate with me in recieveing this money on my behalf.

Also becuase of the finances required in the process of the transaction,my present financial resources as a civil servant may not be sufficient for me to handle the transfer alone succesfully without assistance from a good and a willing pertner abroad On this note, you will be presented as a contractor to NEPA who has executed a contract to a tune of the above sum and has not been paid.

Proposed Sharing Partern (%):

1. 60% for me.
2. 30% for you as a partner/fronting for us.
3. 10% for expenses that may be incurred by both parties during the cause of this transacton. If this proposal interests you, do responed as soon as possible with the following information:

1. The name you wish to use as the beneficiary of the fund.
2. Your Confidential Phone and Fax Numbers.
3. Your account informatiom for the transfer to be made. This account will be presented to the committe for approval/order of payments.
   Further discussion will be centered on how the fund shall be transfer and full details on how to accomplish this project.

Email me your response at this email address below. saintubaji20@yahoo.com

Thank you and God bless.

Best regards,

Engr: Saint Ubaji[1]

- Spur-of-the-moment cons. Example: "I have some material left over from a construction job I am doing down the block, so I can fix your roof for a very special price."
- Buzzword cons. Examples: "free," "sale," "cure," "guaranteed," "easy," "fun," and "hope"—words that should trigger at least a degree of suspicion. Example: You get this item free after paying only for packing and shipping (when the costs for the packing and shipping are inflated to more than cover the cost of the item and produce a profit.)
- Cons that are boldfaced, shameless requests for secret information. Example: a request for passwords and social security numbers in an e-mail that reads, "Your Internet account needs updating and to do so we must have your private password and your mother's maiden name."

Step 4: Identify Your Personal Vulnerability to Being Victimized by Psychopaths

The following discussion is not meant to imply that only people with emotional problems are vulnerable to psychopaths. In fact, psychopaths are expert at knowing how to get almost anyone, healthy as well as unhealthy, honest as well as dishonest, skeptical as well as believing, to fall for their ruses. For example, a man who was an honest seller of a house was seduced into going along with a buyer who asked him to inflate the sales price of the house so that she could get a bigger mortgage from the bank—in turn so that she could have enough left over after the purchase to make a big down payment on another investment property. (When he went along the bank found out about it and canceled the entire transaction, and as a result he lost some good offers that had come in in the meantime.)

Individuals can become less vulnerable to psychopaths when they stop being:

Too Trusting

Overly trusting individuals make bad business people. The opposite of paranoid, they are unable to master what for them would be a healing *basic distrust*. Because they are honest, they assume that everyone else is honest too. Often they go along with someone they hardly know, just based on first impressions. In effect, they judge the book by its cover, willingly and eagerly turning their money over to just anyone based entirely on what the person says and even on how he or she looks. They do not check credentials or insurance policies before hiring someone to work for them. They typically fail to ascertain if a business is reputable before getting involved financially, e.g., they do not check with the Better Business Bureau or buy consumer protection magazines before making important purchasing decisions. They willingly sign binding contracts with people they hardly know, ranging from door-to-door salesmen to just anyone on the Internet. When doing a transaction, they rarely if ever get everything in writing or withhold final payment until the work they order is done completely and to their satisfaction. They rarely read the fine print, e.g., they make balance transfers from credit card to credit card without first finding out how big a penalty is involved. They purchase what are obviously counterfeit goods off the street from vendors they assume are honest, and then actually expect them to work; when they fill up at a gas station they pay the bill without bothering to check the reading at the pump; and when they dine out they pay the tab without first determining if it accurately represents what they owe.

They rarely question the so-called and self-styled experts, especially when these purported experts use the respectable media as their forum. Believing that the respectable media would never support shysters, they go ahead and buy into something just because they heard it advertised on their favorite TV station. For example, they fall for a scheme touted on a respected financial news station: make money in the stock market by buying and selling the same stock over and over again, buying low and selling high. (This only works if the stock follows a friendly pattern of rise and fall and does not tank permanently.)

They typically make bad medical consumers. They might submit to major medical procedures before getting a second opinion. They might pick a hospital because it is close, not because it is good, and they rarely bother to check the hospital's affiliations or the qualifications of its staff. They rarely think to ask themselves if their particular case warrants favoring the use of a physician over a nonphysician, for example, a board-certified orthopedic surgeon over a chiropractor, or a board-certified ophthalmologist over an optometrist, and they employ alternate forms of medicine too freely, unwisely using them not to supplement, but to replace, traditional therapeutic methods. They buy into promises that they will be cured of an illness over the Internet, even when the person in question asks about their problem only after asking for their credit card.

Here are two examples of people who fell hard and fast for smooth shady operators. A well-to-do woman believed her boyfriend when he said he loved her, so she married him and trusted him not to take advantage of her. Even though she had two children to protect, she simply failed to ask him, though he was clearly an opportunist, to sign a prenuptial agreement. She then paid for this oversight by having him walk out on her, taking many of her assets with him. The coffee shop owner discussed throughout hired one psychopath after another because she trusted what they said on their application forms and did not bother to check to see if they were telling the truth. In fact, they all omitted mention of past convictions and jail time, such as time spent in prison for selling drugs and for armed robbery. They needed the job, she needed the help, so she took a chance—only to have more than one of them walk off with the contents of her cash register and, in a final indignity, have one walk off with the register itself.

Overly trusting individuals are often that way out of fear. They are unduly fearful of being assertive. Needing to be liked, they become reluctant to be unpleasant or insulting in any way. They fear demanding their legitimate rights. When making a purchase, they are afraid to ask for a price cut because they anticipate that the shopkeeper will snap at and reject them, along the lines of "This is a store, not an auction house." They want to be liked for being known as individuals who are completely trustworthy and accountable. For example, because they want to be known as persons of their word even when they have a solid reason to change their mind, they fail to use the buyer's regret laws put there to give impulsive individuals like themselves a chance to back out of a deal.

Too Altruistic

Extreme altruists are often that way because they like to be identified as "truly wonderful human beings." Proclaiming "There but for the grace of God go I," they too readily fall for exaggerated hard luck stories, not only out of a real sense of concern for others but also in order to be able to view themselves as saintly people who possess an imputed ability to identify with and pity the underdog. Such individuals are the opposite of psychopathic: just too honest, too fair, too empathic, and too giving for their own good. By nature they are so apt to give and so reluctant to take that they even become lax toward criminal activity in their midst and are unwilling to mete out justice even when they or others have been seriously wronged.

Too Impressionable

Too-impressionable individuals are overly ready to be seduced by charmers. At election time they vote not for the able statesman who has a real plan for needed change but for the phony politician who kisses the most babies, apparently the most intensely and sincerely. They fall for hypocrites with impressive lines, even when they are obviously saying one thing and doing another, e.g., they allow the city council member under fire for taking bribes to convince them that the school board should keep gays and lesbians off the roster because "Homosexuals do not have the moral judgment one needs to serve on such an august body."

Too Naïve

Naïve people buy fake merchandise on the streets because they cannot believe that there are dishonest people in this world—or because they convince themselves that the cops would close these operators down if the merchandise being sold were actually counterfeit.

Too Masochistic

Masochists often deliberately, if unconsciously, arrange to have psychopaths take advantage of them. They like being conned, for they actually get a thrill out of having someone put one over on them. Lacking self-respect, they like to lose because they feel it is just what they deserve, and because losing in one place helps them feel less guilty about some other thing they did someplace else. Out of a sense of guilt, they become excessively altruistic in order to deprive themselves by deliberately disregarding their own needs and abjectly deferring to the needs of others. If they get more pleasure out of giving than out of getting, it is because they feel that they are making the sacrifices they need to make in order to atone for the sins they imagine they did or are about to commit. At times they deliberately do not play to win, and do so just to get the reputation of being a good, not a sore, loser, and/or to get the sympathy vote, which includes bragging rights about how much they have suffered and how self-sacrificial they are.

Hoping to save money, an administrator of a mental hospital asked a doctor who worked there to give shock treatment to patients without first anesthetizing them properly—that is, instead of giving them general anesthesia, as was the custom of the day, he wanted her to just give them a minor (petit mal) seizure to act as the anesthesia for the induced therapeutic major seizure. The doctor wanted to say no, but she thought better of it. She excused her actions as self-preservative, along the lines of "If I don't say yes, my boss will blackball me for the rest of my life and I will never be able to get another job." But in fact, she actually enjoyed her martyrdom. She especially enjoyed receiving sympathy by complaining about her fate to her family, friends, and any of her colleagues who would listen.

Too Permissive

Excessively permissive parents can become victims of children with a conduct disorder. They might let them take over their lives completely, due to a reluctance to discipline them themselves or to get others to do it for them. Excessively permissive spouses might allow a pathologically jealous mate to rule their lives because of a reluctance to take out an order of protection or, when applicable, because they refuse to consider moving and changing their name, even when some such action is absolutely necessary to hide from a mate who is potentially dangerous, or actually homicidal.

Authority may become excessively permissive due to being overly and exclusively preoccupied with matters of social injustice toward the antisocial while being insufficiently concerned about the antisocial's social injustice to others. Randy Cohen, the Ethicist of *The New York Times*, received the following question: "Someone on the block is dealing crystal meth. I believe that the drug laws are overly punitive. What's the morality of narcking on the neighbors?" I disagree with his answer: "If your local drug dealer is merely unsightly, do nothing. . . . the war on drugs does more harm than the drug use it seeks to suppress. I would be reluctant to invoke laws that can be both inflexible and ineffectual. (Indeed, a case can be made against regarding drug use as a criminal rather than a public health matter.)"[2] We can also use his statement as an example of endorsing the "Boston Tea Party" principle gone mad: only enforcing those laws that one happens to personally agree with completely.

Too Narcissistic

Narcissists are prone to fall for unmerited flattery. They might do anything for someone who tells them they look great, and do not look at all their age. When they cannot afford the real thing, they buy shoddy goods as long as they look okay. What they want to accomplish is to get others to envy them for being someone who has it all.

Too Greedy

Greedy victims want it all and need to maintain the appearance of having gotten it. Individuals who are both greedy and dishonest fall prey to the psychopath who promises to help them fulfill their acquisitive desires even when doing so requires that they themselves act in a psychopathic manner.

Too Immature

Immature individuals allow the child inside of them to take over. Now the child who used to believe in Santa Claus becomes the adult who believes that fortune tellers can predict the future, that the used car dealership really is having a blow-out best-ever sale, and that the latest diet guru has a new and better method for losing weight—eating what one wants, without ever having to feel at all hungry.

The term "regression" is still used in some circles to describe the process whereby an adult, often an older person, becomes childlike. Dynamically speaking, however, this is a descriptive term that is imprecise, for two reasons. First, the immature adult does not mimic the normal child exactly. Second, other and perhaps better explanations apply to the perceived phenomenon. As Pinsker (personal communication, 2005) suggests, "We may become childlike due to impaired judgment that is in turn due to loss of inhibiting control or that is due to cognitive dysfunction involving memory storage."

Too Materialistic

Materialistic individuals feel that they cannot live without something and that they must have that something now. So they run up big charges on their credit cards that they cannot afford to pay. Next they readily become targets for loan sharks and other people who promise them easy money, such as the kind that comes from get-rich-quick schemes.

Too Dependent

Dependent people desperately need to be loved, a cornerstone of almost all gullibility. Nowhere is this more of a problem than for the above-mentioned individuals who, just to be liked, eagerly and willingly seek attention and love from shysters, no matter what the cost and regardless of any possible consequences, even when it means saying yes to something to which they clearly should say no.

Too Lonely

Dependent people are often desperately lonely individuals who find themselves tempted to accept any offer of human contact just for the temporary lift it might provide. Instead of just accepting their loneliness and living with it, they go to extremes to eliminate the feeling entirely. Dependent people without a supportive, helpful protective circle of family and friends are particularly vulnerable to being duped by strangers offering human companionship for a price.

An older gay man was a gullible, too-trusting individual. As a consequence, he imagined that when a younger man was interested in him it was because he liked not the older man's money, but father figures. He regularly judged the men he picked up in a bar based on how they looked and the seeming validity of their lines. So instead of getting their phone numbers and meeting them later, he took them right home past the doorman put there to protect him—from everybody but himself. Once, his judgment dulled by smoking marijuana, he picked up a stranger in a bar and took him home even after the stranger acted so suspiciously that he should have known not to put the key into the lock. (The stranger repositioned his car even though they were only going a block away—in retrospect, something that should have clearly been a warning that the pickup was planning to fill up the car with the contents of his mark's apartment.) When they got home the pickup made an odd request: he asked the gay man to pour himself a beer before sex. As it turned out, the pickup was looking not for conviviality but for a vehicle in which to dissolve some knock-out drops. Predictably, after the mark passed out, the pickup stole his money, his credit cards, and his identity.

Not yet having fully learned his lesson, he went on to pick up another stranger who did a sexy dance while asking him to undress. To this day he thinks that he might have been killed if a friend had not come home in the middle of this scene. Not long afterwards he took up with a regular lover about whom he cluelessly complained, "I can't understand why he keeps whining that he isn't any richer after meeting me than he was before we met." After breaking up with this man he felt so lonely that he was willing to risk everything just for some companionship, so he took up with a circle of friends who were manufacturing and selling drugs. Not surprisingly, he refused to follow the advice I gave him: that it is better to be alone and lonely now than to fall prey to psychopaths who might make you feel less lonely now, but ultimately ruin your life forever. He replied: "Having a lover is important to me, and in life there is always some bad that comes with anything good."

Too Impulsive

Impulsive people make snap decisions ranging from what to buy to whom to marry. They rarely get and use a lawyer, even for important complex transactions, and they rarely if ever ask confidantes what they think before taking important personal and financial steps.

Too Frugal

Excessively frugal individuals cannot pass up what appears to be a bargain, even when they know deep down why it is so cheap.

Too Rebellious

Rebellious individuals are brats and rascals who need and like to break the rules and defy authority. As a result they patronize counterfeiters just to spite the real businesses whom they see as the Microsofts of the world—i.e., those who sell overpriced merchandise—and who they believe are fair game because the businesses already have enough money, and more than they need.

Being Elderly

Attempting to answer why the elderly are so gullible, Pinsker (personal communication, 2005) notes that "The elderly are gullible in part because they are easily fatigued to the point that they become readily unfocused and inattentive. Theirs is also a decreased ability to multi-task, so that while listening to a pitch they do not have the simultaneous, protective thought, 'this could be a con.' I suppose judgment involves selecting the best choice out of several. To do this, one must be able to hold several in mind." Pinsker also emphasizes "the loss of associations, probably a frontal lobe matter, so that the elderly begin to notice that they have fewer comments, fewer ideas about things not in their areas of major activity, and do not think of as many possible solutions and outcomes, e.g., 'this person may be a con artist and if I do go along with him or her I'll lose it all.'

Newspaper articles have suggested that with the decrease in relationships in the elderly, there is a hunger for connections, so the friendly thief seems to be filling a need. Certainly the elderly are particularly prone to wanting to appeal to others. Their need to be loved makes them reluctant to act like that difficult, off-putting person who mistrusts and challenges everyone. This need to be loved, and with it the reluctance to be unpleasant, are certainly at work when the elderly give money to a person with a hard luck story about having no money for a ticket home, or gasoline, but these charitable cons work at all ages. Of course, the elderly are no exception to the rule that those who are conned are often excited about the possibility of satisfying a greedy wish." (Clearly, Pinsker would agree that the maxim "You cannot cheat an honest person" applies to the old as well as to the young.)

As Pinsker continues, "Also crucial is a preoccupation with other things like their health and mortality that make it hard for them to focus on important here and now considerations.

Also, some elderly appear to return to child-like feelings and behaviors, e.g., to 'regress.' Child-like longings and wishes that make it difficult to focus on potentially harsh reality may assume greater prominence with age. So may child-like trust. However, there is a significant difference between the trusting child and the conned senior. The child is conditioned to be obedient with adults in order to try to please them. The senior, too, may be regressively motivated to please, but here the motivation is not to be cooperative but to be liked."

Finally, some medications the elderly take can make them high, even manic, and induce a judgment-dulling euphoria. This is true for some antidepressants and other medications too numerous to mention here.

In conclusion, each of the above negative identifying traits implies positive correctives—and these in turn belong with the methods for self-immunization I go on to describe in Step 5.

Step 5: Immunize Yourself to the Psychopaths of Everyday Life

Potential victims can immunize themselves to the psychopaths of every day life in one or more of the following ways:

Become more of an honest individual yourself. Become that honest "man" you cannot cheat. Honest people do not welcome psychopaths into their lives. They avoid the company of bad companions who urge them to defy authority, break the laws, and disregard the basic rules of moral conduct. They do not signal to the psychopath, "Go after me, for I am someone easily led, especially into temptation."

Regulate your self-esteem. Many people suffer from a combination of self-esteem that is at once too low and too high. *Increasing excessively low* self-esteem can help avoid the temptation to abjectly defer to anyone with a good spiel. *Decreasing excessively high* self-esteem can help avoid inappropriately feeling indestructible and thinking that "I am an exception to the rule that complex problems have easy solutions." This type of thinking can lead one to fall under the spell of illusionists, such as the fortune teller who supposedly sees into the future; the guru who offers a way to take complete control of one's life; the healer who offers perfect health without having to take medicine or offers any other easy cure for a difficult and serious medical problem; and the pitchperson who offers that proverbial free lunch—that something for nothing that promises illusive gain without pain, a combination that rarely exists in real life, in or out of the gym.

Master your tendency to be easily hypnotizable. Easily hypnotizable people automatically comply when anyone tells them to do something, even when that something goes against their grain. In the hypnoid state, they let the self-appointed gurus of this world take over, lead, and rule. They become like the composer of an operatic rallying hymn who hears his own song and feels inspired to take up arms against the entirely fictitious enemy forces his librettist wrote into the opera's book. Avoid being mesmerized by those in charge in the belief that higher-ups must have gotten there because they are honest, and otherwise the right person for the job. Be especially certain that an alarm bell rings, sounding the wake-up call, when you hear the hollow promise of someone saying "Trust me."

Identify with the aggressor. Decide if it is right for you to cope with psychopaths by giving them a taste of their own medicine, e.g., by becoming psychopathic yourself—in self-defense and/or just to get revenge. Do not go too far in this direction, however, as did the following patient:

A patient started dealing with telemarketers by retaliating in kind, so that when they called he would say "excuse me for a moment" and then put the phone down in order to let them hang there. He dealt with what he considered to be annoying subscription cards in magazines by returning them blank so that the company had to pay the postage without benefiting. He went on to deal with a psychopathic boss who was overworking him, by foot-dragging and calling out sick, and then, when she passed him over for a promotion she gave to her friend, by regaining a preeminent position in her retinue by becoming her secret agent—gaining the confidence of his coworkers and then reporting back to her what they said about her behind her back. Finally hoping to get back fully in her good graces, even though that meant cheating on his wife and otherwise thoroughly compromising his personal integrity, he started having an affair with her.

Here is a concluding caveat: always be sure to distinguish true psychopaths from people whose unfortunate circumstances compel them to need and to have to do just about anything to make a living.

Step 6: Avoid Enabling Psychopaths and Their Psychopathy

So often those identified as passive victims of psychopaths have actually had some hand in causing others in their lives to become psychopathic—thereby both creating their own victimization and facilitating the victimization of others. Here are some classic enablers—individuals who do not stop psychopaths when they should, or egg them on when they should not. They include:

- Psychiatrists—who enable psychopathy by refusing to judge patients at all, along the lines of "It is not my business to make moral judgments." Mostly they do this subtly, by labeling a patient's willful behavior as the product of emotional illness, as in "He may look 'bad,' but that can be entirely accounted for by the fact that he is 'mad,'" and by calling even the most atrocious actions "maladaptive" (that is, "bad for the individual") rather than "appalling" (that is, "bad for all concerned").

- Lawyers—who make antisocial personalities worse by providing them with a good defense. As Vaillant and Perry note, patients with an Antisocial Personality Disorder "are not helped by [having good lawyers protect them] from their own anxiety or from the consequences of their behavior."[3]

- The Government—by rewarding psychopathic behavior on a large scale, as when the government rewarded a psychiatrist for plagiarizing a good portion of a book she wrote by giving her a major political appointment as head of a relevant government agency.

- The Media—by publicizing psychopathy and psychopaths, as did the publisher who rewarded the just-mentioned psychiatrist by publishing her book on the following topic: "How to protect yourself from psychopaths."

- Families—like the ones discussed throughout who enable psychopathy by refusing to lay down the law with a psychopathic family member. Instead of enforcing good moral behavior in their children, they bring the child up in an anything-goes atmosphere, encouraging the child to self-actualize no matter what. Then, when the child gets into difficulty, they bail him or her out, with the result that the child rarely if ever has to face the consequences of his or her actions. In the news recently was a story of a family who protected a son who was a rapist by arranging for him to escape from the country. Then they supported him in exile just so that he could keep out of the clutches of the United States courts.

- Spouses—like the man who encouraged his wife's prostitution because he had pleasurable fantasies about the other men she went with—fantasies that rescued him from his pallid, humdrum existence; because he liked the scent of evil about her; because he both wanted and needed the money she brought home; and because he liked how her business dealings distracted her from the affair that he was having with her sister.

Here are some of the ways ordinary individuals from all walks of life do their enabling either covertly or overtly:

- By patronizing psychopathic organizations. For example, they buy things spammers sell on the Internet and willingly and eagerly patronize companies who create file sharing software whose only purpose is to steal copyrighted material.

- By siding with and supporting individual psychopaths in small ways, e.g., by giving to the beggar on the subway, even though, or just because, begging on the subway is against the law, and they have decided that they are above the law and therefore entitled to determine for themselves which laws are just.

- By eagerly creating and defending upside-down views that fly in the face of common sense, for example, the view that our Constitution offers and protects unlimited freedom of expression under all circumstances.

- By maintaining and advocating such questionable ideals as "Permissiveness is next to Godliness"; "The highest goal in life involves not deep love but good sex"; or "Winning at poker is the model for winning in life."

- By compromising one's ideals just for the money, saying or doing anything to satisfy the people who pay. Lawyers do this when they take on unjust lawsuits for financial gain, and then disguise their real intent as a love of fairness coupled with deep concern for the victim and the letter of the law.

- By secretly or openly envying and emulating the psychopath's skills at extracting the maximum from others with the minimum of work, easy achievements aspired to along the lines of "I wish I could get something for nothing like she does."

- By secretly admiring and envying psychopathic rebelliousness and wanting to become or actually becoming equally socially defiant.

- By not supporting and protecting potential or actual victims of psychopaths, for example, by joining in a conspiracy of silence with a friend who cheats on a wife he promised to be faithful to, or by sitting back and enjoying the downfall of whistle-blowers, comfortably standing by as they get punished for being "rat-finks." I once had a psychiatric resident who was seducing patient after patient, asking them not "How do you feel today?" but "What shall we try today?" When I found out about it, I felt that I had to report his behavior to my supervisor. Whom did everybody side with? They sided with the resident, not with me. He became the one who was misunderstood and mistreated, and I became the bad guy who was not supporting, but ratting out, a colleague.

- By allowing our own acquisitiveness and pleasure-orientation to lead us to condone the cheating and lying of others—as long as we share in the spoils.

- By making excuses for the psychopath, such as:
  - ✓ He is basically a good person
  - ✓ It's just this once; anyone can make a mistake
  - ✓ Everyone does it
  - ✓ You have to forgive him, for to err is human, to forgive divine
  - ✓ There are worse things in this world than what she did
  - ✓ I would do the same thing myself if given the opportunity
  - ✓ She had a bad childhood
  - ✓ She is going through a temporary life crisis
- By not setting a good example and instead behaving psychopathically ourselves. All of us need to stop being hypocritical, saying one thing and doing another, giving our word and making promises and then breaking our trust and failing to keep them. On the job, all of us need to support honest whistle-blowers by congratulating them for being model citizens and not condemning them for being snitches. We should all think twice about forming anti-management coalitions with coworkers and instead join the boss and work alongside him or her toward the common goal of making the business a success. Away from the job, in our personal lives, we need to avoid being participants in the noisy desperation of conning, manipulating, and scamming that characterizes the life of even the mildest of psychopaths, and instead focus on the core virtues of fairness, honesty, and trustworthiness, however corny these may sound.

True, we should all do what we can to find our place and get ahead in life. But we should do so by dint of effort and hard work, striving to meet our goals through honest methods eagerly sought and quietly pursued, in what has, alas, too often become not only figuratively, but also literally, the "old-fashioned way."

Notes

Chapter 1

1. American Psychiatric Association. (1994). *Diagnostic and statistical manual of mental disorders* (4th ed.). Washington, DC.

2. Stout, M. (2005). *The sociopath next door.* New York: Broadway Books.

3. See American Psychiatric Association, p. 649.

4. Hare, R. D. (1999). *Without conscience: the disturbing world of the psychopaths among us.* New York: The Guilford Press, p. 31.

5. Perring, C. (1999). Review of Hare's *Without conscience: the disturbing world of the psychopaths among us.* Retrieved November 14, 2005. http://mentalhelp.net/books/books.php?type=de&id=65.

6. Lewis, D. O. (1985). Adult antisocial behavior and criminality. In H. I. Kaplan and B. J. Sadock (Eds.), *Comprehensive textbook of psychiatry/IV* (pp. 1865–1870) Baltimore: Williams and Wilkins, p. 1869.

7. See American Psychiatric Association, p. 85.

8. See American Psychiatric Association, p. 649.

9. Millon, T. (1981). *Disorders of personality: DSM-III: Axis III.* New York: John Wiley and Sons, p. 182.

10. Machiavelli, N. (1952). *The prince.* New York: Penguin Books USA.

11. Cleckley, H. (1955). *The mask of sanity.* St. Louis: C. V. Mosby, p. 534.

12. See Lewis, p. 1869.

13. Sadock, B. J. and Sadock, V. A. (2002). In Sadock, J. S. and Sadock, V. A., *Kaplan & Sadock's synopsis of psychiatry: behavioral sciences/clinical psychiatry* (9th ed.) (pp. 807–808). Philadelphia: Lippincott Williams and Wilkins, p. 808.

Chapter 2

1. Toch, H. (2003). Psychopathy or antisocial personality in forensic settings. In T. Millon, E. Simonsen, M. Birket-Smith, and R. D. Davis (Eds.), *Psychopathy* (pp. 144–158). New York: The Guilford Press, p. 155.

2. Black, D. W. (1999). *Bad boys, bad men: confronting antisocial personality disorder.* New York: Oxford University Press, p. 152.

3. See Black, back cover.

4. See Black, p. 152.

5. Hare, R. D. (1999). *Without conscience: the disturbing world of the psychopaths among us.* New York: The Guilford Press, pp. 113–114.

6. See Hare, p. 113.

7. Cleckley, H. (1955). *The mask of sanity.* St. Louis: C. V. Mosby, p. 211.

8. See Cleckley, p. 211.

9. See Cleckley, p. 211.

10. See Cleckley, p. 213.

11. See Cleckley, p. 213.

12. See Cleckley, p. 214.

13. See Cleckley, p. 214.

14. See Cleckley, p. 214.

15. See Cleckley, p. 215.

16. See Cleckley, p. 215.

17. See Cleckley, p. 215.

18. See Cleckley, p. 215.

19. American Psychiatric Association. (1994). *Diagnostic and statistical manual of mental disorders* (4th ed.). Washington, DC.

20. See American Psychiatric Association, p. 633.

21. See American Psychiatric Association, p. 630.

22. Oldham, J. and Morris, L. B. (1995). *The new personality self-portrait.* New York: Bantam Books, p. 21.

23. See American Psychiatric Association.

24. See Cleckley, p. 215.

25. Reich, W. (1949). *Character analysis.* New York: Orgone Institute Press.

26. See Reich, p. 44.

27. Millon, T. (1981). *Disorders of personality: DSM-III: Axis III.* New York: John Wiley and Sons, p. 181.

28. See Hare, p. 102.

29. See Hare, pp. 113–114.

30. See Hare, p. 113.

31. Stout, M. (2005). *The sociopath next door.* New York: Broadway Books.

32. Simon, R. I. (1996). *Bad men do what good men dream.* Washington, DC: American Psychiatric Press, p. 27.

33. See American Psychiatric Association, p. 650.

34. See American Psychiatric Association, pp. 649–650

35. Hansen, H. (2003). Treating the 'untreatable' in Denmark: past and present. In T. Millon, E. Simonsen, M. Birket-Smith, and R. D. Davis (Eds.), *Psychopathy* (pp. 458–462). New York: The Guilford Press, p. 460.

36. See Hansen, p. 460.

37. The Angel Bible, Authorized King James Version. (1996) Grand Rapids, Michigan: World Publishing, p. 63 of the New Testament. Luke 23:34.

38. See American Psychiatric Association, p. 683.

39. See American Psychiatric Association, p. 649.

40. Millon, T., Simonsen, E., and Birket-Smith, M. (2003). Historical conceptions of psychopathy in the United States and Europe. In T. Millon, E. Simonsen, M. Birket-Smith, & R. D. Davis (Eds.), *Psychopathy* (pp. 3–31). New York: The Guilford Press, p. 6.

41. See Millon et al, pp. 5–6.

42. See American Psychiatric Association, p. 649.

43. See American Psychiatric Association, p. 683.

Chapter 3

1. Vaillant, G. E. and Perry, J. C. (1985). Personality disorders. In Kaplan, H. J. and Sadock, B. J. (Eds.), Comprehensive textbook of psychiatry/IV (pp. 958–986). Baltimore: Williams and Wilkins, p. 978.

2. American Psychiatric Association. (1994). *Diagnostic and statistical manual of mental disorders* (4th ed.). Washington, DC: p. 647.

3. Schwarzenegger, A. Quote on a poster.

4. See American Psychiatric Association, p. 649.

5. Freud. S. (1915). Some character-types met with in psycho-analytic work: III criminality from a sense of guilt. In *Collected papers*, John O. Sutherland (Ed.) (pp. 318–344). London: The Hogarth Press, p. 342–344.

6. Machiavelli, N. (1952) *The prince*. New York: Penguin Books USA.

7. See American Psychiatric Association, p. 472.

8. See American Psychiatric Association, pp. 472–473

9. Hare, R. D. (1999). *Without conscience: the disturbing world of the psychopaths among us*. New York: The Guilford Press, p. 31.

Chapter 4

1. Machiavelli, N. (1952) *The prince*. New York: Penguin Books USA.

2. Tallmer, J. (2004, December 8). Retrospective on Pulitzer prize-winning composer: new documentary on Ned Rorem. *Villager*, p. 27.

3. American Psychiatric Association. (1994). *Diagnostic and statistical manual of mental disorders* (4th ed.). Washington, DC: pp. 648–649.

4. Stout, M. (2005). *The sociopath next door*. New York: Broadway Books, p. 187.

Chapter 5

1. Cocheo, S. (1997). The bank robber, the quote, and the final irony. Retrieved November 11, 2005. http://www.banking.com/aba/profile_0397.htm

Chapter 6

1. Cleckley, H. (1955). *The mask of sanity*. St. Louis: C. V. Mosby, p. 390.

2. See Cleckley, p. 390.

3. Eysenck. H. J. (2003). Personality and crime. In T. Millon, E. Simonsen, M. Birket-Smith, and R. D. Davis (Eds.), *Psychopathy* (pp. 40–49). New York: The Guilford Press, p. 46.

4. Millon, T. (1981). *Disorders of personality: DSM-III: Axis III.* New York: John Wiley and Sons, pp. 198–199.

5. Parrat, S. (2005). You are a disgusting example of a man [Letter to the editor]. *TriCity Mail*, 3 March, p. 8.

6. See Cleckley, p. 397.

7. See Cleckley, p. 397.

8. See Millon, p. 102.

9. The Daily Camera (2005). Ward Churchill statement. Retrieved October 7, 2005. http://www.commondreams.org/cgi-bin/print.cgi?file=/headlines05/0201-05.htm.

10. Murphy, T. and Oberlin, L. (2005). *Overcoming passive-aggression: how to stop hidden anger from spoiling your relationships, work, and happiness.* New York: Marlowe and Company, p. 70.

11. See The Daily Camera.

12. Beck. A. T. (1999). *Prisoners of hate.* New York: HarperCollins, p. 127.

13. Perring, C. (1999). Review of Hare's *Without conscience: the disturbing world of the psychopaths among us.* Retrieved November 14, 2005. http://mentalhelp.net/books/books.php?type=de&id=65.

14. W. S. Gilbert. Retrieved November 16, 2005. http://www.lexscripta.com/links/cultural/pinafore.html

15. See Cleckley, p. 395.

16. See Cleckley, p. 395.

17. See Cleckley, pp. 395–396.

18. See Cleckley, p. 396.

Chapter 7

1. Cleckley, H. (1955). *The mask of sanity.* St. Louis: C. V. Mosby, p. 406.

2. American Psychiatric Association. (1994). *Diagnostic and statistical manual of mental disorders* (4th ed.). Washington, DC: p. 650

3. Millon, T. (1981). *Disorders of personality: DSM-III: Axis III.* New York: John Wiley and Sons, p. 187.

4. See Millon, p. 187.

Chapter 8

1. American Psychiatric Association. (1994). *Diagnostic and statistical manual of mental disorders* (4th ed.). Washington, DC: p. 649.

2. Hare, R. D. (1999). *Without conscience: the disturbing world of the psychopaths around us.* New York: The Guilford Press, p. 177.

3. Wolman, B. B. (1999). *Antisocial behavior.* Amherst, New York: Prometheus Books, p. 158.

4. See Wolman, p. 158.

5. See Wolman, p. 154.

6. See Wolman, p. 154.

7. Eysenck. H. J. (2003). Personality and crime. In T. Millon, E. Simonsen, M. Birket-Smith, and R. D. Davis (Eds.), *Psychopathy* (pp. 40–49). New York: The Guilford Press, p. 45.

8. See Eysenck, p. 45.

9. See Eysenck, p. 45.

10. See Eysenck, p. 46.

11. See Eysenck, p. 46.

12. See Eysenck, p. 46.

13. See Eysenck, p. 47.

14. See Eysenck, p. 47.

15. See Eysenck, p. 47.

16. See Eysenck, p. 47.

17. See Eysenck, p. 46.

18. Rozhon, T., and Thorner, R. (2005, May 26). They sell no fake before its time. *The New York Times*, C1–C5.

19. See Rozhon and Thorner, p. C5.

20. Stone, A. (2005, August 8). The line between mad and bad. *Psychiatric Times*, pp. 1,7.

21. Murphy, T. and Oberlin, L. *Overcoming passive-aggression: how to stop hidden anger from spoiling your relationships, work, and happiness.* New York: Marlowe and Company, p. 136.

Chapter 9

1. Millon, T. (1981). *Disorders of personality: DSM-III: Axis III.* New York: John Wiley and Sons, p. 181.

2. See Millon, p. 181.

3. See Millon, p. 181.

4. See Millon, p. 181.

5. See Millon, p. 181.

6. See Millon, p. 182.

Chapter 10

1. Hare, R. D. (1999). *Without conscience: the disturbing world of the psychopaths around us.* New York: The Guilford Press, p. 174.

2. Eysenck. H. J. (2003). Personality and crime. In T. Millon, E. Simonsen, M. Birket-Smith, and R. D. Davis (Eds.), *Psychopathy* (pp. 40–49). New York: The Guilford Press, p. 46.

3. Cocheo, S. (1997). The bank robber, the quote, and the final irony. Retrieved November 11, 2005. http://www.banking.com/aba/profile_0397.htm

4. Cleckley, H. (1955). *The mask of sanity.* St. Louis: C. V. Mosby, p. 431.

5. Dorland, W. A. N. (1954). *The American illustrated medical dictionary.* Philadelphia: W. B. Saunders, p. 116.

6. Saint-Saens, C. (2005). In Britannica student encyclopedia. From *Encyclopaedia Britannica Premium Service.* Retrieved March 17, 2006. http://www.britannica.com/ebi/article-9276858.

7. Millon, T. (1981). *Disorders of personality: DSM-III: Axis III*. New York: John Wiley and Sons, p. 195.

8. Wolman, B. B. (1999). *Antisocial behavior*. Amherst, New York: Prometheus Books, p. 120.

9. See Wolman, p. 110.

10. See Wolman, p. 107.

11. See Cleckley.

12. See Wolman, p. 112.

13. See Wolman, p. 103.

14. See Wolman, p. 108.

15. See Wolman, p. 120.

16. See Wolman, p. 96.

17. See Wolman, p. 109.

18. See Wolman, p. 111.

19. See Wolman, pp. 111–112.

20. See Wolman, p. 108.

21. Machiavelli, N. (1952). *The prince*. New York: Penguin Books USA, p. 93.

22. See Machiavelli, p. 92.

23. See Machiavelli, p. 92.

24. See Machiavelli, p. 95.

25. See Machiavelli, p. 93.

26. See Machiavelli, p. 93.

27. See Machiavelli, p. 97.

28. See Machiavelli, p. 94.

29. See Machiavelli, p. 99.

30. See Machiavelli, p. 99.

31. See Machiavelli, p. 98.

32. See Machiavelli, p. 119.

33. See Machiavelli, p. 119.

34. American Psychiatric Association. (1994). *Diagnostic and statistical manual of mental disorders* (4th ed.). Washington, DC: p. 472.

35. See American Psychiatric Association, pp. 472–473.

36. Hansen, H. (2003). Treating the 'untreatable' in Denmark: past and present. In Millon et al. (pp. 458–462), p. 460.

37. See Hansen, p. 460.

38. The Angel Bible, Authorized King James Version. (1996) Grand Rapids, Michigan: World Publishing, p. 432 of the Old Testament. Ecclesiastes 8:15.

39. John Roberts's Rapid Ascension. (2005). *The New York Times*, p. A26.

40. Rygaard, N. P. (2003). Psychopathic children: indicators of organic dysfunction. In Millon et al. (pp.247–259), p. 249.

41. See Millon, p. 183.

Chapter 11

1. American Psychiatric Association. (1994). *Diagnostic and statistical manual of mental disorders* (4th ed.). Washington, DC: p. 90.

2. Michaels, J. J. (1955). *Disorders of character: persistent eneuresis, juvenile delinquency, and psychopathic personality*. Springfield, Illinois: Charles C. Thomas.

3. See American Psychiatric Association, p. 632.

4. See American Psychiatric Association, p. 632.

Chapter 12

1. Cleckley, H. (1955). *The mask of sanity.* St. Louis: C. V. Mosby, p. 210.

2. Hare, R. D. (1999). *Without conscience: the disturbing world of the psychopaths around us.* New York: The Guilford Press, p. 193.

3. See Hare, p. 199.

4. Kernberg, O. F. (2003). The psychotherapeutic management of psychopathic, narcissistic, and paranoid transferences." In T. Millon, E. Simonsen, M. Birket-Smith, and R. D. Davis (Eds.), *Psychopathy* (pp. 372–392). New York: The Guilford Press, p. 380.

5. Black, D. W. (1999). *Bad boys, bad men: confronting antisocial personality disorder.* New York: Oxford University Press, p. 133.

6. See Black, p. 133.

7. See Black, p. 134.

8. See Black, p. 134.

9. See Black, p. 184.

10. See Black, p. 186.

11. Dolan, B. (1998). Therapeutic community treatment for severe personality disorders. In Millon et al. (pp. 407–430), p. 425.

12. See Kernberg, p. 391.

Chapter 13

1. Saint Ubaji. Received December 10, 2004, from saintubaji20@yahoo.com

2. Cohen, R. (2005, September 4). Dealing With Dealers. *The New York Times,* p. 18.

3. Vaillant, G.E. and Perry, J. C. (1985). Personality disorders. In Kaplan, H. J. and Sadock, B. J. (Eds.), *Comprehensive textbook of psychiatry/IV* (pp. 958–986). Baltimore: Williams and Wilkins, p. 978.

Index

Adaptive evasiveness, 17
Adult antisocial behavior, 25
Affect, 88–89; impoverishment, 88–89
Affirmative therapy, 164–165
Age-appropriate social norms, 35
Aggressiveness, 143
Aggressive personality, 133
Aggressive personality nonantisocial
    type, 18–21
Aggressive promotion of products
    con, 181
Aggressivity, 36–37
Altruism: insufficient, 112
Altruists, extreme: victimization by
    psychopaths, 185
Ambitiousness, 180
Amnesia, 51
Anal manipulators, 42
Anger, 88
Anger management, 171
Animal models, 138–139
Antisocial personality disorder,
    1, 11–13, 18, 123–124; vs. mild
    psychopathy, 24–26
Anxiety, 7; lack of, 7, 37, 146–147
Aphasia, 140
Appeals to pity cons, 181

Appearance: in psychopathy, 30–31, 85
Arbitrary inference, 99
Artists, 62
Assumption of blamelessness, 143
Authors, 62

Bad Boys, Bad Men: Confronting
    Antisocial Personality Disorder: Black,
    Donald W., 12
Basic distrust, 183–184
Bathroom ritual, 147
Beck, Aaron T.: selectivity, 96
Behavior: diagnosis of psychopathy
    and, 29–53; mental status of
    psychopaths, 85
Behavioral characteristics, 179–181
Behavioral constructs, 142–144
Behavioral therapy, 171–172
Berkowitz, David, 1, 5
Biological factors: psychopathy, 137–140
Black, Donald W.: Bad Boys, Bad Men:
    Confronting Antisocial Personality
    Disorder, 12
Blame shifting, 90
Blaming tendency, 180
Blurring of differences between right
    and wrong, 93

Borderline personality disorders,
    118–119
Brinkmanship, 43–44
Bundy, Ted, 1, 5
Business people, 58–60
Buzzword cons, 183

Case vignettes, 73–84
Categorical diagnoses, 14–15
Categorical lying, 49
Cause and effect: switching of, 98
Character armor, 16
Charming, 44–47
Cheating, 75–84
Claiming altruistic motives, 92
Cleckley, Hervey, 8; *The Mask of Sanity*,
    12, 86, 179
Cognitively defined psychopathy, 21
Cognitive therapy, 171
Compensation, 117–118
Compensation disorder, 51, 144
Competitiveness, 119
Con artists, 44–47
Conditionability: poor, 87–88
Conduct disorder, 5, 154; child onset
    type, 75; onset before age 15, 18
Conning, 44–47. *see also* specific Con;
    recognition of, 181–183
Conscience (superego), 145–146;
    dealing with problems, 161
Conservatism: encouragement of
    psychopathy, 128–131
Core personality structure, 85–106
Corruptness, 143
Covertness, 180
Covetousness, 180
Criminality, 38
Criminals, 70–71
Customers, 55–56

Deceitful manipulativeness, 143
Defensive character mechanisms, 19
Defensiveness, 94
Demotic or popular speech, 33
Denial, 149
Dependent individuals: victimization
    by psychopaths, 188
Depression, 117–118

Dichotomous thinking, 99
Differential diagnosis: associated and
    overlapping disorders, 107–122
Difficult to ascertain/incomprehensible
    motivation, 86–87
Dimensional diagnosis, 14–15
Disability benefits, 52
Disinterest in loving relationships, 180
Disloyalty, 35–36, 106, 143
*Disorders of Character: Persistent
    Eneuresis, Juvenile Delinquency, and
    Psychopathic Personality:* Michaels,
    Joseph J., 153
Displacement, 149
Dissociation, 96, 150
Distortive lying, 49
Don Juan character, 67–68, 119
Drop-that-name cons, 181
Dynamically defined psychopathy, 21

Easy money cons, 181
Educational therapy/coaching, 165–166
Educators, 57–58
Ego, 146–151; problems, 163
Ego dystonic traits, 16
Ego-ideal, 151–152; dealing with
    problems, 161–162
Ego syntonic traits, 16
Elderly persons: victimization by
    psychopaths, 189–190
Elegant/polished speech, 33
Emotional causes: psychopathy, 7
Emotional illness: in psychopathy, 50–51
Emotionally caused physical illness, 51
Emotional speech, 33
Entitlement: narcissistic, 113
Evasion, 100
Evilness, 143
Expressive therapy, 172
Eysenck, H. J., 87, 126

Factitious Disorder With
    Predominantly Psychological Signs
    and Symptoms, 51
Family, 62–63; enabling psychopathy,
    192
Family therapy, 167–169
Feelings of centrality, 113

Femme fatale character, 67–68, 119
Fictional characters, 71
Flamboyant sexuality, 38–39, 67–68
Forgetfulness, 102
Freud, Sigmund, 37
Friends, 63–64
Frugal individuals: victimization by psychopaths, 189

Ganser's syndrome, 51, 143
Get-rich schemes, 180
Government: enabling psychopathy, 192
Grandiosity, 114
Greedy individuals: victimization by psychopaths, 187
Guilt, 7; by association, 98; capacity to feel, 18; lack of, 37
Gym people, 64

Hare, Robert D., 5; *Without Conscience: The Disturbing World of the Psychopaths Among Us,* 13, 126
Health professionals, 56–57
Hedonism, 7, 112
High-class displays, 180
Histrionic personality disorder, 51, 119–120
Hyperalertness to danger, 143
Hyperbole: in psychopathy, 32
Hypermnesis, 51
Hypersexuality, 67–68
Hypocrisy, 40
Hypocritical thinking, 90
Hypomania, 89, 107–109
Hypomnesis, 51

Identification, 150
Id (instincts and impulsivity), 145; problems, 163
Immature individuals: victimization by psychopaths, 187
Immaturity, 181
Impressionable individuals: victimization by psychopaths, 185–186
Impulsiveness, 35, 181; victimization by psychopaths, 189
Inattention, 98

Indulged psychopath, 140–141
Inpatient treatment, 169–170
Insanity defense, 6
Insight, 101
Instincts and impulsivity (Id), 145–146
Instinct theories, 137–138
Insufficiently altruistic individuals, 112
Intelligence, 102
Interpersonally defined psychopathy, 21
Interpersonal relationships: capacity for, 103–106
In-your-face charm, 179

Judgment, 102

Kernberg, Otto F., 157

Lawyers, 60–61; enabling psychopathy, 192
Lax superego, 162–163
Laziness, 112
Learning theory, 142–144
Lewis, Dorothy Otnow, 5
Liberalism: encouragement of psychopathy, 128–131
Loneliness: victimization by psychopaths, 188–189
Love: capacity to feel, 18
Lying, 47–53; by therapists, 177–178

Machiavelli: *The Prince,* 7, 42
Maladaptive behavior, 13
Maladaptive evasiveness, 17
Maladaptive traits: discontinuous use, 20; sublimation of, 20
Malapropisms, 32
Malingering, 50–52
Manipulation, 40
Manipulative disenfranchised individuals and groups, 66
Manipulative paranoia, 109
Masochism, 7
Masochistic determinism, 60
Masochistic individuals: victimization by psychopaths, 186
Materialistic individuals: victimization by psychopaths, 188

Media: enabling psychopathy, 192; people, 57
Medical profession, 56–57
Memory, 101–102
Mental illness: vs personality stype, 18
Michaels, Joseph J.: *Disorders of Character: Persistent Eneuresis, Juvenile Delinquency, and Psychopathic Personality*, 153
Mild psychopathy, 4. *see also* Psychopathy; case history, 75–84
Milieu therapy/group therapy, 170–171
Millon, Theodore, 6, 133
Minimization, 98–99
Minimizing immorality, 92
Mistreatment of children, 181
Mistreatment of pets, 181
Motivation: difficult to ascertain/incomprehensible, 86–87
Multiple Personality Disorder, 33
Münchausen Syndrome, 143

Naïve individuals: victimization by psychopaths, 186
Name-calling, 180
Narcissism, 91, 105–106, 111–116, 180; aggressive, 115; entitlement, 113; feelings of centrality, 113; unsuccessful *vs.* successful, 111
Narcissistic individuals: victimization by psychopaths, 187
Narcissistic mode of speech, 32–33
Negative countertransference, 173–177
Neighbors, 63
Neologisms, 32
Nonaffirmative therapy, 165
Nonantisocial aggressive types, 133
Normal or conformist speech, 33
Normal personality: determination of, 16; structure of, 16–18

Obsessive compulsive neurosis, 24
Obsessive compulsive personality disorder, 24, 147
Oldham, John M., 15
Omniscience, 99, 180
Omniscience *rechthaberei*, 99
Oral manipulators (wheedlers), 40–42

Organic aphasia, 140
Organic causes, 139–140; psychopathy, 7
Orientation, 101–102
Outsiders in society, 26
Overgratification: in psychopathy, 7; by therapists, 177
Overly harsh superego, 163

Paradoxical therapy, 172
Paranoia, 91, 109–111
Parental unpredictability, 142
Passive-aggressive, 147
Passive psychopaths, 18
Pastoral counseling and therapy, 172
Patients, 56–57
Permissive individuals: victimization by psychopaths, 186
Perring, Christian, 5
Perry, J. Christopher, 29
Personal injury compensation, 52
Personality differences, 15
Personality style: quantity, 15; *vs.* personality disorder, 14–15
Personality traits, 16; adaptive evasiveness, 17; combinations of, 17; maladaptive evasiveness, 17; selection, 17
Phallic manipulators, 42–44
Physical disorder, 51
Pinsker, Henry, 12
Pity, skill for eliciting, 180
Politicians, 61
Poor conditionability, 87–88
Poor prognosis: assumption by therapists, 177
Positive countertransference, 176–177
Posttraumatic stress disorder, 5, 120–122, 143
Practitioner syndromes, 56
Previously existent but mild physical disorder, 51–52
Prichard, J. C., 24
Prison psychosis, 51
Projection, 151
Promised reciprocation cons, 181
Pseudo-activists, 66–67
Pseudologia fantastica, 50
Psychiatrists: enabling psychopathy, 192

Psychoanalytically oriented psychotherapy, 166–167
Psychological tests: trick questions, 52
Psychopathic consumers, 4
Psychopathology of everyday life, 14–21
Psychopathy (psychopathic personality disorder), 58–60; as an actual disorder, 5–6; associated and overlapping disorders, 107–122; behavioral constructs, 142–144; behavioral manifestations, 29–53; causes, 137–152; composite cases, 73–84; considerations of id, ego, and superego, 144–152; controversy about causes and dynamics, 7–8; controversy about description, 6–7; controversy about treatment, 8–9; coping with, 179–186; course and prognosis, 153–156; defined behaviorally, 21–24; defined by core characteristics, 21; developmental theories, 140–142; difficulty of evaluation, 5; elusiveness, 5; enabling of, 128–131, 192–194; everyday life, 24–28, 55–72; goals of treatment, 172–173; identification in everyday life, 179–181; identify personal vulnerability to victimization, 183–186; immunization against being a victim, 190–192; improvement in, 25–26; learning about, 179; mild: successful, 133–135; therapy, 157–178; vs. antisocial personality disorder, 24–26; vs. severe, 11–14; outsiders in society, 26; social causation, 125–128; social concepts, 5; specific pathology, 161–163; therapeutic errors, 177–178; therapy, 157–178
Psychosis, 11

Rationalization (spin), 92, 150–151
Reaction formation, 149
Reactive psychopathic disorder, 20
Rebelliousness, 128; victimization by psychopaths, 189

Reduction ad absurdum, 98
Regression theories, 138
Religious leaders, 58
Remorse: lack of, 37
Repression, 149
Right and wrong: blurring the differences, 93
Rights violations: in psychopathy, 34

Sadock, Benjamin James, 8
Sadock, Virginia Alcott, 8
Sadomasochism, 116–117
Salvation cons, 181
Savior identity, 180
Schizotypal personality disorder, 119
Secret information cons, 183
Selective abstraction, 96
Selective inattention, 98
Selectivity, 96
Self-absorption, 180
Self-indulgence, 111
Selfishness, 111
Self-love, 111
Self-pride, 151–152
Self-promotion, 180
Self-reliance, 143
Seminormal personality, 18–21
Sexual disorders, 118
Sexual franticness and wildness, 180
Sexuality: flamboyant, 38–39, 67–68
Shady or illegal dealings, 180
Shrewdness, 143
Similar things are the same thing, 95
Simon, Robert I., 18
Single-minded goal direction, 143
Social concepts: psychopathy, 5
Social issues, 123–131; serious problem with all social theories, 128; too-conservative and repressive society, 127–128; too-liberal and too-permissive society, 126–127
Social liberalism and conservatism: as cause for psychopathy, 8
Sociopathy, 124–125
Speech: in psychopathy, 32–34
Spiels, sweet-talking, 179
Spin (rationalization), 92
Splitting, 150

Spoiled, 112
Spouses: enabling psychopathy,
    192–193
Spur-of-the-moment cons, 183
Students, 57–58
Subcriminal psychopaths, 18
Substance abuse, 68–70, 107
Successful psychopaths, 18, 133–135
Superego (conscience), 145–146;
    dealing with problems, 161; lax,
    162–163; overly harsh, 163
Supportive therapy, 163–164
Switching figure and ground (cause
    and effect), 98

Tenants, 64–65
The Mask of Sanity: Cleckley, 12
The Prince: Machiavelli, 7, 42
Therapeutic impatience, 178
Therapists: errors made with
    psychopathic patients, 177–178
Therapy of the mild psychopath, 157;
    additional approaches, 171–172;
    family, patient, milieu, and group
    therapy, 167–171; general principles,
    158–163; general rule, 159; goals of
    treatment, 172–173; individual
    approaches, 163–167; mastering
    one's negative countertransference,
    173–177; opening salvos, 159–161;

specific pathology, 161–163;
    therapeutic errors, 177–178
Thought content disorder, 89–94
Thought process disorder, 94–101
Toch, Hans, 12
Too-conservative and repressive
    society, 127–128
Too-good-to-be-true cons, 181
Too-liberal and too-permissive society,
    126–127
Transference cons, 178
Treachery, 35
Trusting individuals: victimization by
    psychopaths, 183–184

Undergratification: in psychopathy, 7
Unempathetic individuals, 112
Unreliability, 35, 180
Upbringing, 140–141

Vaillant, George E., 29
Victimization: by psychopaths, 183–194
Violations of rights of others, 34

Wheedlers (oral manipulators), 40–42
White-collar psychopaths, 18
*Without Conscience: The Disturbing
    World of the Psychopaths Among Us:*
    Hare, Robert D., 13
Workers, 65–66

About the Author

MARTIN KANTOR, M.D., is a psychiatrist who has been in private practice in Boston and New York City, and active in residency training programs at hospitals, including Massachusetts General and Beth Israel. He served as Assistant Clinical Professor of Psychiatry at Mount Sinai Medical School and as Clinical Professor of Psychiatry at the University of Medicine and Dentistry of New Jersey, New Jersey Medical School. He is the author of 15 books, including *Understanding Paranoia: A Guide for Professionals, Families and Sufferers* (Praeger, 2004); *Distancing: Avoidant Personality Disorder, Revised and Expanded* (Praeger, 2003); *Passive-Aggression: A Guide for the Therapist, the Patient and the Victim* (Praeger, 2002); and *Homophobia* (Praeger, 1998).